A Cast-Iron Will

The true legacy of Fred Dibnah

Sheila Dibnah

2QT Limited (Publishing)

First Edition published 2013 by
2QT Limited (Publishing)
Dalton Lane, Burton In Kendal
Cumbria LA6 1NJ

Re-print Edition 2013

Cover Design by Robbie Associates Ltd
Photographs supplied by S. Dibnah

Publisher Disclaimer:
The events in this memoir are described according to the Author's recollection;
recognition and understanding of the events and individuals mentioned and are
in no way intended to mislead or offend. As such the Publisher does not hold any
responsibility for any inaccuracies or opinions expressed by the author.
Every effort has been made to acknowledge and gain any permission from
organisations and persons mentioned in this book. Any enquiries should be directed
to the author.

Printed in the UK on behalf of Latitude Press Limited

A CIP catalogue record for this book is available
from the British Library
ISBN 978-1-908098-825

I dedicate this book to my wonderful son Nathan.
And anyone who has lost true love.

Never knowing or fully understanding why —
but loving all the same...

FOREWORD

Aelish Michael's bitter-sweet drama, *The Demolition Man*, premiered to a packed house on the 7th April 2011 at the Octagon Theatre, Bolton, Lancashire. It received an excellent public response and favourable reviews from the national media throughout its sell-out four-week run. It was allegedly the second best-selling production in the history of the theatre, surpassed only by Bill Naughton's highly-acclaimed stage play *Spring and Port Wine*.

With foundations rooted in truth, *The Demolition Man* starred the gifted Colin Connor as an eccentric, kind-hearted but flawed Fred Dibnah, and feisty television soap-star actress Michelle Collins as me, his third wife, Sheila. It is partly based on the following personal memoirs that I kept for many years during my marriage. The personal can of worms the play opened suddenly became public for the first time in almost seven years, since my famous husband passed away. I found myself giving candid radio and press interviews about 'what happened' at the end of his life.

Like any rivetingly good drama, however, the whole account is also humorous in parts, since the man the public celebrated as 'Our Fred' was a naturally funny, friendly, approachable, sincere, open and down-to-earth character. To the end, he remained a brilliant orator and a skilled advocate of Britain's industrial past. Colin Connor captured that quality beautifully in his role as Dr Frederick Dibnah MBE, the celebrity steeplejack who died in Bolton Hospice from cancer of the bladder on 6th November 2004.

After I met Fred in October 1996, I came to realise that despite the public image of 'what you see is what you get', there was a far greater depth and sensitivity to this colourful, complex character who was seemingly at odds with our modern way of life. There was a lot more to the man than the popular, working-class flat-capped northern image he tended to portray on television.

Aelish Michael met Fred once at a steam rally and was inspired by him. After an introduction to me through a mutual friend, cameraman Nick Wilding, she began to explore ideas of where the story would lead and developed several drafts of the play in an effort to find what we both considered a fair balance. I stipulated this must not show Fred wrongly as some kind of boorish ogre, hell-bent on causing his wife grief purely for the sake of it. I wanted to show the stark reality of a vulnerable but larger-than-life man under a great deal of stress, and fearful of what was happening, over a period of several years. Aelish and I became good friends as she slowly began to unravel the many complexities of the 'warts and all' scenarios in my memoirs and discovered that it was essentially a love story that went wrong.

A talented playwright, Aelish used artistic licence and certain dramatic devices to move the plot along to its tearful, gripping, heart-felt climax. Here Fred is seen by the audience being manipulated into signing a new will just days before he dies. Actors John McArdle, Mike Burnside and Richard Heap portray three fictional amalgamations of real people who surrounded Fred in life, but are known simply as Malc, Bert and Keith in the play.

As a gullible Fred becomes increasingly confused through fear, medication and interference, he relies on the support of friends and confides in his mentor, the great Victorian engineer Isambard Kingdom Brunel, played by Huw Higginson, who appears in his shed as a vision to guide him through increasingly troubled professional and private times.

In reality it happened slightly differently, but the end result was exactly the same: *I was cut out of my husband's Will just days before he died.*

The play captures the essence of my marriage and many scenes are true, such as my father getting killed in a terrible accident at my parents' home the same day we learned that Fred had terminal cancer.

It is not merely a story for Fred Dibnah fans and neither is it some tacky 'kiss and tell' account, for I respect my late husband. But I still feel upset that he had no peace at all towards the end of his life.

Aimed at the 6.5 million people who enjoyed Fred's BBC programmes at the height of his career, it is also for those who know what it is like to suffer at the hands of others and feel helpless. It deals not only with the strange concept of celebrity status but also the dynamics of a marriage under stress; it is a human-interest narrative which will touch anybody who has ever nursed or lost a loved one and has endured grief as a consequence.

Despite previous and various well-documented memoirs published by scores of people claiming to be lifelong friends and acquaintances, primarily aimed at stalwart Fred Dibnah fans, it's pretty clear to me that not many of them fully understood or appreciated exactly what made the man in front of the camera tick as a human being.

Fred was essentially a loner who lived obsessively for his work. Influences which went far beyond his interest in all things mechanical ultimately shaped his expectations of some of those closest to him; it wasn't easy at times to live with those ideals. Fred was his own man.

A man of Victorian values.

During my time as his third wife, he was influenced by events beyond his control such as the consequences of his increasing fame from 1998 onwards and, later, serious illness. As things became complicated and he experienced a growing feeling of helplessness during the latter years of his life, his public image and our private life together gradually grew further apart.

The dreadful news that cancer had touched us meant things had to change. Like the true fighter he was, Fred regarded the immediate shock and side-effects of this illness as a direct challenge to get his beloved steam tractor up and running under its own head of steam. The oily gauntlet was down and nothing could distract or dissuade him from this mammoth task; his superhuman strength and determination knew no bounds. In the face of adversity, he finally completed the job – as I knew he surely would.

But it came at a price to Fred: his health and, ultimately, our marriage.

It's a terrible tragedy that in July 2010, almost six years after his death, the marvellous traction engine he'd laboured on for more than twenty years was auctioned off by the Estate. This action concluded a very bitter and pro-tracted legal battle that resulted from him cutting me out of his Will literally days before he died in Bolton Hospice, full of fear, pumped up on morphine, apparently hating me.

I never thought it would end like that and neither did Fred.

This is my story.

The most personal one you will *ever* read.

It gives you a rare insight into two soul mates...

...and, like the play, it's a tale that is as funny in parts as it is ultimately tragic...

So, let me share my knowledge of the wonderfully brave man with vowels as flat as his familiar, well-worn oily cap and take you deep inside our married lives; the emotional upheavals through the years – good and bad. The story is set against an ever-changing backdrop to a life that could be regarded as

'*Steam Heaven*' ... or later, '*Steam Hell*'; a life which moved faster than any main

line locomotive, from when we first met in 1996 to its tragic, untimely end in

Bolton Hospice on 6th November 2004.

'I've always been intrigued by relationships between unlikely couples; Fred was a TV personality but I often wondered about the real man behind the public persona. I thought maybe there is a story that hasn't been told. Film maker Nick Wilding introduced me to Sheila Dibnah and the idea for the play was born.'

Aelish Michael, playwright, The Demolition Man (2011).

'The story leaves the reader satisfied that the legacy "Our Fred" left to his thousands of fans remains intact and that our love continues to this day, despite the cast-iron will of some whom I truly believe tried so desperately hard to destroy me and unwittingly maligned a great man in the process.'

Sheila Dibnah, widow of Dr Fred Dibnah MBE.

I made another garden, yea,

For my new love;

I left the dead rose where it lay,

And set the new above.

Why did the summer not begin?

Why did my heart not haste?

My old love came and walked therein,

And laid the garden waste.

She entered with her weary smile,

Just as of old;

She looked around a little while,

And shivered at the cold.

Her passing touch was death to all,

Her passing look a blight:

She made the white rose petals fall,

And turned the red rose white.

Her pale robe, clinging to the grass,

Seemed like a snake

That bit the grass and ground, alas!

And a sad trail did make.

She went up slowly to the gate;

And there, just as of yore,

She turned back at the last to wait,

And say farewell once more.

*(Victorian poet, Arthur William Edgar O'Shaughnessy, b. 1844,
who knew a thing or two about love and loss.)*

PROLOGUE

Bolton, Lancashire. A busy town twelve miles from Manchester in the once-industrial north of England. It's a cold and grey mid-November morning; crowds are already gathering under dull skies, oblivious to the fine rain which threatens this bleak occasion.

The wide pavements of Bolton, my home town and that of my late husband Fred, are lined with well-wishers: fans, journalists, television crews. There are hundreds of cameras held by scores of curious locals and visitors from far away, all jostling for better views to preserve this moment for posterity. They are waiting for the funeral cortège which will soon wend its way from our home in Radcliffe Road to Bolton Parish Church.

This will mark the loss of the town's famous son, Dr Frederick Dibnah, MBE. Our quaint Victorian gatehouse, my husband's much-loved home of some thirty-five years, is surrounded by a sea of glum-faced people, some grasping colourful umbrellas, their vivid nylon covers at odds with the grey skies above and pallid faces below. Meanwhile, out in the back yard Fred's two sons, Jack and Roger, and a few of my late husband's friends busy themselves getting his beloved traction engines in steam for this, the most important of days.

Each person goes about their business with a sort of grim determination.

Other people are present in the famous back yard: fans and faithful followers, hoping to be a useful part of this unforgettable day. They mill around the two green engines anxiously, offering to carry out mundane tasks in a collective attempt to dull the pain they all share in an effort to do 'Our Fred' proud on this, his last sad journey…

His rope and red ladder festoon the light-oak coffin, with its shiny brass handles; Fred's trademark oily flat cap is perched firmly on top. The coffin sits majestically on a large, flat-bed trailer. It will soon be pulled to the Parish Church by the highly polished tractor, in full steam, followed by a procession of other vehicles in a convoy headed by his steamroller. After the remembrance service, the procession will slowly wend its way through the crowded town to a final resting place in Tonge Cemetery where Fred's granddad and grandmother are buried, not far away at the bottom of our back yard.

Fred is to be accompanied by a loud fanfare of steam whistles as he is lowered into the cold, hard ground. It's what he wanted, you see (though sadly, he never told me so).

But now, for the time being at least, the yard is still packed out, crawling with men – some familiar faces, some not – all united by this single, heartfelt grief. A sense of oneness, emptiness and change; a loss that suggests nothing will ever be quite the same again. The very ethos of the place has been transformed; it has morphed into this stark wilderness of dead machinery without its vital star who once shone so brightly over this quaint northern empire.

The King is dead.

The place is cold and dead too.

The implication makes me feel giddy and strange. Indoors, I stand dressed in my smart funeral attire but feel like a dazed stranger as I contemplate the scene through the kitchen window. I recall the lively, charismatic man with dancing blue eyes, my 'Hippo', whom once I loved deeply and who loved me in return, before he was taken away by illness and prejudice. I ponder the task which lies ahead. I knew thousands of people would attend this Victorian-style showman's funeral but now, feeling empty and hollow, I must steel myself away from all negative thought. Apart from my son, Nathan, other members of my family and a small group of trusted close friends and confidants, I know that I must face this particular grim battle alone.

I have to be brave here. Don't let them see...

No time for tears just yet – those will come much later in private.

Not here, not now...

To most people, I am raw with grief and rightly deserve their kindness and sympathy. To a certain few, however, I have no hope of their sympathy – for they don't know the full story, and have no compassion ... some even hate me!

The show must go on. I fully understood the day's agenda; I saw what was happening a long time ago. It is exactly as I'd expected and precisely what I feared would happen: I wasn't in charge.

Fred had seen to that shortly before he died.

Except the day wasn't about me — my grief, love, fears.

None of it really made much sense, but then, over the past three years since my husband was first diagnosed with terminal illness and its suffocating grip took hold, squeezing the very soul out of our marriage — none of it really had.

My loving husband, the man I adored, was lost to me forever on the 29th day of October 2001.

Today, as I leave the house and finally face the crowds on this dreary, damp 16th day of November 2004, I am burying a famous stranger.

Contents

Chapter 1	A working-class background	1
Chapter 2	Meeting Fred	12
Chapter 3	'Thanks for the – Memory!'	34
Chapter 4	The higher they climb...	49
Chapter 5	Bricks, spanners and the final knot	71
Chapter 6	Have wives - will travel!	95
Chapter 7	We're all going on a summer holiday	115
Chapter 8	'Mr Frederick Dibnah, Famous Raconteur And Chimney Murderer!'	141
Chapter 9	The height of bad manners...	167
Chapter 10	'Dr Dibnah, I presume?'	187
Chapter 11	'It's bad news, I'm afraid...'	215
Chapter 12	Fred and the steam mafia	230
Chapter 13	News of a gong ... and the final chimney drop	253
Chapter 14	'MBE ... My Bloody Empire!'	286
Chapter 15	Love and hate	305
Chapter 16	Alone...	321
Chapter 17	Life without Fred	349

CHAPTER 1
A working-class background

'Wait until I tell you, cock, and then press down hard...'

I fidgeted with the big steering wheel and gazed around at the multi-coloured gates lining the narrow, red-brick street. A tabby cat from across the road sat on top of a wall, languidly scratching itself in the warm summer sun as I popped my head out of the window to see what was happening.

'Not yet, luv ... only when I tell you ... whoa!'

A grease-covered hand, no stranger to hard work, appeared from under the bonnet of the small car and began waving frantically around. 'Right! Go on then – whoa! Bit more ... go on cock, a bit more.'

I obliged by pressing down hard on the pedal, pumping slowly with all my slender might.

'Bit more, luv – again, go on!' bellowed my dad's voice.

I was helping to bleed the brakes on our Ford Anglia. It was the summer of 1967 and car maintenance was my favourite pastime. The previous week we'd changed the vehicle's carburettor to a twin one, which Dad explained would make it go faster. I examined some oily pink cardboard gaskets, turning them round and round in my grimy hand, getting gunk on my striped summer dress.

Dad said he wanted me to fetch a 'sturtump' from the toolbox. That was my name for spanners.

He worked as a milkman for the Co-operative Society but liked to tinker with cars in his spare time and this two-tone Ford Anglia, with its sky-blue bodywork, white-wall tyres and jaunty white roof, was his pride and joy. When Dad resprayed the damaged right wing with a cellulose paint aerosol, I'd sprayed some of my collection of model cars and, into the bargain, the shelf of my mum's kitchenette – a curious, tall cabinet used for storing food which inadvertently ended up the same colour as our family transport!

I enjoyed finding small nuggets of discarded cast-iron lying around in our back street, which must have been 'slag' from a local foundry. I collected them to make obstacles to crash my toy cars into (hence the cars needed spraying). I loved their feel and acrid smell. I soon discovered that the small round covers of water stopcocks located outside the neighbours' houses, cast with the letters of BCWW which stood for Bolton Corporation Water Works, were made of this stuff.

I was thrilled to find the covers could easily be removed so I could examine the criss-crossed spiders' webs in the dark, musty-smelling hole beneath. This brought about a few good clouts round the ear from my mum, who couldn't understand why I wasn't content playing with my green and cream Silver Cross doll's pram – a generous present from Santa – instead of toy cars, spanners, dirty grid-lids and grubby little boys.

Neville and Ricky, mischievous brothers from down the bottom of our street, were my best pals. I seemed to get along with boys so much better than girls and enjoyed the rough and tumble of their games. Between us, we swapped toy cars, shared grazed knees and picked on smaller kids.

I was fascinated with the romance of pit-head gears, chimneys and empty factories. There was an old plastic factory at the bottom of our front street where we played regularly. The three of us would crawl in through a broken window around the back and play amid the rusty machinery, discarded bits of plastic offcuts and other stuff, smelling the strange polymer reek, pretending we were on an adventure in some kind of netherworld where we were the only three human adventurers alive.

However, despite my love of cast-iron and mucky old places, my childhood in the late fifties didn't have a lot in common with Fred's perception of a working-class childhood in this same northern mill town of Bolton. By the time I was born in 1957, the halcyon days of the textile industry were grinding wearily to a halt. Most people now expected an improved standard of living, better wages and safer working conditions than their parents and grandparents could ever have dreamed of.

Big mill chimneys no longer dominated the town's horizon like so many industrial cathedrals to worshipping capitalists. Gaudy cars with American styling now travelled on thick tyres over cobblestones where once only tired workers had wearily trodden their way home in clogs after their daily shift in the factories. Children were taller, healthier, better educated; clothes were more fashionable, more available. The endless lines of terraced homes were brightly furnished with all the latest affordable fads – gaudy, laminate creations of tubular steel and colourful plastic, seen by young newly-weds as the last word in style.

These consumer goods were working-class aspirations to modern life, and our family was no exception. Early supermarkets were springing up everywhere and tastes had changed: like my peers, my parents absolutely hated tripe and onions, black puddings and pigs' trotters. Sometimes, just to confirm that our lives were indeed better, we'd take foreign holidays to Majorca – all unheard of in my granny's day. She still firmly believed in charabanc travel because flying led to blood disorders!

Fred and I were born twenty years apart at the same local hospital in Farnworth, just outside Bolton. My family lived within a few feet of a dye-works factory chimney, which he later repaired and maintained. The age gap between us – some would later say the chasm – meant he was working as a time-served joiner, which he'd done since leaving school at the age of fifteen, whilst I was gurgling away happily in my pram. My earliest memories are of the last few remaining tall, sooty chimneys that Fred loved, and seeking them out whilst riding with my dad on the milk truck during the school holidays and at weekends.

I was fascinated with manhole covers, with their raised patterns and designs, which my parents found highly amusing in their little girl. Mostly though, these were unremarkable days, lived out in the innocence of youth. Like most of the neighbourhood kids, my little world revolved around our cobbled back street, resplendent with a single gas lamp located conveniently opposite our back gate. I was seven when I happened upon square boxes scattered around the base of the lamp stating on the lid: The Whelmar Gas Mantle. I began another collection of these strange objects to accompany my precious cast-iron nuggets, folding flat each little white box with loving care.

I was fascinated by this hissy cast-iron thing that lit up our back street and I often spent the cold, windy nights sitting at my bedroom window, staring out at its weak, yellow-green light. The way the flame danced across the iridescent mantle kept me up way past bedtime, transfixed with innocent childish wonderment late into the night.

I loved anything old and rusty and my memories of that back street, my own little piece of the industrial north, eventually formed the basis of a relationship with the most unique exponent of 'King Cotton's' glorious heyday: Steeplejack Fred Dibnah.

The year was 1978. At twenty-one, I was working in Blackpool alongside Master Hypnotist Peter Casson as his stage and public relations assistant.

Peter was a clever academic who had gone on to become a showman. He was the only layman to have lectured at the illustrious Huntarian Society, the oldest and most prestigious medical society in the world, which was founded in 1819 by Dr William Cooke. Peter had studied psychology during the 1950s and at one time owned a clinic in London. Now, having owned two nightclubs in Yorkshire for a number of years, he worked as a stage hypnotist.

I'd met Peter at Blackpool Tower in the summer of 1977 when I was working as a window dresser for the Bolton Co-op, doing part-time modelling for the Lucy Clayton Agency in Manchester and also taking dancing and singing lessons. He was presenting his cabaret show 'Hypnotic Phantasy' in the Tower Ocean Room and had problems finding a suitable stage assistant. He asked me to consider the post as we chatted at the bar after the show.

I'd gradually fallen in love with this distinguished, educated, older man. He had an amazing personality, a calm, well-spoken voice and a pair of twinkling blue eyes that dazzled me. It was a completely new life for me. Peter was forever trying to make me more sophisticated – and I succumbed, becoming more polished and worldly-wise with his Svengali-like guidance.

During the year following the summer season, we worked on board Fred Olsen's cruise liner the *Black Watch*, sailing to Madeira, Tenerife, Lanzarote, and then immediately afterwards on the *QE2* for six weeks. We sailed to New York and back several times on the luxurious liner and also visited the Caribbean over the next two months.

I spent the next four years of my life living and travelling with Peter before working with another stage hypnotist called Andrew Newton. By then, Peter had gone back into medical research in America, serving as an adviser to the Neurology Department of Wake Forest University in North Carolina. We remained close friends until he died of leukaemia in 1995. Aged seventy, he gave a magnificent final performance at the London Palladium, filling the theatre.

Meeting Peter started me on a stage career that lasted a lifetime. Aged six, I'd seen Frank Ifield live on stage during his summer season show at the ABC Theatre in Blackpool. I never forgot the glamour of The Tiller Girls. Sitting on the front row, I could smell their perfume as the curtain came up and see their dazzling blue costumes draped in diamanté, their long legs covered in bronze fishnet panty-hose as they kicked up high on silver heels. They were beautiful and I wanted to be a showgirl too one day. It was my dream, but my parents thought it wasn't for the likes of us and my dad wouldn't hear of wasting time going to drama school or anything like that. In ordinary working-class families from industrialised areas of northern England it wasn't done or expected in those days.

But I eventually toured the world as a jobbing entertainer, working with other hypnotists and starring as a partner in the illusionist act 'Duo Magicana' working mostly in Geneva and across Europe. I began singing in nightclubs, dancing finally as a glamorous showgirl on stage and eventually, much later in life, became an award-winning public speaker after my time with Fred.

But all that was in the future. For now, Peter and I toured abroad regularly as well as presenting the show in theatres and cabarets throughout Britain. On this particular occasion, we'd just returned from Morocco and a letter from Mum was waiting. Tanned, tired and feeling the cooler climate, I disappeared into the kitchen to make a much-needed cup of English tea and left the letter aside.

This recent trip had been amazing. As I began opening the envelope, I thought about our visit to Marrakech and the Kasbah, where wrinkled old men, wrapped in flowing white robes with skin the colour of old copper, tried to cajole us into buying live chickens, spices or gaudy rugs and garments. The experience had been fantastic: drinking mint tea and sharing food with friends Peter and I had made, digging in with our hands, scooping up lemon chicken couscous from giant, colourful ceramic dishes, soaking up a different culture and style of living amidst the sensual aromas of musk, spices and warm, scented evening breezes.

Now we were back in wet, windy Blackpool.

The letter was a cheery one with all the latest family gossip. A large newspaper cutting fluttered out, depicting a cheeky, flat-capped, middle-aged man wearing a red checked shirt, holding a cigarette and smiling at the camera. I picked it up and studied the face. Here we go, I thought: she's on about that Fred Dibnah again! This was the year that Fred first appeared on TV and it seemed that every time we spoke she was on about this odd little chap who climbed chimneys and steeples for a living and had a steamroller in his back garden.

Mum automatically assumed I'd be interested in hearing about Fred because he was from Bolton, so I quickly scanned the clipping and studied the grainy photo. It seemed we'd arrived back in time to catch him on telly. So at 8pm, Peter and I flopped down just as the opening credits came on: 'Honk-honk, honk-honk,' a loud hooter blared out. 'It's going! It's going!' Startled, a jubilant Fred, decked out in trademark cap and shabby striped sweater, shot off to avoid flying bricks from the falling masonry. 'It's done fer!' he quipped, just as the chimney crashed to the ground. Then he turned to face the camera, beaming that smile and shouted, 'DID YER LIKE THAT?'

In the next shot, a haunting tune called 'The Carnival of Venice' accompanied him as he swung from his boson's chair on the side of a 200ft brick chimney. Sitting there, shuddering at the sight of him scaling the heights of a familiar landmark, I can't say I was enthralled by what I saw. Being a young showgirl, I was acutely aware of my awkward Boltonian accent and mannerisms which Fred, irritatingly, seemed to accentuate.

'Are you all right then, cock?' he enquired of an older man who was helping to pull some ladders up from the bottom of the chimney.

I had tried hard to distance myself from what I now considered a dreary, humdrum lifestyle in Bolton and hated my accent with a vengeance!

I was ready to fly and Bolton wasn't on the map as far as I was concerned. I had retained my liking for traditional things but my outlook these days centred on the heady world of glamour. I was far too busy dressing up my long blonde hair and painting my talon-like fingernails red in readiness for some glitzy showbiz gathering, such as the annual Grand Order of the Water Rats Ball. I was too busy meeting people like Cliff Richard, Les Dawson, David Nixon, Bob Monkhouse and Freddie Starr ever to be bothered about life in Bolton again ... *or* Fred Dibnah.

The voice did it: that deep, gravelly, nasal twang with its twisted dipthongs and double negatives, all wrapped in a thick, northern accent, the chocolate tones of which growled in the direction of his long-suffering wife Alison and their three restless young daughters.

'The kids are hungry Fred...' moaned the very pretty, yet weary, Alison. Standing there in the bar of some pub they had stopped off at whilst out on the steamroller was the indomitable, larger-than-life Fred Dibnah.

Oddly compelling, covered in grimy soot, wearing an oily flat cap, holding on to a fag between thumb and forefinger, noisily swilling beer down his throat, he piped up: 'Well then, cock, gerrum a bag o' cheese n' onion crisps then.' Then he carried on draining the glass between long drags on his fag as a dejected Alison and her three girls looked on. The camera gradually panned close up. They all shuffled around, glancing glumly at Fred, hoping he might say something like, 'Come on dear, let's be on our way and find the children something substantial to eat then...'

I jumped up out of the chair and flicked over the channel, complaining to Peter, 'Ugh! No wonder they all think we still walk about wearing a shawl and clogs up north with this sort of stuff on telly! *How* obnoxious! What a male chauvinist pig he is. Did you see *that*?!'

It was the first time I had seen the pint-sized, charismatic Fred Dibnah in action. I had no reason to suppose it wouldn't be the last...

CHAPTER 2
Meeting Fred

'...I thought: "Well, she's a bit different this one."'

I t was now late October 1996 and Fred was back on telly.

Still living in Blackpool, I had a job working as a tape duplication engineer at Astra Productions Recording Studios owned by my fiancé of four years, keyboard player Kelvin Futers.

Kelvin was a talented Geordie musician and all-round nice guy who lived with me and my son Nathan. He regularly appeared during the summer season at the Horseshoe Show Bar at Blackpool Pleasure Beach and owned Astra Productions. We had met through a mutual friend when I was part of a singing group called The Songbirds. The relationship with Kelvin, who I loved with all my heart, was not going too well due to the fact that I disliked his mother intensely. I thought she was clingy and highly controlling. We argued constantly about her and she always came first in Kelvin's eyes – despite him being in his early forties. Eventually, after four years, the relationship disintegrated when I thought he was seeing someone else and he moved out that summer to move back in with his mum – or ' Marm' as he called her.

Nathan was seven and was keen to know about steam engines. I had videoed a Fred Dibnah programme for him one evening. We put it on next day, watching as Fred expertly demolished the Dart Mill tower in Bolton. We were enthralled by the fearless way he went inside the fragile tower, held up with nothing but cut-down telegraph poles. Then he started knocking against the stout wood with a hammer, like playing a massive xylophone. Gradually, he lit the fire at the base of the tower. We both laughed when, exasperated, Fred exclaimed, 'What's wrong with the thing – what's holding it up then?' as the tower stayed up, unexpectedly defiant under the raging fire. I taped more programmes and became hooked on Fred's gritty humour as I watched them with Nathan.

My parents still lived in Bolton and sometimes we held our family 'heritage trail' when I visited them. My old school – near Fred's house – was on the list. We'd reminisce about my favourite cast-iron manhole covers nearby. My parents would point to a spot in the crazed tarmac where, as a kid, I was once fascinated by a magnificently detailed oval manhole cover with splendid raised designs. We would discuss 'Keck lamps'; these to me were the ancient cast-iron road-menders' paraffin lamps which flamed at the side of the road in foggy weather when I was a child, warning passing motorists to beware of danger. Or we'd see the cast-iron weighbridge I liked, intrigued by the patterns, dates and name embossed into its rugged surface in a nearby quarry. A cast-iron pipe range on a factory wall had also sparked my childish curiosity; that was not far from Fred's home.

'Is this where Fred Dibnah lives, then?' asked Nathan during one such outing. There it was.

We stopped outside. There was a peculiar, green wooden living van on painted red wheels parked outside the rusty iron gates. Inside the gates was a cross between Steptoe's scrapyard and an industrial works from bygone times. There was a smell of burning timber, the noise of flapping belts; all sorts of odd, angular shapes made out of iron and stone jutted out. Wood, pulleys, wheels and lines were juxtaposed against a backdrop of stark, wintry trees.

We climbed out of the car and walked closer to the iron railings.

There was lots of activity going on – whirring machinery, hissing, clattering and a general sense of 'getting things done'. We peered tentatively inside the top gates, which were wide open, and spotted Fred wearing his flat cap and well-worn pullover. Despite his dirty, oily appearance he gave a genuine pleased-to-see-you smile. He was holding a metal pail in his left hand and waved it unthreateningly at us. 'Come on down, mate – you're alright. Have a look round!'

We went sheepishly down the driveway and Fred gave us an informative guided tour. When I muttered something about being sorry for the interruption, he dismissed my apology, saying he always had a lot of visitors on a Sunday. He explained how he'd come across all the machinery and restored it.

I listened with interest, noting how animated he'd become, but I failed to spot Fred's misery at recently being left alone after the sad demise of his second marriage. It should have been obvious from the way he was talking at that time that he was very hurt inside. 'Aye ... she's buggered off like – a divorce sorta style – but Jack's still here...'

Fred recalled our visit to his friends later.

This tall, slim lady came down the path, with her mum, dad and little lad. I thought: 'Well, she's a bit different this one...' She impressed me with her interest in the back garden. If I liked 'em – I'd invite them into the house! She really opened my eyes when she mentioned the galleries on oil-lamps: how do I get them so clean, and all of that? She told me she'd got five at home, but couldn't get them clean...

'How do you go on for getting good coal?' I asked her what she meant and she mentioned she'd got a coal fire in her house in Blackpool. There were other things, like – on my mantlepiece she spotted a little cardboard box with 'The Kildark Gas Mantle' written on it, and nearly went wild looking at this box. She told me all about when she was a kid,

and about a gas lamp she liked in her back street! I told her about me having a box full of mantles in me shed!

Her reaction made me think 'Bloody hell ... you are different!'

Anyway, time to say goodbye had arrived, and they'd gone...

I have a Visitors' Book, and I always get people to sign it. When I looked in the book, it had Mr & Mrs Grundy, Miss Sheila Grundy – and Nathan Yates. And I thought, this lady's had a bit of bother, you can see it in her face. She's evidently the product of a recent divorce. Well, they've gone now ... I can hardly ring up her mam, and say 'How's your daughter going on, like?' or summat like that, can I? So I never bothered – just thought about it. Then one day, a letter arrived. A little thank you note, which said: 'Thanks for a lovely day – and we really did enjoy our recent visit to see your sheds.'

On the bottom of the note, she'd mentioned she comes over to Bolton to see her mum and dad regularly, and could they call again sometime – really enjoyed our visit – 'n' all of that.

I wrote back, and said, yeah ... why not!

I was surprised to receive a letter from Fred, in his beautiful copperplate handwriting (I've left the spelling as he wrote it):

Dear Sheila,

Thanks very much for your letter it really cheered me up. I rememberd you very well the long blond hair Mum dad and little lad. I would like to say you are very welcome to

come and see me and my yard anytime you want also as you can see I am not very good at

letter writing and spelling it really whould be nice to see you for a chat and a cup of tea

and a look round the yard wenhever you wishe to come round just give me a ring on Bolton

531303

> *yours,*
>
> *Fred Dibnah.*

Fred breathed fresh new interest into my life. We spoke on the phone for hours and I'd visit him most weekends now that Kelvin had left me. He was real: a man's man, very chatty, animated – and, like me, emotionally hurt. We talked about everything and anything. We'd attended the same school, The Bolton School of Art and Design, and even shared the same driving instructor!

One slight niggling apprehension was Fred's son, Jack...

Fred's second wife, Sue, had left him in charge of Jack and taken their youngest son, Roger, with her to the Isle of Man to live with her new boy-friend. It was obvious that Jack ruled the roost; he seemed to be running wild and kind-hearted, gentle Fred constantly fretted that he was somehow responsible for the boy's unhappiness. He didn't seem able to offer any kind of parental discipline for fear of upsetting him. Also, Fred's ability to look after Jack as far as food was concerned was open to much criticism, since main meals seemed mainly to consist of meat pies, fish and chips, beans, burgers, sausages and endless packets of crisps and Twix bars, washed down with the healthiest thing in his diet: fresh orange juice.

I continued my visits, but another female on the scene so soon after his mum had left was an unwanted complication for Jack. Fred, ever the perfect gent, never made any improper suggestions so we enjoyed each other's company and once Jack had finally gone to bed we would relax with a pint or two of Guinness in the parlour.

I saw Fred as my great friend; he made me laugh with tales of his interesting life, impressing me with his knowledge of history of how things worked, sharing his love of old things such as oil lamps. On one occasion I commented on his rugged hands and, as he beamed that familiar, charismatic smile, he took great delight in showing me his many calluses. He banged his hand down hard on the table, proclaiming: 'Everything I like in life is heavy, dirty or dangerous – bu-bum!'

He shared his views on women, perplexedly at times, lifting his cap, rubbing his bald pate, saying it was strange how a young woman like me was so interested in the stuff he was interested in. He admitted that he had never understood women: 'Too complicated,' he said.

On one occasion, I visited his home and hardly recognised him.

My dad Arnold worked for most of his life as a milkman for the Co-operative Dairy based in Kay Street, Bolton. He eventually became Assistant Manager – a job he loved.

© *Sheila Dibnah Collection*

My earliest memories are of our back street in Elgin Street in the Halliwell Road area of Bolton. My love of all things cast-iron stems from the Bolton Corporation Water Works stop-cock covers (which you can see in this picture to my right). I named these 'my grids'. When I turned 21 and the street was ready for demolition, I used a screwdriver and rescued them from the scrap yard! I still have them today and love them now as much as I always did.

© *Sheila Dibnah Collection*

As a child, I loved playing with toy cars. Here I am on holiday in Cornwall at the side of our Ford Anglia with its newly-fitted twin carburettor, which made it go faster. The car was always prepared for weeks before the trip, and I used to get very excited helping my dad as he worked 'fettling' it. I would get covered in gunk and enjoy collecting spanners, which I dressed as dolls.

© *Sheila Dibnah Collection*

My dad was a keen photographer as he got older and took this picture of me during Christmas spent at my parents' home in 1982.

Taken during my days working as a showgirl. I never thought one day I would fall in love with a man who had dirt under his fingernails!

Working for Master Hypnotist Peter Casson. I was his Stage and Public Relations Officer.

FULLY INSURED

F. DIBNAH

STEEPLEJACK

8 ALFRED STREET, BURNDEN PARK, BOLTON

REPAIRERS OF CHIMNEYS AND CHURCH SPIRES, LIGHTNING CONDUCTORS ERECTED, FLAG POLES PAINTED
AND REPAIRED, CHIMNEYS HOOPED, RAISED AND REPOINTED, IRON CHIMNEYS PAINTED AND REPAIRED

Mr. F. T. WEBSTER   3rd May 19 63.

	£	s.	d.

No. 15.

Timber Merchants Spa Road
Bolton.

Dear Sir,
    I thank you for your enquiry
for repairs to your water tower
I am pleased to quote for the
job as follows, —

The fixing of wooden gutters to
water tower, repairs to roof
of water tower, painting of cast
iron R.W.P. and gutter
Painting of ridge tiles on roof
of tower.

    Yours faithfully.

    F. Dibnah,

| | 50 | 0 | 0 |

✓

© *Sheila Dibnah Collection*

One of Fred's early letter-heads. It shows his beautiful copper-plate handwriting.

He'd got himself spruced up, and sat in the corner of the room on his green leather chair, looking uncomfortable without his trademark cap. I asked why he hadn't got it on; bashfully he replied, 'Well, it's not polite when you have a young lady coming along to see you, to wear your work clothes in the parlour!' When I said I didn't mind him wearing his cap indoors, he looked pleased and said, 'Hmmm ... right then!' and immediately shot off upstairs to retrieve it.

When he returned he took it off again, smelling it and inhaling deeply as he continued his chat-up line: 'Ahhh, that's better ... SMELL mi' cap, love!' he urged.

On other occasions he had me in fits of laugher when he mentioned the 'sex-files' – letters and saucy suggestions from various women of all ages from up and down the country eager to get acquainted with him. He showed me the more curious ones, and we laughed about one lady in particular whom he referred to as 'Miss Two Parrots' because she kept two macaws. Each time she rang up, just as she set about whispering sweet nothings in his ear to light the flames of passion, the birds would start to holler in the background. Fred would pipe up, 'Yer what, cock? What did you say? You'll have to speak up louder – I'm a bit DEAF and I can't hear you for them bloody budgies!'

We talked and talked and talked; his candour knew no limits. His break up with his second wife, Sue, had all but destroyed him. Being surprisingly sensitive when it came to affairs of the heart, Fred was not able to cope with the emotional fallout. But his single biggest regret was losing his two boys, and he would cry openly with me about this for hours to exorcise his inner demons and the loneliness he felt without them in his life.

Then one night in Blackpool I got a telephone call. 'Hiya, cock! It's me, Fred. I were wondering, like, if you'd fancy coming on a steam rally with me an' the kids next weekend in South Wales?'

With it being the school holidays, he added that Nathan might enjoy it. By now both Fred's boys lived full time on the Isle of Man with their mother and her new boyfriend, and were over in Bolton to see their dad for the holidays.

'Nowt funny, like – you don't have to worry, cock.'

'Yes! We would love to!'

Fred explained that we'd all go down on the train but I suggested hiring a car. 'Hmmm ... could you manage to drive the thing, though? I mean – a strange car 'n' all, it is a long way! I don't like driving 'owt modern and fast myself. You'd have to do it, cock!'

'Well, Fred, it's going to be very expensive on the train for five of us if we don't ... then all the luggage and what have you...'

Nathan and I set off in my little Austin Metro from Blackpool for Bolton and pulled into the driveway of his home the following Friday. We parked up behind a brand-new silver Peugeot 406, fully equipped with power steering, air-conditioning, turbo diesel engine and one worried (temporary) owner – Fred! He was sauntering around, tentatively examining it, mumbling something about was I *still* sure I wanted to drive this bloody shiny thing, as he didn't realise they made cars this big.

'Product of the modern world, the combustion engine – too fast for me – give me a steam engine any day!' he said, as he stood frowning at the strange electronic key in his hand.

Within the hour, we'd loaded everything into the car's cavernous boot, ready for the long journey ahead. We reached the M6 and Fred started to relax. Only the increasingly grim, cloudy weather was something of a disappointment, but we enjoyed the journey.

Until we eventually reached the outskirts of Wales...

I asked Fred for directions.

He hadn't a *clue* where we were supposed to be heading – all Fred sheepishly remembered was that the town had an odd-sounding Welsh name, and was 'somewhere near Cardiff...'

'Did you not bring a contract with you, or anything?' I asked.

'Oh – bloody 'ell, I'm hopeless at this sort o' stuff, me, like!'

We stopped the car wondering what to do next.

A thought occurred: we would ring and ask a mate whom he'd told about the trip. He would hopefully be able to provide details.

We drove around searching for a phone box: 'Eeee, I'm reet sorry – I shouldn't be allowed to do stuff like this, me,' Fred said.

But what with the Welsh name, and Fred being a bit deaf and a slow writer, the money ran out long before he'd managed to get all the details down, turning the exercise into a bit of an ordeal.

'You'll have to speak up, mate – can't hear you!' Fred shouted into the handset. 'Yer what – say it again, ah this bloody thing – I can't hear you!'

Eventually, armed with the necessary information, we sallied forth wondering what we would have done had his mate not answered the telephone. The rain was a downpour by now but we hoped for nicer weather for the next two days of the rally.

We found the venue; it was a veritable *sea* of mud.

Our gang of kids started grumbling about being hungry. Everyone around us was tramping through wet grass and mud, wrapped up in padded jackets and hats – and the wind kept rising. I reflected on the flimsy leather jacket I was wearing: where on earth would we get warm and dry? Fred, impervious to the weather conditions, set off looking for his steamroller 'Betsy', tromping big, sloppy, army-boot prints in his wake, moaning, 'Oh, could I do with a couple of pints after this bloody performance!'

We trudged behind him as the mud sucked at our feet and found Betsy looking cold, forlorn and dejected, too. The engine had been transported down by low-loader the previous day and now she stood there, her front iron rollers all rusty red, stuck in mud.

'Right – well then, at least we know where the engine is.'

'Yeah – we'd better see the organiser and find out about food and digs.'

The 'food' turned out to be an endless supply of unpalatable greasy bags of chips, with charred burgers thrown in for Jack and Roger. Being vegetarians, Nathan and I were considered something of an oddity by the catering van staff, as we stood muttering at the front of a trailer, wondering what to eat.

An organiser came to find us and guided us to a tatty caravan with flat, disintegrating rubber tyres, which had been used as a showroom-cum-office for promotional work at some earlier stage. Further inspection inside revealed a musty interior with no beds, toilet, hot water, or gas ... nothing – only lots of drawing pins, dust and filth!

We were ready to jump into the car and head off back home as three friendly-looking people came across and introduced themselves as the organisers.

'There's no bloody beds in here, mate. We've got two adults, three kids, and no bloody beds!' retorted Fred.

The rain poured down continually. 'What about putting us up in a local pub or hotel then, mate?' Fred went on, visibly annoyed. 'This is no bloody good, is it?'

The organisers frowned. 'Oh, we can't do that – we've overspent on the budget as it is!' Then they added, 'Don't worry, Fred, we'll sort something out.'

They wandered off to try and arrange something with the other members of the committee. Minutes ticked by; we stood in the damp caravan waiting to see what would happen next.

I'd decided to head back to the car. Fred strolled over to where I was sitting and stuck his head in through the open window. 'Don't know why I bloody bother coming to these things sometimes, when it's like this. Fancy coming all this way ... no beds! Its ruddy ridiculous!' he fumed. Then, as he leant forwards to reach an opened packet of mints off the dashboard, he added more softly, 'Bloody hell, I'm sorry, love; it's not usually as bad as this – sorry, love, your first rally 'n' all. I'm reet sorry.'

The three people were coming back in our direction. One of them shouted, 'It's OK – all sorted! We've got a tent for the kids to sleep in, and we're finding a couple of beds for the caravan.'

Fred looked at me and shrugged as if to say, 'Well, whaddaya think?'

'Well – it will be a bit of adventure for them, they'll have fun. It'll be like camping out, I suppose,' I said.

I decided I needed a coffee and went off in search of a Styrofoam cup full of hot, tasteless murk that nearly took the skin off the roof of my mouth and stripped my tongue like a pile of stewed mahogany wood shavings. When I returned to the group, I noticed they had erected the promised tent next to the uncomfortable caravan and an argument had broken out amongst the three boys and Fred. Having seen the tiny, green, two-man tent, they were all flatly refusing to sleep in it.

'I'm too big anyway,' piped up Nathan to Roger.

'Yeah ... and Jack will squash me!' Roger said.

'No I won't! You'll put your stinky feet in my face, Roger!' shouted Jack in return, and gave him a hard shove for good measure. Roger hit back – hard.

'Boys, boys – please – FOR HEAVEN'S SAKE!' spluttered Fred.

'Well, I'm not sleeping in *that*!' retorted Jack, and stormed off – just as the beds for the tent arrived. The organisers were now unceremoniously shoving two battered and tatty old bus seats inside the tent.

'It's OK, we'll sleep in the tent,' I wearily informed everyone.

Fred looked relieved, and stroked his chin, pondering what to do next. 'Hmmm ... I need a pint after this bloody lot. Where's the beer tent, mate?'

By now, the boys' accommodation was completed by the addition of two tatty white plywood signs, with faded writing, tentatively balanced across the caravan seats to form hard, springy wooden beds. But at least for now it had stopped raining. Taking advantage of the welcome change, we gathered all the sleeping bags and our meagre possessions from the car in readiness for the next two nights' stay on the cold, muddy field.

A bag of chips and a trip to the beer tent later, and we were ready for anything! Fred contemplated getting drunk to deaden the situation. Instead, I cheerily asked him to look on the bright side of things.

'Yeah – you're dead right,' he agreed, glowing from about four pints of beer. 'This ale's not too bad after all either ... quite good actually.'

Later, as the evening wore on, coloured lights strung around the beer tent glowed defiantly into the misty night. There were more showers of rain and the bleak field was pervaded by the pungent smell of cooking, carried by the frequent gusts of wind into the makeshift bar: fried onions, burgers, chips. The sound of gaiety, laughter and taped music drifted further across the field from the tannoy system.

Booze dulls the pain and lightens the mood, and I felt quite merry as Fred regaled a group of boisterous steam men and fans with his wondrous tales.

Nearly time to retire to our humble accommodation!

But I was left wondering how on earth I would be able to brush my four-foot long blonde hair in one of those awful chemical portaloos strategically placed near the beer tent.

The kids had settled down to a night without the benefit of mattresses but eventually ended up having great fun, as predicted. Back at our own humble tent, I crawled inside and watched as Fred followed into the darkness on all fours, slithering around like some giant slug.

'Oh bloody 'ell, love – hey – I'm reet sorry about all of this.'

He was convinced it would be the final time he'd get me to visit a rally and kept repeating as he slid inside his sleeping bag: 'Sorry, love – oh gawd ... I'm sorry.'

We lay squashed together due to the sloping angle of the bus seats and the lack of space in the tent. As the driving rain pitter-pattered onto the thin fabric, I felt a sense of excitement. Cold, damp, cramped, a dank, musty smell coming from the makeshift beds – but I could see Fred's bald head shining softy in the weak light that escaped from nearby security lamps, and hear his regular breathing.

If anyone had predicted back in the late seventies that one day I would be sleeping in a tent in the middle of a wet field, with no facilities to wash or clean my teeth – or even a convenient toilet – *with Fred Dibnah at the side of me on an old bus seat*, I would have shrieked and recoiled with horror!

As the rain continued, I snuggled down and gave Fred's bald head another affectionate rub. We both chuckled, seeing the farcical side, until our bellies ached with laughter and we gradually drifted off into a light sleep, keeping each other warm with the heat of our bodies.

Next morning, I awoke early. Fred was already awake, lying on his back, arms tucked firmly behind his head, staring up at the fabric roof of the tent.

'Good morning, Freddie!' I chirped

'Gawd! This is terrible, love. I've had a horrible night ... these damned bus seats...' He groaned as if to prove the point. He said he'd felt cold and had to sleep in his engine driver's jacket and cap.

Outside, the morning was still dull and dreary but at least the rain had stopped. It was still only 7.30 a.m. and several people were already ambling about, passing our tent with water carriers and cups of hot, steaming liquid. I could hear that our three children were up already. Jack had started on the engine early, lighting the fire and stoking it up and so Betsy was nearly in full steam.

I stepped outside to find some breakfast, but first made a trip to the caravan to spruce up. Friendly steam engine owners – rugged men already covered in oil, soot and whatever else splattered forth from their mechanical contraptions – were standing around discussing various traction engines, sipping hot tea, smoking fags and looking forward to enjoying some of the 'craic' again with Fred over a pint or two in the beer tent later.

'Morning, love!' one shouted across, waving his coffee cup.

'Oh – morning!' I replied, with a nonchalant wave back.

'Both sleep alright in there last night?' the man enquired. Knowing looks flitted across mischievous faces: 'Wink – wink!' Clutching my toilet bag to my chest like a shield, I continued sheepishly to the flimsy metal door of the caravan thankfully left half-open by the kids.

The steam men began to laugh again, punctuated by grunts and snorts of various kinds, and I overheard something like: 'He's a lucky old bugger...'

I surveyed the black mascara and red lipstick in the bag. It would have to do for now, and I coped with brushing my hair in the cramped confines of the four-berth caravan – now thankfully free of excited kids.

But nothing prepared me for what lay ahead...

Show Time!

The public started to arrive on the field by 9am. Slowly at first, then crowds of families appeared. The rain continued to fall softly – and still they came.

The organisers had set up a white canopy nearby beneath which were a long table and two chairs. I offered to give Fred a hand with selling videos called *The Ups and Downs of Chimneys* and *All Steamed Up*, and colour-printed postcards, which he would autograph and sell. It soon became obvious that he needed help, as he was busy with the 'talking side of the operation' as he put it.

A fairground organ piped up somewhere not far way, groaning out its tired, familiar melodies throughout the rest of the day. At first, a small number of people trickled over. 'Hi Fred, we've been watching your programmes. How about signing a card for us, then?'

'Course I will ... you're alright, mate. Give this lass here yer money ... that'll be 50p.' He picked up his pen, asking which name to sign.

A woman stepped forward. 'Fred! Smile for the camera – do you mind signing my autograph book, eh?' A treasured, dog-eared book was produced out of a wet anorak and placed on the table. Fred winked and replied, 'Aye cock, but you'll 'ave to wait a mo while I see to this lady here, first, like.'

The first woman spoke as I took the money and Fred handed her the signed card. 'Thanks Fred – I've always wanted to meet you.'

Click! The second woman caught him as he signed his famous scrawl: 'To Nancy, with best wishes.'

Pictures, fans and well-wishers: a very long queue had developed. I tried to keep the line moving but it was difficult, partly because Fred talked incessantly, often going off at a tangent.

'Here's a pint for you, Fred!' (What, it's only 10.30 a.m.?)

'Here – will you hold little Johnny? He likes you better than the Teletubbies or Thomas the Tank!'

Johnny began to wail, not impressed at all by the sight of Fred. 'Ooh – come on sweetie, its FRED – Fred from the telly ... y'know, you've seen him, haven't you?' Johnny clapped eyes on the oily cap and burst into tears.

'How-do, Fred.' A ruddy-faced man with a shock of white hair proffered his hand in a more formal greeting. 'We're down on holiday from near you – Yorkshire – can we have a video as well? How much are they?'

I spoke up above the noise of the public-address system and the man gave me two notes as he continued speaking with Fred, who replied: ''Eck ... Yorkshire, eh? Now there wer' a great big chimney disaster there once a long time ago, at a place called Cleckheaton... "The Great Cleckheaton Chimney Disaster"! It was in eighteen hundred and odd, and a big tall, thin chimney fell down. The steeplejacks decided to go up higher with it to get a better draught. Aye, poor buggers, they put too many bricks on – built it one coursework too high. It fell down and crushed a few sheds, like...'

A diehard steam fan, complete with a smattering of oil, silently came up to the front of the queue and handed Fred a picture taken a long time ago at another rally in Lancashire. Fred tapped at the photo with the pen. 'Hell, man, before the telly came along, there's no way I'd 'ave ever been down 'ere wi' me engine, like – I mean, it takes a fair bit of money to move one of these things around the land...'

People came in droves. There seemed to be no end to the queue and despite the weather they waited patiently to meet their hero: the pint-sized steeplejack from Bolton whom they had all seen on telly. He was kindness itself, this unlikely star, and had time for everyone. It seemed to matter to

Fred that each and every person didn't feel cheated about the amount of time they could spend talking with him.

I was frantically trying to cope with all the attention it brought, fumbling with money whilst people clicked pictures of me too. 'Who's this then? Have you got one of your daughters with you today, Fred?'

'Bugger off, it's me new girlfriend!'

One keen lady, in her lovely Welsh lilt, enquired of me: 'How are you, love? Shame about the blummin rain, eh – still he's worth waiting for, aren't you dear?' She turned to Fred. 'Oh, go on – give us a kiss then, go on!' to which he obliged, looking at me in a theatrical way as if to say 'You'll kill me'. His audience lapped it up, rewarding him with a hearty, collective laugh.

'Fred! I've seen all your programmes ... I like the ones where you climb up the chimneys – still climbing up them, then, eh?'

'Too bloody right I am, mate – need the money!'

It was not bad going, for someone I had mistakenly assumed was not particularly well-known outside a fifty-mile radius of Bolton!

By noon, I had a bit of a headache and was ready for a break. Fred said he fancied a trip to the beer tent. Having packed all the merchandise back in the car, I willingly accompanied him and, after a bag of chips, we both gulped down pints of real ale, quickly ordering another two. My mind was still in a bit of a whirl as I slurped down the cool liquid. There was still no escape. In the tent, people were still coming up to us all the time, shaking Fred's hand, asking about the television.

'Can I have your autograph, please – I've watched all –' a young man tussled with a rucksack, looking for a suitable piece of paper.

Fred interjected, not unkindly: 'We're just having a bit of a break, cock, won't be long. See that table out there? Well ... I'll be scribbling me name down again over there later, and I'll tell you about me new engine that by rights should be here now – its twenty-two years and two divorces, still not finished though...'

All around us, people were staring, talking and pointing and the ubiquitous cameras were constantly aimed in our direction. Fred drank, smiled, continued to talk and gesticulate, becoming very animated when he met a thin little man from an engineering works, wearing a similar cap and speaking about the technical points of a lathe with the same amount of enthusiasm as himself.

Then a member of the press stepped forward to do an interview. 'Tell us what you think of your trip to Wales, Mr Dibnah,' he asked.

'Very wet!' declared a giggling, mischievous Fred.

He melted my heart on that cold field that summer.

CHAPTER 3
'Thanks for the – memory!'

'Yeah ... when you are hurt by divorce an' all that, your brain goes a bit haywire, like'

*T*hey say opposites attract and in our case that was true. The opposite of all that I had grown accustomed to over the years, Fred was tireless, unafraid of showing raw emotion, a bit on the wild side, funny, open and talkative but above all he was his *own man*! At a modest five feet six inches tall, he was certainly confident enough to handle me being a few inches taller at a statuesque five feet ten.

The twenty years age difference between us meant nothing.

He knew about life, did not mind taking risks and getting dirty. Life was too full and too interesting for Fred to be concerned about the minutiae. You only lived once, and he was determined to take full advantage of that fact. He knew with absolute certainty he could never offer me the same world to which I had previously belonged, but out there somewhere was adventure and good times waiting for us both. It meant me giving up such things as going out shopping together, eating in some cosy, quaint tea room – or holidays abroad. Life in my own, more 'modern' world of cinema, pizza restaurants, bright lights, nightclubs, theatres, parties, Sunday rides out in the car and everything else taken for granted over the years, would be a thing of the past. It was a lot to give up.

Would I be able to accept a radically different lifestyle?

It would also mean moving if things progressed between us...

Another problem: I knew inside that I wasn't nearly ready to trust another man after Kelvin. My only security lay in knowing with *absolute certainty* that Fred knew how it felt to be let down, destroyed and left to pick up the pieces of an empty life. He would not get involved with someone lightly after all that had happened to him. I didn't see the harm in us spending time together as friends at first – and we could take it from there – *if* the situation developed. He would also need practical help.

Left alone after Sue had departed, Fred unsuccessfully tried managing after-dinner bookings and steam rally dates, and vast amounts of paperwork mounted up at an alarming rate. He had quickly gotten into a muddle. One day, Fred even managed a double-booking by accident.

Yeah ... when you are hurt by divorce an' all that, by worry and everything – your brain goes a bit haywire, like. I had bits of paper everywhere with things written on, that

I had forgotten what they were. I would write telephone numbers down, but no names, like. I were in a right bloody mess...

I had managed to somehow do this 'double-booking' by accident. I should have been at Eastnor Castle, in Herefordshire. Instead, I'm booked to be on a school playing field with the engine at Nelson, near Colne in Lancashire! I thought – how am I going to wriggle out of this one? So I reckoned the best thing to do, is introduce each party to the other, and let them sort it out!

Anyway, I did ... and to cut a long story short, Eastnor Castle only needed me from about lunchtime on Sunday, until about four in the afternoon. The other guy at Nelson had booked me for all weekend, with my steamroller. We'd got the steamroller there, and all Saturday we chuffed round the field and made everybody happy. On Sunday morning, we got a lookalike to drive the engine around the field on Sunday afternoon! A helicopter came and landed on a nearby school sports ground, and me, Jack and Roger sneaked off, jumped in the helicopter, and flew all the way down to Herefordshire! It was quite an exciting flight too because helicopters don't go very high in the sky, and we could see all the various landmarks as we went along...

As the relationship with Fred continued, I could tell by the twinkle in his mischievous eye that he'd always been a devil, a bit on the wild side – and I loved him for it. Now we were ready for the next step. This was to be the very first night we had spent together as a 'proper couple' in his big, shiny Victorian brass bedstead, lovingly polished especially for the occasion, he told me later!

The next morning, I travelled along with my exciting new lover in the Land Rover to see the work in progress on the Barnoldswick chimney he was working on. An independent film producer called Nick Wilding, who would go on to capture the last ten years of Fred's life on film, was at work. On this particular day Fred and his assistant were replacing some iron bands.

We were both smiling and giggling like a couple of kids, standing at the base of the chimney as he got ready for filming. Nick, who was wiring him up with a tiny microphone, joined in and caught the happy mood. In due course, it was time for Fred to ascend the ladders. He would follow up the chimney with the camera, filming as he clamped the iron bands in position and secured them firmly.

A warm, balmy day, a light breeze, with the sun beating down. I happily went off for a walk around the area. Peace and tranquillity – with only the distant *ti-clunk ti-clunk ti-clunk* from Fred's hammer against the solid, red Accrington bricks. I smiled to myself, blithely soaking up the sun on my back, contemplating a small babbling brook that glittered in the sunlight, and giving in to the warm, new, unfamiliar sensation of being cheerfully happy and contented at last. Life was good again. I was happy.

When I arrived back, Fred was leaning against his ancient red Land Rover having a bit of a break, not far from the base of the chimney. No sign of the other two; no harm then in going across for a bit of a kiss and a cuddle...

We were both locked into our own intimate world, expressing all the sloppy and erotic things new lovers might say to each other, which Fred – at the time once voted as possibly the least romantic man in Britain – eventually vocalised in his own indomitable style:

'Thanks for the lovely screw last night, love, it was–'

He stopped dead in his tracks.

Concerned, I followed the direction of Fred's startled glance. Looming out from behind the chimney was Nick with Fred's steeplejacking assistant. They both wore big grins and started sniggering, bending over double and clutching their sides as they came nearer to where we were standing.

'What the – ?' Fred groaned and slapped the top of his head 'Oh 'ell... No ... I don't bloody believe it, noooo!'

I quickly caught on.

Fred was still wired up to the small radio microphone, worn on his jacket lapel for filming. We'd totally forgotten about it, and left the switch in the 'open' position throughout the *entire* conversation!

The two men had heard every single declaration of lust through the headphones!

'Oh Gawd, noooo, purleeze!'

I shrieked and put both hands up to my flaming red cheeks. The pair of them continued falling about, guffawing, their eyes shiny with tears of merriment. At least Fred had the decency to look embarrassed: 'You rotten buggers!' he exclaimed. 'You could 'ave told us. Eh up, yer won't show all that on't video, like – will yer?'

Fred and I attended more steam rallies and various outings during the summer months. These were halcyon days; we had many good laughs with his accurate, un-politically correct powers of observation and sometimes caustic wit.

I liked rallies, except for the bother of putting up with the dreaded caravan accommodation. It wasn't easy to find nutritious food, or enjoy a good scrub after the oil and soot of the day. The other thing I didn't really care for was the total lack of privacy and relaxation away from crowds of people. The attention was relentless and, after a while, I began to feel a bit resentful of all the various knocks on our caravan door, followed by a singsong: 'Yoo-hoo! Are you in there, Fred?'

But as far as business opportunities go, we took it to the wire.

Fred signed countless autographs, with me standing at the side of him from mid-morning until about 6pm – sometimes later – selling and constantly plugging merchandise, spieling like some hardened market stallholder, promoting further sales. It was mind-numbing, but became like a drug to see how much business we could do. Public attention demanded Fred, so we diligently worked longer and harder on every rally, sometimes without a break. I eventually introduced pens, car stickers, certificates, engine drivers' jackets similar to his, model vans and various books. We also charged a nominal cover price for the signing of brochures and books not supplied by us on the day, which I put towards Fred's 'Guinness Fund' for the weekend.

It was rewarding; we were selling more videos and postcards than ever before. It was better organised too, so fans could spend a little more time chatting, getting autographs, photographs or videos – and although they sometimes had to queue for more than half an hour to get to him, he was always there, near the steam engine area and easy to find. It had never been organised to this degree before but, if Fred and I were going to relax together one day when he retired, we had to ensure we were financially secure.

The size of the queue sometimes became unwieldy and unmanageable, and we had to appoint marshals on the field to cull the numbers. For this purpose, and partly due to Fred being hard of hearing, I would send rider contracts to organisers stipulating that we shouldn't be placed near the tannoy system or any loud music, so Fred could hear the public speaking to him.

It sounded pedantic to some committee members who commented, 'She's bossy, isn't she, Fred?' when we arrived and found the rider had not been adhered to. I put my foot down, but in general things were much better and Fred had a secret chuckle about my ability to get things done. We were praised by some event organisers, who admired our sheer tenacity and stamina at getting through the day! Fred got return bookings, sometimes because his effort attracted crowds to their organised events; more than 100,000 people per rally at the bigger ones got time to spend with Fred if they wished. And profits steadily grew as Fred was becoming an instantly recognisable household name.

By the time 6.00 p.m. comes around, after standing all day long without even a break for lunch, your mind starts to become fuddled and you sometimes end up feeling stressed-out with anything, including each other. Some of our best rows were when we were tired after a long rally day, screeching at each other like two tomcats! You need peace, solitude and quiet, away from the din of voices still constantly resonating inside your head. It's extremely draining and you definitely need to relax with a bottle of wine and a hot bath. Evidently, this was not going to be possible with the present accommodation arrangements – sleeping in caravans on the rally field.

I complained to Fred, who didn't seem too bothered; eventually, though, even he felt the need to escape at times, so I would bundle him into the car and we'd zip off to some country pub for our tea. Fred had become used to all the attention, but what with the revised way of working and his increasingly high profile, the pressure increased and a part of him didn't like it, despite what the public and steam faction thought.

For him, a rally was no longer just an excuse for a boozy get together with fellow engine drivers, travelling at a leisurely pace with the family and living in the green 'shed-on-wheels', getting drunk all day long in the beer tent. Of course Fred wanted to meet his fans and spend time with them, but he needed rest afterwards.

The public became almost predatory and, besieged by fans towards the end of a show when we'd simply had as much as we could possibly take, we would end up hiding in the caravan, giggling like a couple of kids with the curtains pulled together. People circled around the caravan, waiting for signs of life, like birds of prey all eagerly ready to pounce with cameras, autograph books, pens. It was a strange sensation.

Then, after the show, other exhibitors and steam-engine owners would come and expect to have a chat with Fred, or attempt to whisk him off to the beer tent to get him inebriated. They didn't take into account that he was no longer a young man or realise how draining the day had been. It all became too much – for both of us. But Fred wouldn't readily admit to it, because it was letting people down, admitting he was only human after all...

Things gradually came to a head over accommodation.

Fred was booked to appear at a steam rally in Banchory, Aberdeenshire. For very long distances, we were still hiring what was now my favourite car – a dark blue Peugeot 406 christened 'Linky'.

Betsy the steamroller was going up to Aberdeenshire on a low-loader. Jack and Roger were over for a visit during the school holidays, so we all set off on the long journey early in the day. I thought to myself as we neared Glasgow: 'Oh good – we're in Scotland. Not too far to go now.'

I didn't realise it was nearly as far again!

On the outskirts of the beautiful granite city of Aberdeen we found the rally field ... and saw the caravan, our makeshift home for the following two nights.

Like in Wales – only with beds included this time.

No lights, no water.

Even the kids were fed-up ... and the *size* of this caravan.

Tiny.

The novelty about camping out had most definitely worn off. I couldn't understand why Fred should be subjected to this and be expected to put up with it; after all – wasn't he supposed to be a *'celebrity attraction'* or something like that? I tackled the organisers myself this time, but it was too late: no alternative accommodation was available. As in Wales, Fred stood there frowning, lifting his cap and scratching his head, perplexed – but this time, to save face for Fred, I took charge and complained to the officials.

After the Aberdeen incident, caravan digs would have to go. In future, I stipulated we would not stay on the rally field and would require accommodation elsewhere. Hotels: hot baths, healthy, well-balanced meals, clean sheets, decent breakfasts and above all – *most importantly* – total relaxation in private for Fred after an exhausting day.

I learned much later that this move had caused dissent amongst certain steam-engine owners and a few rally organisers who thought I was making Fred into '*something above his station*' and taking him away from their rallies.

By now, we had become an item. I was despondent whenever I had to leave Bolton and return to Blackpool. I longed for and missed Fred so much throughout the week.

I had fallen totally in love with him in a different way, not based on all the things I previously imagined I knew about love. I now knew excitement and recklessness, as well as fire and passion; he had an element of the unknown and it all made perfect sense. It was real.

I still had a long way to go before finally casting off all my bitter pain about losing Kelvin, and a lesser man would possibly have felt I was seeking momentary comfort after being crushed by another man. But not Fred; he knew with certainty that I would eventually respond with all my heart and trust as things developed between us.

One evening, as we were sitting in the parlour on the green leather chesterfield sofa, listening to music, sipping red wine and speaking about the past, present and future, he turned to me with tears in his eyes. He stroked my face and said, 'You know I'll never do owt to hurt you, cock. I'm not like that — I'd never hurt you.' I trusted him, accepting the moment and the security it brought.

I still believe what he said to this day and that he meant it, too. We were calm, happy and contented. I had a man who loved me and I now enjoyed an exciting lifestyle that was free of any trouble.

It was late summer of 1997, and the busy steam rally season was almost at an end. The last one we attended was the Grand Henham Steam Rally, near Ipswich in Suffolk.

We arrived at the Angel Inn in the nearby village of Wangford. The next morning, we went off for a hard day as usual. The rally was one of the best we had attended and we sold more videos than usual. By about lunchtime, I was getting concerned about the number we had left to sell. Experience told us that if Saturday was *this* good, tomorrow would be phenomenal. By noon, we had run out of videos. Before leaving Bolton, Fred had been left in charge of loading the car and had only packed a few. It seemed probable that we would run short at some point during the weekend.

By the middle of Saturday afternoon we had none left and were enduring complaints from disgruntled fans eager to purchase a video. We packed up signing postcards quite late in the day, about 6.00 p.m., and headed back to the hotel for a quick wash and brush up before our evening meal. Fred and I were downhearted, wondering how we would cope the next day without any merchandise to sell. He resigned himself to signing autographs instead, just chatting to people.

By 8.00 p.m., I had hatched a plan. What if I returned to Bolton, loaded up the car and travelled back to Suffolk through the night? I knew it was a long way and a rather hellish journey. I mentioned it to Fred, who said I was 'bloody barmy' and tried to dissuade me from the idea.

But I was determined. My greatest enemy would be fatigue, and Fred worried mostly about this aspect. However, I couldn't be dissuaded and so at 8.30 p.m. I headed off back to Bolton at the wheel of Linky. Fred stayed behind at the hotel with Nathan.

I arrived in Bolton at 1.00 a.m., and loaded up as many videos as I could, plus more postcards for good measure, and set forth again in Linky for the return journey. I was enjoying it immensely ... the music on loud, plenty to eat, pop and crisps on the passenger seat to keep me well fuelled. There is something unreal about late-night driving alone. The dark open road stretched out before me, bathed in pale, languid moonlight; the stillness mingled with ambient dusky odours of dark empty fields and scent of dank summer woods drifting in through open vents as the sleepy towns and cities rolled by...

By 4.00 a.m., I was getting a bit weary but was thrilled by the wondrous sight of rabbits, seemingly in dozens, hopping along the sides of the quiet Suffolk roads. I had to concentrate hard on my driving and slow right down as I dreaded the prospect of any fatalities of the cute, fluffy kind. The film *Watership Down* came into my mind as bunnies hopped across the road in front of me, staring into the headlights as if to say: 'What are you doing out at this time?'

I had not very far to go now, and could easily trace my way back to Wangford. Fatigued, the vast quantities of rabbits disoriented and confused me. Just before 5.00 a.m., I pulled Linky into the gravel driveway and looked up at our hotel bedroom window. I had gone off without a key; how on earth would I manage to attract Fred's attention, alerting him to let me indoors? It was pointless throwing pebbles up at the window – what with him being half deaf, I would need to smash the damned thing with half a brick before he could hear anything, much less wake up!

At that point, the bedroom window flooded with soft yellow light, and a half-dressed Fred slid the net curtain across the pane and quickly heaved up the sash, revealing his round, naked belly.

'Eee, love, I've never slept a wink all night, worrying about you, an' that's a fact!' His booming northern tones rang clear; decibels resounding, disturbing the stillness of twilight for those light sleepers all around us.

'Shhh ... just throw down the key,' I urged in a soft voice.

'EH? Yer what, love? Can't hear you...'

'SHHHH!' I made a mime as if to open a lock.

'What's up with you, eh?'

'The key, Fred – to the front door. Let me in.'

'Huh? Oh aye – just a minute, cock, I'll get 'em!'

Within minutes, I was back inside the cosy room I had left all those hours before. I had been driving non-stop for almost eight hours.

When I eventually drifted off to sleep wrapped in my 'Hippo's' arms, it felt as though my mind was playing a ghostly video recording of a road stretching out endlessly before me, the movement of the car still real ... the rabbits ran in front of my eyelids...

Then all too soon it was breakfast time again.

At the rally the day progressed just as we predicted. We sold every single video I'd brought back from Bolton.

Fred signed and signed for hours without a break until he could no longer hold the pen. After hauling Betsy up onto the low-loader after the rally, we set off in Linky with me wearily at the wheel, retracing the previous night's journey all the way back to Bolton.

CHAPTER 4
The higher they climb...

'They'll be thinkin' how does an old boy like me keep getting them young dollies?'

I t was approaching the 2nd October, my fortieth birthday; Fred was arranging a surprise party for me down at our local pub and inviting along some of our family and friends. But the most exciting time was when he asked me to marry him.

There was no getting down on one knee; it was more like coming back home from the pub and him saying, 'Hey up, cock, we can always get wed if you fancy – well, I need someone to look after me, like.'

I was ecstatic!

We decided that we should treat the party as a double celebration to celebrate my birthday and our engagement. It was a lovely gathering and Fred, not normally known for being romantic, arranged an exquisite cake decorated with my name and presented me with a diamond engagement ring.

We decided on a longish engagement as neither one of us wanted to rush into anything and we planned on tying the knot about a year later – hopefully by that time, we would know for sure if everything we felt about each other was what we both really wanted. I would have to move to Bolton, bringing Nathan out of school, and decide what to do with my own house. I loved Blackpool and had lived there for twenty years; I would miss the breezy resort.

The press had caught wind of our relationship when I accompanied Fred to Bolton's law courts for his 'wood-burning' appearance. I smiled, Fred rubbed his chin and we ended up in the local paper, the *Bolton Evening News*, and were also filmed for a local TV news item, which appeared later on that day. The next day the pictures appeared in some of the national papers as well.

Our local paper approached me, wanting to do a feature about all the things Fred and I had in common. They printed an article about gas lamps, mantles and, emblazoned in a column on the front page a colour photograph of me under a red banner which read: '*Exclusive – why I fell for Fred, see page 19*'.

Having been on stage during my showgirl days I was used to a bit of attention and didn't mind the resulting interest in my 'affairs of the heart' with the famous Fred.

He viewed it all with much amusement: 'They'll be thinkin' how does an old boy like me keep getting them young dollies?'

In autumn and winter, he got requests to do after-dinner speaking. I was amazed the first time I saw him in a smart dinner suit for a black-tie soirée, decked out with colourful waistcoat, gold watch chain, white shirt, bow tie, shiny black shoes – and clean cloth cap!

I enjoyed going along to these events. For fun during these trips, Fred and I would sometimes buy each other little surprise gifts, plastic ducks and such like, presenting them whenever one of us was in the hotel bath or shower – or we'd play pranks on each other by squirting water like a couple of kids.

It wasn't unknown for Fred to attend a function with his flat cap all wet because it had somehow got into the bathroom and been soaked through by the shower. One day I'd brought with us some trick black soap from a joke shop and left it wrapped up on the sink in readiness for our bathroom games. Fred began getting ready for the function and unwittingly used the soap. I could hear him complaining, 'Oh bloody hell, what's WRONG with this damned soap ... nah ... why don't they provide summat proper, like, at these prices?'

I stepped into the bathroom, expecting to see him covered with black suds, but instead he merely moaned about its lathering qualities! He was indeed wearing a beard of dark grey suds, but because he was so used to grimy washing conditions it was normal to him! He never even noticed that part until the white fluffy towel was discoloured. He said they'd think a set of bloody mucky buggers had been staying in the room that night...

I liked to open a bottle of wine, enjoy room service and then watch telly until Fred came back after the event. One night I'd fallen asleep before his return, and awoke in the early hours to the sound of someone shuffling around. It was Fred. He'd come back very late and hadn't wanted to wake me up by putting the light on. However, he'd had a little too much to drink and couldn't remember where the bathroom was. He was just attempting to get into the wardrobe. 'I'm bursting for a pee, an' all. Where's the bloody bathroom door in this joint, eh?' (Thank goodness I caught him in time!)

We would often stop off for a leisurely lunch at some nice country pub on the way home and if anything was worth seeing in the area, such as a nice windmill, engineering works or heritage site, we'd visit that too. But the outward journey always held an air of mystery; we'd look forward to finding the smart hotel we were staying at and making the most of it. On one occasion, Fred was booked to do an after-dinner talk at the prestigious Belfry Hotel near Birmingham where the open golf tournaments are held.

The morning after the event, we set out for breakfast. Fred was in his usual garb of flat cap, engine driver's jacket, granddad shirt, and black baggy trousers – complete with gold watch chain dangling from his striped waistcoat. I suppose we did look a bit of an unlikely couple as we approached the restaurant. A dark-clad, well-groomed young woman at the entrance stood ready to direct us to a table. 'Can I take your room number please?' she asked

politely.

'Room 301,' I replied.

She looked at Fred, then me, looked at Fred once more, giving him a

head-to-toe cursory glance and, realising room 301 was a double, politely

said: 'Is that the *same* room, madam?'

Fred just grinned. 'Aye, flower, that's right,' he said. 'Same room, cock –

left me zimmer back there, but yer alright, can just about manage without it

fer now...'

'Now come on, dearest, you are OK – go easy,' I said, enjoying the joke.

"Ave yer got me pills – me PILLS, you know!' He began dithering theatri-

cally, looking like Walter from that old television sit-com *Nearest and Dearest*. I

joined in the fun. 'Have you beeeen, Fred, have you beeeeen?' Turning to the

woman, I winked and added, 'It's me dad, you see, he can't control himself

when he sees a pretty face ... he really shouldn't be out in public. He doesn't

get out much these days.'

I guided his arm and we toddled off shakily towards the breakfast table,

as Fred carried on, 'Urrrahh uraahh, what day is it, cock? Where are we?'

The girl looked nonplussed, a bit uneasy and confused, not exactly sure

how to take us.

'Ooooh me pills – must 'ave me Viagra...' he continued rambling.

'Now come on, Dad...' I cautioned. We both fell about laughing!

It was lovely to be so happy and in love and this was to be a memorable year for two reasons. We had set our wedding for the 26th of September 1998. Then David Hall returned with definite financial backing from the BBC to produce a series of six programmes.

David would, in due course, turn around our lives since Fred was to be a television presenter for the first time, and it would prove to be a highly successful formula. Offering his skills and knowledge on the rich legacy of our industrial past, Fred demonstrated much of what still remains and is available for us to appreciate today.

This first series was to be entitled *Fred Dibnah's Industrial Age*.

I had lots to organise with the wedding plans so we decided to move to Bolton to give Nathan a chance to settle into his new school before the main summer holidays started. I would retain my own house in Blackpool and rent it out.

Easter was looming and I was spending the holidays with Fred. He was currently mending a factory chimney in an area of Bolton called Breightmet. The top of the chimney was dangerous and crumbly; he and Simon Warner were at the stage of pointing and repairing the final few feet. I had been curious for some time about how it must feel to climb up a vertical ladder. I'd inadvertently thrown down the gauntlet when I'd commented to Simon that any bugger could climb up a chimney – it's what you do when you get there – in other words, the skills employed in mending it are what counts. Now I had to prove my point of view...

It was a memorable Easter Monday.

Nick Wilding, the cameraman, was filming it, which somehow made matters worse. Suppose I chickened out, then what?

It was like the time I visited the Coliseum in Rome, pondering the fate of humble Christians being thrown to the lions...

Now it was my turn.

A red brick beast awaited...

Sunny, a bit breezy and quite cool – I was clutching my bulky fake-fur leopard-skin jacket. If I made it to the top, I knew it would be extremely chilly and cold up there...

(But I would be shivering and shaking enough already!)

We arrived, and like the time before at the Bancroft Mill in Barnoldswick, Nick began rigging us out with microphones ready for the climb. Fred suggested I wear a harness with a massive hook attached, in case I 'froze' on the ladder on the way up. I could then hook myself to a rung, he said, until I was either composed enough to carry on – up or down – or perhaps be rescued by him!

I took further instruction that I shouldn't grip the ladder too tightly (he's gotta be kidding, surely!). He called it 'the grip of death' when people did that, because they got pins and needles and couldn't move.

Just as I was being fitted with the microphone, a gust of wind took hold of Fred's cap, suddenly whipping the prized possession off his head and landing it in the top of a big sycamore tree. Fred scaled a high brick wall so he could reach the bottom branches, and then he was away like some monkey up a tree to retrieve it. He stayed there in the tree regaining his breath, swinging about like King Kong as he stuck the cap firmly back in place, shouting: 'Aye, I've got it, I've got the bastard.'

It was time...

For what seemed like forever, I stood at the base of the chimney gazing skywards. The sturdy wooden ladders petered out into a thin red stripe right up to the top. They were lashed together with blue nylon rope, wrapped neatly around iron 'dogs' or hooks knocked firmly into the joints of the ancient brickwork, the very fabric of the chimney. At the top few feet, high above us, were two sets of tubular scaffolding staging, bearing 'lolly stick' planks of wood laid around it in a big square shape, just like you see on television.

It all looked very flimsy against the broken blue sky as Fred confidently demonstrated the way I should ascend the ladder by holding on to the sides and not the rungs. Apparently, he pointed out, if a rung broke you had slightly more chance of avoiding plunging to your demise since you would have something to grab on to, in case of an accident!

He told me of a steeplejack long ago who had fallen off a ladder holding onto it like this, flailing the flesh off both his hands right down to the bare bone through terrible friction burns on the way down.

Better to lose your skin to the bone than get scraped up on a shovel, he said. I got the impression Fred was enjoying himself.

My nerves were steadied by young Jack who, like Fred, seemed born to climb; it was almost second nature. He was going up to the top of the chimney as well. He'd been up once when he was nine and several times since; he said: 'It's really great, Sheila – you'll love it.'

I managed a weak smile.

Simon bounded off up the ladder first, carrying my fake-fur jacket and Nick's heavy camera on his back, followed enthusiastically by Jack and finally Nick himself. I knew this was the moment of truth... My impression of the scene was wonderful and awful at the same time. The first few rungs seemed OK. Then a few more and then more still ... not as bad as I thought it might be, and Fred was behind me. He kept on shouting up: 'Go on, cock – you'll be all right – just keep going.'

I had got up to about the halfway stage and couldn't resist having a peek down. I know people say you should never do this, but it was just too tempting. Only halfway up, and the sight was unimaginable! Cars looked like Dinky toys, the roads narrowed off into dark lines, lined with Monopoly houses and the view was terrific. A strange feeling comes over you, something like a mixture of horror and uncertainty, as if in some way you cannot fully trust yourself not to go berserk, jumping off, screaming: 'WHEEE ... LOOK – see! I can FLYIEEE...'

Slight giddiness took hold as that thought crossed my mind.

The wind whistled around my ears and I plodded on slowly; in mid-air by now, thoughts of sky, land, hard ground and gravity. I was panting, out of breath, my mouth was dry and my lungs hurt. My arms and hands were weary, and I had a touch of pins and needles coming on in my wrists. I called to Fred about this frightening sensation. Not surprised, he shouted up, 'It's the grip of death like I told you about. Let go a bit and you'll be alright.'

Let go a bit? Was he serious?

He kept telling me to relax a bit more ... not hold onto the ladder so hard, lean away from it slightly.

The guardians of my mortal soul were watching intently...

My legs were fine and taking the strain well. But I was getting a bit worried about my wrists and, as we approached the first set of staging, they were feeling very numb indeed. I shuddered at the prospect of not being able to hold on much longer, visualised the shovel he'd mentioned, and tried to put it out of my mind. I gazed down … the red line of ladders now petered out in reverse: down towards the narrow base of the chimney.

In some of his earlier films I had seen Fred wrap a leg around the ladder so he could remain there, fixed, whilst his arms moved freely doing something else, and he gave me a 'dee-monster-ation' as he called it.

I reached the first set of staging; the ladder continued up the chimney wall behind the plank at chest level. Fred came up behind me, standing on the next rung down, and explained how I should proceed. I had to let go with my right hand, he instructed, and grip the ladder just above the plank, and do the same again with the left hand. I had to compose myself and work up enough courage simply to let go of the ladder with one hand.

I had by now managed successfully to get both hands above the level of the plank. Fred then instructed me to go up a few more rungs, leaving just my right foot on the rung; I should swing my left knee onto the plank. I had to transfer all my weight onto that knee, hoisting myself up with both hands onto the plank. Then I had to take my right foot away from the relative safety of the ladder and slither as best I could on to a couple of narrow wooden planks two hundred foot up from the ground.

It was all very disorientating; I felt light-headed.

Eventually I jostled myself into a sitting position with my back flat up against the brick chimney, gazing in awe all around me. My feet were dangling off the edge of the plank, hanging free in space. It was like floating. The lingering feeling I might at any moment turn weird and suddenly jump off still remained, but I was able to relax slightly now that I'd finally got up there.

The worst thing so far about the entire experience was the disconcerting way the staging wobbled with every vibration each time a member of our group moved around. It did not feel safe or stable, although common sense told me it must be, as long as I didn't do 'owt daft'.

I placed my entire trust in Fred's thirty-odd years career as a steeplejack and tried to stop worrying about the movement and capture the moment instead. Everyone else decided to climb up to the next set of staging a few feet above our heads to the very top of the chimney. I knew I would have to attempt this after bravely coming this far. Fred again advised and instructed me what to do...

Another encounter with the ladders. The same process again to get up onto the next staging, so I got back onto the ladder lashed up against the chimney. And I did it!

I succeeded in standing up this time on the second stage of planking, making a lunge for the brickwork around the top of the chimney, wanting to cling on like grim death. But Fred immediately shouted: 'Whoaaa! Be bloody careful, you'll bring the whole lot down, cock!'

He was referring to the brickwork which was unstable and very crumbly indeed. I scrutinised the masonry; like Fred had advised, it looked dangerous with pockets of light showing through the joints. It was liable to be dislodged easily. I moved further, walking with caution, grasping the cold, grey scaffolding tubes for all I was worth. Up at the top of the chimney it was scary, freezing cold and very windy – but exhilarating too.

I glanced over towards Simon for my coat, but Fred – full of devilment as usual – had taken it and was wearing it himself: 'Bloody lovely this thing – could have done with one YEARS ago for this job, nice and soft and a pocket for your fags too!' There he was ... fit for a part in *Dynasty*, poised to rival Joan Collins togged out in fake leopard-skin, big padded shoulders, demonstrating what the very best dressed steeplejack should be wearing this season ... complete with jaunty, oily flat cap!

I managed to whip out my camera for some superb shots not only of Fred in his glamorous new apparel, but the surrounding scenery as well. We stayed up there for a while. Nick got his footage, Jack was having a great time, and Fred still insisted on parading around showing off in my jacket to the sky above ... uninhibited, funny and completely confident in his domain.

Then, eventually, it was time to go down.

That part was much, *much* worse, believe me.

You have to kneel down at the very edge of the plank, dangling one foot in space, blindly seeking for a rung on the unseen ladder. I tried a couple of times but I was frightened of overbalancing and toppling off.

Fred got onto the ladder first and guided my foot towards the nearest available rung under the staging. As he got my foot in the right position, there came the terrifying moment when I had to place my entire weight on that foot, swing down with my other leg and find another rung, which I couldn't see. It took a while, but finally I was perched on the ladder. Then I had to repeat the performance of letting go with one hand to grasp the ladder under the plank. It seemed far trickier and more alarming than on the way up. I had to repeat this performance on the lower staging, fear not diminished by any kind of familiarity.

A sigh of relief when, finally, I was able to descend. We were just over halfway down, when Fred chirped up, 'Look over there, love – that's your shadow – see that little bump?' I turned my head to catch sight of the long dark shadow of the chimney cast in a nearby field and it looked absolutely massive! Both our shadows were on the side of the chimney: tiny blobs, barely visible. I realised the enormity of the situation and suddenly froze for a moment or two. Fred coaxed me; within a short while, I was able to continue down the ladder and we were off again. Several feet from the ground, I got quite confident, and quickly stepped up the pace. Then, I felt something different underfoot and heard Fred protest strongly, 'Ow! Go easy, cock... Yer've stood on me bloody 'ed, like!'

I was extremely relieved to leap off the last rung, and looked up again.

I could not believe what I had done! What an amazing experience... I later went on the Pepsi Max Big One in Blackpool with Fred, but it was *nothing* compared to this for thrills and an adrenaline rush. It was truly a white-knuckle chimney climb, and it was amazing to think that Fred had done this almost daily for most of his life.

Around now, Fred and I were wrapped up in anticipation of our wedding and the new television series due to start filming soon. As expected, he left all the planning to me, flatly stating, 'I'm bloody useless at owt like that!'

I had thought up a novel idea and Fred was all for it. As mentioned previously, since I was a little girl spanners – or 'sturtumps' as I called them – have always intrigued me. I love the curves and symmetry of all the different sizes and used to pinch them from my dad's toolbox and dress them up like little dolls in outfits.

During my many foraging expeditions into Fred's workshed, I had come across dozens and dozens of spanners, all stacked up inside grey metal filing-cabinet drawers. These had fired my imagination, along with some massive nuts and bolts I had found from many of the iron bands around the big mill chimneys which Fred had repaired over the years.

I had a quirky idea to feature these in our wedding reception as table decorations and carry a big 'sturtump' with silk flowers wrapped around it as my bridal bouquet. But first, everything had to be prepared by some cleaning. Fred set up a cement mixer in the back yard and placed the carefully chosen 'sturtumps' inside with some abrasive stuff he'd found. It worked like a charm and gradually they all came out free of oil, grease, grime, rust and all the other stuff I didn't want marking the white damask tablecloths on our big day.

Next, Fred tackled the nuts and bolts in the same way, ready for the next stage: *painting everything gold!*

With the whole lot hanging up on a wire, we sprayed them with gold paint and left them drying resplendently in the sunlight, like strange, new-found treasure.

A local mill owner in Bolton, whose property was due for demolition, had given Fred a number of old bricks. They were lovely, unusual quaint old ones, with a sort of 'leg' attached at each corner. Their purpose was originally for use in the mill cellar, where they lay abandoned. In the halcyon days of the textile industry, they were used for stacking large bales of raw cotton which were placed on the floor in a flooded cellar to keep the cotton damp and humid. These cute brick legs held up the bales and kept them dry.

An idea dawned: they were destined to be table decorations at our wedding. I named them my 'Geevor bricks' (after an old Cornish tin mine Fred was to visit on the *Industrial Age* series).

The Geevor bricks were soon ready for decoration with candles and silk flowers, after I'd used a thin coat of clear matt varnish to bring out their terracotta beauty. Fred drilled a small hole in the top of each one and inserted a stiff copper wire. With this in place, he drilled each church candle and placed it down hard on the heated copper wire, making the bricks into candle bases.

My best pal, Christine Jones, whom I had known since we were window dressers together many years before, volunteered to do the flowers. I dropped off about sixty spanners, dozens of nuts and bolts, the Geevor bricks – oh, and the special, rather large 'sturtump' destined to be my bouquet – at her house on the outskirts of Bolton and left her to this seemingly impossible task.

As usual, Christine despaired of me and my funny ways. She showed me a photo album of her sister's wedding, where she had done all the beautiful flower arrangements. I think she was half hoping I may just change my mind about using the raw building materials and iron tools, which were now sprawled all over her front room carpet!

May 1998 was a lovely time. I was caught up in the wedding plans and often travelled around the country with Fred.

Filming of *Fred Dibnah's Industrial Age* was to begin a month later, continuing over a number of weeks into July, August and the beginning of September. The dates had to be planned around work commitments like steam rallies.

I looked at this remarkable man and what he was wearing shortly before the start of filming. A worn and faded red-checked work shirt with rolled up sleeves, the usual faded blue engine driver's jacket full of rips and holes, sometimes a saggy, badly bobbled 'train spotter' sweater underneath – which he'd had for about eighteen years. Plus his own unmistakeable trademark: a disgusting slimy and smelly old cloth cap, full of oil and other unmentionables. The curious way his trouser legs always seemed to be at odds with each other, hanging 'one-in-one-out' of grimy, black army work boots, tied up with laces knotted in several places, wouldn't pass muster either. I remarked about it, and decided we would have to do something a bit different for the programmes without ruining his image, smartening him up – or worse – *modernising* him.

We kept the old cap for use in the workshops but set off in search of a new one. Entering into the spirit of the occasion, he splashed out and bought three at once; one was going to be saved for our wedding. I didn't mind that he was going to wear a flat cap on our big day – in fact I expected it – but insisted it would have to be a new, clean one. As it turned out, Fred reverted to wearing his 'fried mushroom' oily lookalike (as I called it) for his first debut as a TV presenter ... but it was firmly banned from the wedding on pain of death!

I discussed an idea I had for a good television image with him. If he dressed up similar to men in some of the old photographs in his industrial books, he would not only look the part but would feel very comfortable. So we went shopping, first to the place that made his engine drivers' jackets, and ordered several smart dark blue ones with a mandarin-style collar. The jackets would be made out of polyester instead of the usual faded cotton. I suggested a granddad-style collarless striped shirt in pale blue fabric with a waistcoat and watch chain, just like they had worn in the old days. Because Fred said Brunel had always worn moleskin trousers, I chose black jeans in brushed fabric. I found a cheap clothing outlet in Blackpool and bought three of the type of shirts from a bargain rail. The young shop assistant chewed gum and casually remarked as she packed the bag: 'They're out of fashion now, these, love – that's why they are reduced.'

I thought to myself, 'Blimey! If only you knew!'

Fred was booked to attend a rail festival in Doncaster. Betsy was low-loaded to her destination, and we set off in the car as usual. Nathan, Jack and Roger were with us. Jack was looking forward to the trip very much because of his great interest in steam trains, and we relished the usual fare of pop, crisps and chocolate as we headed eagerly over the hills to our destination.

It was a gathering to commemorate the sixtieth anniversary of the famous A4 class locomotive *Mallard* breaking the world speed record on 3rd July 1938.

It was midday, and all five of us had been invited to a civic lunchtime function held in honour of the town's council and local dignitaries. The mayor would be in attendance, with Fred as the guest of honour. The function was a few miles from the site and we decided, for the sake of the local press, that we would arrive at the venue on Betsy.

We all clung on as she trundled on along the roads, hissing and finding what seemed to be every manhole and cat's eye in the surface of the bumpy tarmac. A police escort helped stop the traffic at roundabouts, all of which Fred thought was a waste of time. He quipped sarcastically, 'If you see this big lumbering ten ton of iron coming at you, you'll bloody stop if you've any sense.'

Hooting her steam whistle, people responded with a friendly 'beep-beep' as they passed by in their cars. I had learned the hard way just how black you become when travelling on the engine – even on a short ride – so I was glad that I'd tied my hair back and was wearing a dark outfit. By now the lads all resembled juvenile chimney sweeps from the Victorian era and Fred – as usual – was covered from head to toe in coal dust and oil, loving each minute as we rumbled on.

We arrived at the venue in a cloud of spewing black sulphur and white-hot steam. A bright red carpet, rolled out for the guests, soon fell prey to uneven black spots of soot issuing forth from the engine's funnel. Fred skilfully parked up behind a new Vauxhall Cavalier, the driver of which jumped out, fearful of the big green iron thing looming up in his rear-view mirror and the unfamiliar hiss of steam in the next parking bay. 'Yer alright, mate – it won't move forward any,' Fred shouted above the din. Frowning, the man did not look convinced and hopped back into his car and hit forward gear, pulling quickly out into the road with a blink of his right indicator.

It had started drizzling and we were soaked as well as covered in soot and oil. We looked wet 'n' wild, like a bunch of half-crazed travellers, as all five of us plodded up the soiled carpet ready to be greeted by the waiting crowds sheltering from the rain just inside the double doors.

Fred prepared to hold court. Men in their best suits, pressed shirts, silk ties and with creamy white hands stepped forward. Ladies dressed in pale pastel colours, formal elegance befitting any mother of the bride at a smart wedding, wore hats, accessories and sophistication. Everyone jostled for a better view of Fred, eager to make his acquaintance, and we were handed glasses of champagne as we entered the foyer. Smiles all round, irrespective of the sight and state of us. I woefully noticed one of my ex-army boots had left clear impressions of oil and soot on the carpet. Young Roger had innocently done the same on the polished bevelled glass of the mahogany door with his oily hands.

The ripe, opulent smell of perfume and cigar smoke wafted above the sound of excited voices as we were accompanied to the large room where the luncheon buffet was laid out. There was an air of ceremony as speeches and toasts were read out to the seated crowd. Responses were made, and the buffet finally declared open by the mayor. Hungrily, we herded forward like starving urchins in need of food and sustenance, leaving behind the smell of engineering industries of a bygone era.

Afterwards, as usual, Fred again held court.

He heartily shook many of the proffered clean, well-manicured hands; no one seemed to mind a bit but I did wonder about the inevitable cleaning bill afterwards. And about the effects of small sooty hands on the pristine, white damask tablecloths of the banqueting tables as Jack, Roger and Nathan wiped their dirty fingers after eating cream cakes!

Finally, we all clambered aboard Betsy to return to the rail festival for the rest of the day.

CHAPTER 5
Bricks, spanners and
the final knot

'Sheila and Fred married at Mere Hall, September 26th 1998.'

*I*t was a busy time; I was rushing around preparing for our final move to Bolton, between more engagements and driving around the country with Fred. There seemed to be no end to it. Filming was due to start and Fred would be away from home on location for five days at a time, in between doing steam rallies at weekends.

Then one day Fred had a mishap...

Disaster! Cleaning my teeth was never one of my strong points when I were a kid; so of course I've ended up with many sets of plastic ones over the years. They have all ended up in quite a state, busted and all that. And on this particular occasion, the BBC were coming to pick me up, and take me off filming in Yorkshire for the new Industrial Age series. So I decided I would polish up the plastic that morning, ready for it.

I'm up in the bathroom, polishing away with the toothbrush and the toothpaste – and

I dropped the buggers in the sink – and they broke into two halves! It's now something like quarter-past eight in a morning and I only had a bit of time before they all arrived. Bloody hell ... I didn't know what to do. I hadn't any spare ones! I mean, it's not like a pair of glasses that you can possibly do without, is it?

Anyway, there's many dental laboratories around Bolton, so I got the Yellow Pages out, and I selected one or two of 'em. I rang the first one – no reply.

Desperation's now setting in!

I rang another one, and the person came on and said: 'Oh yeah ... we are at such-and-such a place, come now and we'll do them for you.' I set off in my Land Rover, and had difficulty in finding this place. You always imagine dental laboratories to be places of a fairly hygienic condition! Well, the only place I could find – they hadn't even got a number on the door – was the most unbelievable scruffy place, with the filthiest door and windows you've ever seen. It looked like semi-derelict! I thought, 'Well, this has gotta be it...' I knocked on the door and nothing happened for a bit, then the door opened, and this filthy carpet was revealed. I thought, 'No, this can't be it!'

I stood there and said, 'Is this such-and-such dental laboratory?'

'Oh yeah ... I'll go and get the man who is in charge.'

He opened another door, and the vision got even worse, with the filth and what have you. I thought to myself, 'Teeth or no bloody teeth – I'm not having mine mended here!' So I just legged it quick and got in the Land Rover. Then I went to another place and they couldn't do it, by which time it's getting towards nine. I rang Sheila and asked her to get ready to give David a ring on his mobile, and tell him what had happened, in case I couldn't get them fixed until later. Anyway, I eventually ended up finding one that did emergency repairs and I explained I needed them because I was going to be on the telly. After that, we managed to get off to do the filming, without much delay!

It was Friday, and Fred was due to return from location to attend another rally over the weekend. Nathan and I were to accompany him as usual. It was Nathan's thirteenth birthday on the 25th of June, also his last day at his old school in Blackpool. I packed up our final few things into the car, picked him up from school and headed off for our new life in Bolton.

By late summer, I was getting a bit cheesed-off with going to steam rallies each weekend. Fred and I had not much time to ourselves lately but, thankfully, the end of filming and the rally season was not that far off.

There were also a few after-dinner talks to attend and life became a whirr of travel, filming, interviews and personal appearances for Fred. He took it all in his stride as usual and arrived back home after the filming, ready to do another rally in mid-Wales. It was the school holidays, and Jack and Roger were over for a visit from the Isle of Man.

By now, I saw to it that the rallies were very well organised for us, including a courtesy caravan on site for our exclusive use so we could have a break. We could also store merchandise safely under lock and key before returning to the comfort of a hotel each evening. We drew up alongside the low-loader carrying Betsy and were directed to the caravan by one of the field marshals, who told us that it was unlocked and ready for us.

Nathan went off to seek out the caravan, whilst Fred and I chatted away. The rally looked quite a small affair, perched up on top of a broad, flat plain, which the cruel wind blew across relentlessly. I was thinking how glad I was to have brought a jumper with me when Nathan suddenly returned. 'Hey, Mom!' he said. 'There's a naked bloke having a wash in our caravan!'

Inquisitively, I trailed behind him to find a middle-aged man without teeth, naked from the waist up, dripping in grey suds, rubbing a purple towel around the back of his broad, pock-marked neck. 'Won't be long, sweetheart – you can bring your gear in about ten minutes.'

'Don't call me sweetheart, and why are you here?'

'They said I can use this place. I'm sleeping in here tonight, love.'

I enquired as to how this had come about and stood my ground as he explained that the organisers had mentioned the caravan would not be used by us at night. So they deemed it fit to give permission for him to sleep amidst hundreds of pounds worth of our merchandise and be trusted with a key at the same time, did they? I noticed all the camping paraphernalia scattered haphazardly around and caught a strong whiff of stale booze hanging in the air.

I told the man it would not be possible to remain in the caravan, that it was booked subject to contract solely for our own use. A row broke out, and he got the lot – both guns blazing. I endured a bit of return abuse before storming off in search of someone in charge.

My first introduction to the organisers was full of hostility. I informed them we required exclusive use of the caravan at all times. I could see them thinking 'we've got a right awkward one here'. I tried to make them appreciate how we couldn't trust a complete stranger to oversee the safety of many hundreds of pounds' worth of merchandise. Someone eventually offered the man alternative digs for the night and resolved the matter amicably – and since the other caravan was closer to the beer tent that somehow seemed to make everything all right!

We left the field to search for our hotel and found it, a quaint white pub called The Fostressle Arms (we later named it The Stressful Arms), a little up the road from the rally field.

'Hello, you have a booking for the next two nights,' I said to the landlord.

He recoiled, seeming a bit puzzled. He glanced at each of us in turn, shuffling about a bit from foot to foot. 'We didn't expect three children as well,' he said. 'We can put them in a room near yours, but it's not very nice...'

All five of us were escorted through the unremarkable lounge area of the pub and up some narrow stairs at the side of the bar. I was sober as a judge at the prospect of what lay ahead. The stale reek of tobacco hung like fog in the thick air, and Fred and I were shown into a large dingy room which had been cheaply furnished back in the sixties. It was waiting for the next hapless occupants.

By now, Fred was highly tuned to my outspoken ways and, as he saw my face, he murmured, 'Don't start – it's only for a couple of nights. Don't cause a row, cock.' I pulled a face at him.

The smaller room across from ours held two single, saggy beds, covered in faded pink and yellow candlewick bedspreads. A battered old worktop ran along one side with disused paint cans perched on top and, a dirty, narrow sash window cloaked in bleached-out curtains let in some pale light. The room had at some point been used as a small kitchenette and was now a storeroom-cum-emergency bedroom. A big, ugly three-phase meter hummed noisily away in the corner nearest the door.

Roger, aged seven, started crying, fearful of the sound and sight of the meter and the horrible room. Then Jack started up: 'I want to sleep with you, Dad, in your room.'

'I do too, Dad – this place gives me the creeps!'

Before long, both boys were in full protest about the sleeping arrangements – and we still hadn't sorted out a third bed for Nathan!

The landlord shifted about, bewildered, and waited for a gap in conversation as we all continued to protest loudly. He mentioned a guest-house over the back of the car park, where they would put up one of the children. Anyone would think we had suggested sending them to an enemy encampment and Jack and Roger objected noisily. Being the oldest of the three boys, Nathan bravely volunteered, saying he really didn't mind. Both of the youngest continued with a full-scale paddy and Fred and I escaped back downstairs for a well-earned drink.

After junior World War Three had finally ended, teatime arrived.

'What have you got in the vegetarian line?' I enquired.

'Well, we can do you some chips and salad.'

'I'll have chips and salad then.'

We managed to placate the boys around bedtime, and snuggled them down in the rickety beds. Roger wanted Fred's cap, and drifted off to sleep sniffing the familiar smells of oil and daddy for comfort and reassurance. I went with Nathan across to the guesthouse which turned out to be run by a lovely old Welsh lady with snowy-white hair.

Fred and I finally settled down in our brown Formica time-warp for any-thing but a peaceful night's kip. Music and male singing blared out from downstairs for what seemed like half the night. I got up and opened a win-dow as wide as it would go to disperse the evil stench of dozens of cig-arettes wafting up to our room and threatening to gas us in our – so far

– elusive sleep. Why anyone should want to fill healthy, clean lungs with that evil poison is beyond me, and Fred said he was glad he didn't smoke anymore ... unromantically adding that the reason he had stopped was because his ex-wife had offered him 'extra nookie' on a Thursday night as a bribe!

Somewhere in the distance, when all was mercifully quiet at around 1.30am, the loud, tinny intermittent 'tink' of a fire alarm needing a new battery frazzled our nerves even further. We had also discovered that the room did not possess any running water or a lock on the door ... and someone had stepped into the room during the course of the night, mumbling, 'Ooops! Sorry, pal...'

The rally went along like most rallies those days, and was successful for the organisers and for us. We spied our chance early on Sunday and ventured out for a bit of a walk around the exhibitors' stalls, selling everything from army surplus to teapots and second-hand scrap car parts. Fred spotted an old cast-iron oil lamp base on one stall, made from opaque cream glass and brass blackened through storage and age, and enquired: 'How much, mate?'

'Give us a tenner.'

'I'll buy you that, cock!' he offered as he examined the raised casting on the base of the lamp. 'Do it up for you and make it rather beautiful.'

Eyes shining like a small excited boy, several weeks later he came indoors covered in muck from 'fettling' it and proudly presented it to me. This was so typical of Fred; he would show his love by doing something like this instead of buying a box of chocolates or flowers.

'Any daft bugger can buy a bunch of bloody flowers or mass-produced cards,' he'd often say.

He was right!

The wedding plans were going well. Christine had nearly finished the flower arrangements. My wedding bouquet, the 'sturtumps' and Geevor bricks all decked out in gold, cream and burgundy silk flowers.

We were to be married at the new registry office in Bolton. Mere Hall is situated in parkland and was built originally by the Dobson family as their home in 1837. I remember the house from my childhood in the mid-sixties. Mum used to take me to play on the slides, swings and roundabouts in the grassy area close to the big house, which was then a public park and playground. The dark stone house of my childhood always appeared rather neglected and a bit scary. Now, by comparison, it stood magnificently transformed into an idyllic location worthy of any couple's most important day.

The elegant hall is set amidst lovingly tended gardens, lawns, shrubbery and trees. As a child, I wore simple white sandals, tartan ribbons and a seersucker, rock-candy pink striped frock as my mum pushed me high on the swings near the big hall. I never once guessed that as an adult I would occupy almost the same spot, standing tall and radiant, dressed in an exquisite cream gown on my wedding day.

Fred had expressed an interest in arriving on his steamroller. I wondered about the effects on his formal smart black suit and jazzy waistcoat. There was no shortage of ideas for this wedding. Both liking foraging – disregarding the odd cut finger or two – we'd enjoy a good root around amidst the various weighed-in metals and alloys at the local non-ferrous scrapyard. I came across a heavy brass nut, about five inches in diameter.

At first, Fred was a bit reluctant about buying it, not realising what I wanted it for. He moaned that it might cost about ten quid or so because it was heavy, saying, 'What the bloody hell do you want THAT THING for?' But I had the idea of polishing it up and stamping the sides with our names, the date and location of our wedding. A *real* keepsake and it would make the most excellent centrepiece and talking point for our top table! We paid for it, Fred relieved that it had only cost three quid, and brought it home where he tackled the task of polishing and stamping the relevant information on it.

It was breathtakingly beautiful when he'd finished and said on the side: *'Sheila and Fred Married at Mere Hall, September 26th 1998.'* I was delighted.

The industrial theme continued, with some striking wedding stationary depicting the names of Jack, Roger and Nathan, a chimney – complete with scaffolding – with Fred ascending a ladder to me, his bride. Steam engines, gas lamps, everything was on there that mattered to Fred and me.

A few weeks before our wedding, Nathan went to Ibiza on holiday with his grandparents for a fortnight. So, at David's invitation, I was able to travel around on location with Fred for the last two weeks of filming *Industrial Age*.

We visited many places during that memorable fortnight. Everything was such a whirl, but as I recall, the general routine went something like this. We would get up about 7.00 a.m., have breakfast, and be out on location by about 8.30 to 9.00 a.m. If we were lucky, we got a quick break for a bite to eat at lunchtime and then filming would continue until teatime. The next location could be miles away in another town, maybe in another part of the country, so we would set off for our destination, arriving hopefully at the next hotel before 8.00 or 9.00 p.m. We would then quickly get washed and changed, going down for dinner at around 9.30 p.m. Bedtime was around midnight, and next day we would repeat the procedure.

On one particular occasion we were travelling to North Wales to film at the Welsh Slate Museum at Llanberris, in Caernarfon, Gwynedd. Fred and I had been touring in my humble little blue Metro, which had done a remarkable job ferrying us around, albeit at a slightly slower pace than the film crew with their fast cars. David was driving a powerful car; it could easily outstrip my Metro and I had a difficult time keeping up sometimes. Mostly, we would just arrange to meet up at the allocated hotel. (We were *always* last to arrive!)

We set off for Gwynedd. David and the crew zipped off. As usual, we plodded on along the road in our modest transport. Routes into parts of Wales are winding and full of sharp bends and eventually we caught up with David, with his red brake light on every few yards. Now, one outstanding feature about that little blue Metro was the way it could nip into a tight bend much better than a big car. Mischievously, I thought we would make up for always being last. I soon managed to overtake David and from there on drove like a rally driver, negotiating bends, expertly accelerating into them, Fred grasping tightly onto his seatbelt as I continued whipping us round without losing revs.

We arrived at our destination chuckling like a couple of excited kids, and once checked in, we bounded upstairs with the luggage. We had arrived before anyone else on this occasion and were going to have a bit of fun! Downstairs in the bar, ready to outdo David, we quickly got drinks and sat in two comfy chairs, recovering from the thrill of the drive. Within minutes the camera and sound crew arrived, highly amused that we were first there for a change. 'W-ayah, look who's here!' one of them said in jest.

Then David arrived. Surprised, he blinked as he entered and saw us seated, seemingly relaxed and having drinks. I piped up nonchalantly, 'Hiya, David, what took you so long – we've been here ages, haven't we, Fred?'

'Aye, we've been waiting ages for you, mate,' Fred joined in.

© *The Oliver Collection*

Our wedding invitations, designed and kindly donated by The Oliver Collection, Redruth, Cornwall.

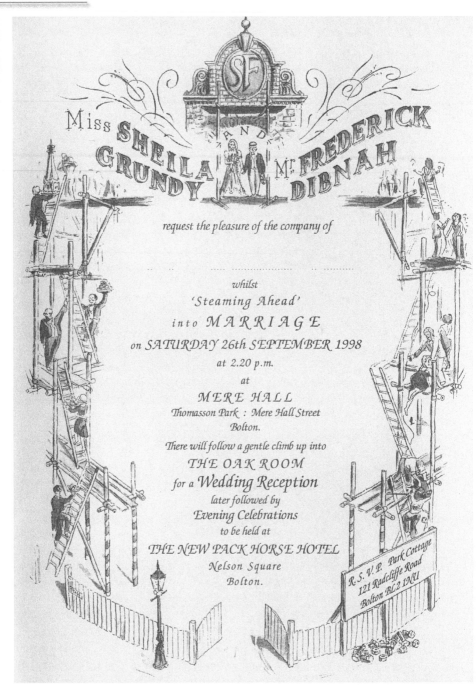

Miss SHEILA GRUNDY AND Mr FREDERICK DIBNAH

request the pleasure of the company of

....

whilst
'Steaming Ahead'
into *MARRIAGE*
on *SATURDAY 26th SEPTEMBER 1998*
at 2.20 p.m.
at
MERE HALL
Thomasson Park : Mere Hall Street
Bolton.

There will follow a gentle climb up into
THE OAK ROOM
for a *Wedding Reception*
later followed by
Evening Celebrations
to be held at
THE NEW PACK HORSE HOTEL
Nelson Square
Bolton.

R.S.V.P. Park Cottage
121 Radcliffe Road
Bolton BL2 1NU

Inside the wedding invitation, you can see the beautiful attention to detail.

A happy day. 26th September 1998. To the left, is my lovely lifelong friend and bridesmaid Christine Jones. Christine and I worked together as window dressers at the Bolton Co-Op in Oxford Street, at the side of the Town Hall. I first noticed Fred before he became famous, working on the Town Hall clock as I looked up one day.

Note my big 'Sturtump', a spanner carried as a bouquet. I have loved spanners since being a little girl, and they made the day complete at our wedding reception as table decorations, along with giant nuts and bolts and bricks as candle holders!

Fred was getting impatient with all the photographers and said to me whilst posing for this picture 'I wish they'd bloody hurry up, I'm dying for a pint now after all that lot'.

Fred designed our wedding cake himself, based on 'The Iron Church' in Bolton. It was so heavy it took two men to lift it, and we were eating fruit cake for months afterwards. Note me sitting on the staging awaiting my bridegroom, as Fred ascends the ladder.

Fred had an intense dislike of dancing and had been worrying about the first dance more than getting married again for the third time!

Fred always liked his wife to light the fire at chimney felling jobs. From this close, the cracks in the structure were very visible and I was always terrified in case it collapsed. Fred accomplished more than 90 successful chimney-felling jobs in his career as a steeplejack.

My chimney climb in 1998, the year we were married. I think Fred was proud of me on that day – but I often wondered later how he had managed to do this job for more than 35 years.

On my way up, I suddenly realised what I'd let myself in for. Fred was on the ladder beneath me and kept urging me to go faster. Unless you have ever climbed a vertical ladder, you don't realise how difficult it is.

I made it to the top – 'LOOK NO HANDS'!!

I made it and look proud of my
220ft climb!

The wonderful lady whom I
call my guardian angel, my
good friend and agent Jennie
Storr of The Speakers Agency
based in Lincoln. As I fought
a six year battle against Fred's
estate on the grounds of
'reasonable provision' Jennie
had faith in me and secured
bookings as an after dinner
speaker.

David replied offhandedly, not seeing the humour: 'Well ... it's not really a difficult journey, is it? And there's no real rush is there?'

But the most memorable event of the filming was going down the shaft at Big Pit Mining Museum in Blaenavon, South Wales. Located in the north-eastern corner of the coalfield, to the west of Afon Lwyd, the Big Pit, originally sunk in 1860, is open for guided tours and is incredible. A working coal mine until 1980, it remains very similar to how it must have been back then. We went down into the bowels of the earth for three hundred feet or so, escorted by two guides who had originally been miners, and got out of the iron cage at the bottom of the shaft. We learned that it was the opening of the Blaenavon Ironworks in 1789 that first created a demand for coal in this area; indeed, the sweeping valleys mean nature is all around. We walked along one tunnel, sampling the same atmosphere generations of miners must have dreamt about during a short night's rest, imagining conditions families could only have feared for their loved ones.

A wide, visible seam of glistening black lucre, immovable bands of it set in the timeless rock. Artefacts here too: ancient and modern tools and machinery waiting, almost, for the return of umpteen pairs of capable hands to set them in motion again. Dark stable stalls, where miserable pit ponies lived out their short, cruel lives until as late as 1967, still bearing cheery names of the long-dead animals. A forgotten steam winch once used to pull the heavy and now rusted pit-tubs along the underground tracks.

And everywhere the palpable feel of toil and struggle.

Back on the surface, the preserved winding engine house engrossed Fred, although the steam winding engine made by Fowler of Leeds had sadly been removed in 1952. The current engine consists of a cylinder drum, nine feet in diameter, arranged in two halves and driven through gearing by a 340bhp Metropolitan Vickers induction motor. An eerie, almost melancholy screeching sound emitted and echoed over the surrounding valleys as each drum, with its own powerful braking calliper, wailed out as the cages descended the shaft into the Welsh earth or returned to the surface.

I liked the marvellously preserved pit-baths, imagining miners mucky, exhausted and aching from a weary shift, gratefully scrubbing away at the black dust covering their skins. It is a great privilege to stand on the spot where some of the bravest men in Britain once earned their crust. You can sense your own mortality in a place like this, and I was left with a profound impression of what life for a Welsh coal miner must have been like back then. Tough men indeed: the museum is a token of respect for them, their families, and all they endured. It is a wonderful and awesome place.

Fred had always been interested in the engineering aspect of mining coal: the dark glamour of extracting the black stuff, the danger it represented and the visual images it produced on the landscape.

My two weeks spent travelling around the country gave an insight into how programmes are produced as well as how versatile Fred could be. He took it all in his stride and was never bothered by all the attention.

There was no time to lose when we returned home. The wedding was in a few days' time. Fred decided to drive his steamroller to Mere Hall. An idea of using a white, disposable overall to cover up his wedding suit was suggested, which prompted some wag to shout loudly on his arrival: 'And how was your day at the abattoir, Mr Dibnah?' I was relieved that my transport would be something a little more traditional: a cream-coloured vintage Rolls-Royce.

The day before the wedding, I went to pick up the table decorations from Christine's house. My Metro groaned a bit, loaded down with beautified bricks, spanners, nuts and bolts, and we parked outside the hotel's main door. A helpful young porter supplied us with a two-tiered trolley, grinning and scratching his head as we piled on some of the bricks from the hatchback car. I wheeled them into the foyer towards the reception area. Standing behind the counter was a slightly plump, smartly-attired but sour-faced receptionist talking on the telephone. She replaced the receiver and turned round, eyeing me up and down. She looked at the trolley then unsmilingly at me again and in that best singsong voice, which some hotel receptionists seem to acquire as part of their job, said, 'Can I help you, Madam?'

I explained what I was doing and a look of astonishment crossed her face.

She pointed the way to the storeroom and when Christine and I returned, she enquired somewhat unkindly: 'What do you want bricks and spanners for on your wedding tables?' Unaccustomed to anything out of the ordinary, she laboured on about the strangeness of my wedding decorations. Knowing she thought I was some kind of nutcase, and not feeling like explaining myself further, I just mentioned it might be a bit different...

An odd vacuous look clouded her features and her mouth went down at the corners. Shaking her head, she carried on: 'Humph! Well ... I can't see it myself, but I suppose it takes all sorts.'

(It certainly does, madam!)

I had arranged to spend my last night as a spinster over at Christine's house. I didn't want the bother of having a hen party but had a few quiet drinks with some friends there instead.

I prayed the weather would stay nice for the following day.

Next morning arrived. I had hardly slept and a tight knot of nerves coiled into action as soon as I opened my eyes. Christine nipped off to the hairdressers, whilst I fumbled with my long hair and fretted about which cosmetics to use: gold or brown eye shadow, pink or burgundy lipstick? All too soon, our elegant cream horseless carriage arrived and Christine and I began the ten-minute ride to my destiny.

As we rode up the wide driveway to Mere Hall, the sun came out – although it was a bit overcast – and shone through the trees, making the scene like something from one of the glossy wedding magazines that I'd been diligently thumbing through for the past several months. I could see Fred had already arrived. Unattended, the steamroller chuffed away contentedly at the bottom of the drive, festooned in bows and white ribbons and flanked on either side by onlookers and admirers with cameras.

As our car pulled up near the stone steps leading up to the open doorway, Christine and I were greeted by a crowd of fans and newspaper photographers. Overwhelmed, we both got out of the car and stood posing for pictures. Many requests for smiles later, we were led inside; I was now in a state of wild panic, signalled by the dreaded blotchy red-neck syndrome, which contrasted nicely with my pearl and gold choker.

We were led to a small room so that I could give my personal details to the registrar. Christine acted as my witness for the marriage and all was entered in the large, leather-bound book.

Soon, it was time. I was led into a finely decorated room with cream, gold and red brocade curtains hanging up at the large bay windows I'd only ever viewed before from outside. Fred was standing expectantly before the registrar, looking as nervous as I was feeling; he turned to see me and made a gesture of approval. As I took my place at his side, it gradually began to feel very natural and I relaxed a little. We exchanged our marriage vows, placed a ring on each other's finger, and soon it was time to leave through double doors leading out into the gardens, as *Mr and Mrs Dibnah!*

The fans and photographers were out in full force and the sun was shining for us. It put me in mind of an old saying, 'Everyone will be famous for fifteen minutes'. I thought of that saying as I stood there having pictures taken, everyone shouting their good wishes, throwing confetti and shaking Fred's hand, congratulating him. I looked at Fred, and he was so very happy, grinning from ear to ear.

I mouthed, 'I love you.'

His whole face lit up. 'I love you too, as well, cock!' he replied.

We were the centre of attention; it reminded me of an occasion a few weeks earlier at an event we attended together...

Fred had been invited to the opening night of the new Warner Brothers' cinema at Horwich, on the outskirts of Bolton. It was to be a prestigious event. Actress Shirley Anne Field had been invited; Dame Edna Everage (the alter-ego of Barry Humphries) and Rick Mayall were there, and celebrities from various soaps. We arrived in a taxi to be greeted by an opulent red carpet leading into the building, with metal barriers and rails down each side to keep back the huge crowds. Hundreds of people had turned up to the event. It looked like something from a dazzling Hollywood Oscar party. As we slowly walked up the red carpet, escorted by liveried attendants, a huge cheer suddenly went up. Arms and flags started waving and camera flashes flickered, hands were outstretched – people were pushing and clamouring to get to the front as the press deftly manoeuvred themselves into position.

I turned to see who had arrived after us, thinking it must be some internationally known movie star or singer.

The crowds were all cheering for 'Our Fred'!

'Over here, Fred! Give us your autograph...'

'Here, mate – sign the back of my hand...'

'This way, Fred – thank you!'

Rik Mayall was much harder to approach than Dame Edna, with whom we'd had a nice long chat earlier, but I wanted Rik's autograph for Nathan who was a big fan of *The Young Ones* and *Bottom*. To no avail, I'd spent time trying to get past Rik's entourage and PR assistants. Then, Fred blurted out, 'Here, give me that bloody pen, cock.' He barged right past Rik's followers, approached the man himself and said, ' 'Ere you are, mate, stick yer mark on this paper for me little lad, Nathan!'

By way of explanation, some suit came rushing up to Rik, quickly stating, 'This is Fred Dibnah, the famous steeplejack.'

Rik gazed blankly for a few seconds and distractedly took hold of the proffered paper, saying loudly in his own distinctive style as he began to write: 'To Fred with love, kiss-kiss-kiss.'

'Eh? Yer wot, mate?' Fred immediately snatched the paper without further ado. 'Bloody 'ell an' all,' he said, and quickly strutted back to me, loudly stating: 'Oh, Christ! What kind of unbelievable world is this we live in where blokes are throwing kisses at other blokes? What kind of bloke is he anyway? He's summat else, baby, that guy, I can tell you. Christ almighty!'

As I stood next to my new husband on my wedding day, we paused for similar requests from adoring fans. Finally, we went off together in the cream Rolls-Royce, Fred exchanging the rich smell of oil for the comfort of leather, all the way to the reception at The Pack Horse Hotel. On our arrival outside the hotel, another flock of people bearing cameras, autograph books and good wishes had gathered. The manager brought some champagne flutes out into the street on a silver tray and we posed again for the press in front of Betsy, giggling like a couple of daft kids.

Fred designed our wedding cake himself. It stood nearly four feet tall; a white fondant church steeple, with a clock and gold weather vane, complete with full staging and ladders up the side. It had an edible Fred figure, topped off with flat cap, climbing up a ladder, and in resplendent edibility, sitting on the edge of the staging in a replica of my wedding dress, was me – waiting for my Hippo! The highly detailed steeple was modelled on a local one in Bolton, taken from photographs. Fred wondered whether to climb it or cut it when the time came!

The meal was demolished, the speeches well received and Fred told everyone gathered how he had only £600 in the bank when he first met me and
thanked me glowingly for all the help I'd given him by arranging and taking
over his business affairs.

Eventually, it was time for the evening reception.

I managed to get Fred on the dance floor, which was something of a miracle, as normally he hated it – I think by that time he'd had a good few pints
to aid his two left feet!

I had spent ages – as any bride does – painstakingly getting ready for
the big day. Everything was carefully planned right down to the last detail.
Under my pale golden-beige gown, I wore matching silk and lace underwear.
Fred liked stockings and suspenders, so I had really gone to town on a wed-
ding-night surprise for him: fine, expensive, gauzy stockings with alluring
frilly tops held up by suspenders; exquisitely designed lacy silk bra and deli-
cate matching panties – the full decadent and extravagant lot!

The evening wore on until about two in the morning. I chatted to the last
few remaining guests, scanning around the room to locate my new husband.
Both Fred and I – though hardly the blushing bride – were now ready to
head off towards the bridal suite for our first night together as man and wife.
Tired, but elated after the marvellous day, we entered our suite: I walked,
Fred staggered. We were all alone, with a strategically placed bottle of bubbly

on ice at the side of the bed.

'I'll just freshen up darling,' (they always say that in films, don't they?) I said as I entered the mirrored bathroom, and slipped out of my wedding dress, admiring and adjusting the fine trimmings of my underwear, in anticipation of Fred's tactile approval. Striking a pose in stiletto heels, I sauntered back into the suite. Fred was lying across the bed half-undressed, chuckling as I came through the door. He looked delighted, and said, 'Bloody hell, cock – what's all this then, eh? Phwarrr!'

Unfortunately perfume, lace and smooth female flesh could not compete with the heady effects of about ten gallons of Boddingtons bitter...

We ended the perfect day – sprawled out on the bed! The only thing we could raise between us was a smile, then a chuckle, followed by full-scale hysterical laughter as we writhed together, sniggering and snorting at Fred's drunken inability to do anything other than to keep on laughing. We both fell asleep eventually on top of the bed, until early morning and his resulting hangover. (I had learned my lesson back in Aberdeen, and hadn't imbibed as much alcohol as my new husband.)

So much for 'sexy undies' on your wedding night... I could have worn his blue long-johns full of holes, oil stains and bobbles, and it would not have made one iota of difference. What a wedding night. I needed a miracle to get *him* all steamed up!

Deciding not to go away on honeymoon, we opted to stay at home and renovate the kitchen. Fred had built an extension on the side of the house back in 1983 to accommodate a new kitchen, but since that time it had held only various traction engine parts that were complained about by the two previous Mrs Dibnahs. Being used primarily as a workshop-cum-storeroom, it now contained four large wheels from his Aveling and Porter steam tractor and boxes of old steam engine parts, all of which Fred had been working on for many years. I decided that the wheels and all the rest of the paraphernalia would just have to go elsewhere.

The present kitchen was a small, dark, poorly-ventilated hovel with a super-low stainless steel sink designed for folk less than five feet tall. I christened it 'The Black Hole'. It also sported dingy wall cupboards with sliding glass doors circa the early 1960s, black and white checkerboard tiles and a drab old gas cooker, which any social history museum would have been very proud to own. There was no air extraction to speak of – except to leave the back door open – and a cold grey stone floor completed the vision. With hardly room to swing the proverbial cat in, it was a recipe for hell's kitchen.

Fred looked as though he was about to have kittens when I told him that this particular Mrs Dibnah *most definitely* required a dishwasher, and all new-fangled appliances in her large, new kitchen, which he was going to complete sooner rather than later!

We ordered a smart maroon-coloured, gas-fired Rayburn to run the central heating. Fred went about making a base for it to stand on. We had discussed the possibility of having the front of a Lancashire boiler set into the wall in our new kitchen, near the seating area, complete with water gauges and polished 'legend ring' which gave the age and make of the boiler. Fred's old mate, master boilermaker Alan McEwen, had one in his kitchen.

Fred found two fancy cast-iron pillars from an old mill that was being demolished and adapted and restored them; he placed one upright each side of the base for the Rayburn. They supported a big old heavy beam of wood, which he'd 'adzed' with a special axe, giving it the appearance of having been there forever. Being the craftsman that he was, it looked like a masterpiece when he had finished.

We ordered oak kitchen units and traditional Minton tiles completed the look, with a big iron plaque Fred had always loved off an old mill engine in Bolton.

CHAPTER 6
Have wives - will travel!

'But what do I do if she asks why they all buggered off, eh?'

M arch 1999 was the first time Fred appeared as a presenter on television. What would they make of this new approach?

Letters started to arrive from all over the country, congratulating him on his style of presentation and content of the new programmes. The BBC released a book to accompany the series and organised a signing tour to promote sales. Travelling far and wide, sitting down in bookshops in one or other location, Fred was required to do a bit of a talk first. These 'introductory talks' sometimes lasted well over an hour – and many books were eagerly sought afterwards – all with Fred's copperplate signature.

The BBC also organised other stuff before the showing of *Industrial Age*. Fred was to meet and appear with Vanessa Feltz on *The Vanessa Show*. They arranged for us to stay in a hotel near the studios in Shepherd's Bush. I looked forward to the trip, unlike Fred, whose first reaction was, 'Bloody hell – what do they want me on there for, eh?'

We set off for London on the train, travelling first class as arranged. As the Virgin train sped along, high-powered commuters busied themselves with various laptops and mobile phones, ignoring Fred's loud verbal observations: 'Christ! I couldn't put up with this lark every day. Why the hell does everybody have to go at an unbelievable pace and hundreds of miles to their jobs? Once, a bloke only had to walk down to some works at the end of his street to earn a crust – and now this! Christ – the country's bloody knackered, nobody makes owt these days, daft buggers, and we're raising a generation of morons; half of 'em can afford smart new £20,000 motor cars, but haven't got a clue how it bloody well works!'

A chauffeured car – one of those classy £20,000 numbers – arrived next day for the trip to the studio. I had a little pep-talk with Fred on the way about his tendency to wear his heart on his sleeve in public and warned him to forego the subject of ex-wives, or discussing why they had left.

Now, the only criticism I often had of Fred was his sheer thoughtlessness. He could be unwittingly blunt with some of his trite comments; he didn't mean to be hurtful but they were pretty sexist. His views on women appeared Victorian at best, and he seemed to consider marrying (and divorcing) younger women made him into some kind of swaggering Henry VIII type of character. Sometimes for effect he referred to 'All my wives' or worse still, 'This is the current one, here'. He would also sometimes go into lengthy, private details about his two ex-wives and their new husbands.

He was puzzled why he shouldn't mention the fact that they'd both buggered off. He regaled me with stories about the time when Alison had left and went on to say how 'dolly-birds' had often stopped to eye him up as he parked his Land Rover outside the off-licence when he went for his Guinness!

'I were off women for a bit, then, like,' he mused in a reflective mood. 'Stick to yer bloody steam engines, Fred, keep it in yer pants from now on, I thought to mi'sel, an' all.'

'Well, Fred, stick to your steam engines today if Vanessa asks any personal questions,' I instructed. But knowing he couldn't keep anything to himself, I didn't suppose it would work. Fred always liked the honest and simple truth.

'What shall I say if she asks all about my private life then, eh?'

'Just say you're happily married now and leave it at that!'

'Yeah ... but it's that sort of show where they ask about...'

'No, Fred! Just stick to the other stuff. Nothing about sex.'

'But what do I do if she asks why they all buggered off, eh?'

'For Chrissake, Fred – leave it will you!'

'Oh, bloody hell, woman, stop grumbling at me, will you!'

We were shown to the studio where Vanessa was waiting. She greeted us cheerily and carried on with her preparations for the morning show. A dressing room had been set aside for Fred and we were shown to a communal rest room, where hot coffee and breakfast refreshments were waiting.

Eventually, half-way through telling the stage crew a long story about our neighbour with whom he had an ongoing feud over smoke emissions, Fred was asked to return to the studio floor to run through the interview schedule. Vanessa informed him roughly, about what sort of questions she would be asking.

The show began. Fred and Vanessa both sat in comfortable leather chairs for the rehearsal, talking under the glare of studio lighting before the audience was admitted. She got to the part about his preoccupation with steam engines. 'So, Fred, what does your wife think about your passionate interest in steam engines, then?'

'Oh, she's great, she doesn't mind at all. She likes them!'

The assistant floor manager and crew grinned benevolently and winked at me, standing with Nathan in the wings. The conversation moved swiftly on to other topics; finally, Vanessa rounded off, ready for the next guest's rehearsal.

Fred was instructed what the transmission time would be, and we headed off back towards the dressing room.

We were soon summoned by a girl holding a clipboard. Trailing behind her to the studio, Nathan and I gazed about, waiting for the show to begin. In the wings we were surrounded by cables resembling thick red pipes, similar to ones used by the fire brigade. The crew and sound technicians buzzed around; the cameraman on his crane was poised ready for the opening shots. The credits rolled by and the show was live on air. The magic of television in the making, waiting until it was Fred's turn.

'Please welcome Fred Dibnah, steeplejack!' Vanessa announced.

He shuffled on, a vision in his blue engine driver's jacket and flat cap, beaming that wide grin as usual, raising his hand in a jaunty wave as the audience applauded. Nathan and I watched the interview through a monitor perched on a high trolley. The rapport with the audience was good; the interview was going fine, Vanessa looked radiant and Fred quickly relaxed into the flow of things.

Then we got to it.

Vanessa: 'So then Fred, what does your wife think about your passionate interest in steam engines?'

Fred: 'Well, aye, they all keep BUGGERING OFF and leaving me, don't they!' He swaggered, looking pleased with his statement like a mischievous schoolboy waiting for a reaction.

I swear everybody looked round for a reaction from me. I could have merrily killed him, and was worried in case he went further into the juicy bits of how he'd divorced his second wife for adultery.

All I could think about was why did he have to wear his heart on his sleeve in public like this? It was so typical of him.

We both saw the funny side of it later. 'Well, they do – they all keep buggering off, don't they ... you wouldn't be here if they hadn't, eh?'

'Any wonder, you daft, big Hippo!' I exclaimed. Being candid was just part of his charm, but it was a lot to put up with at times when he got onto the subject of his ex-wives and the reasons for his two divorces.

Fred later undertook many interviews with national and regional newspapers and various radio stations, chatting about his life, passions and interests instead of why he considered his two ex-wives had 'buggered off'! Letters arrived at our home in piles; on average we were now receiving more than a hundred a week. It was a full-time job trying to answer them all, and so I became something of a personal secretary for my husband as well.

Fred depicted as a knowledgeable presenter somewhat diminished the concept in certain sectors of him being a 'fat-bellied, beer-swilling steeplejack' who at times liked nothing more than being a bit of a daft bugger. Some people who, perhaps as a result of earlier programmes, rejected him as being slightly 'ignorant' and a bit of a self-opinionated know-it-all now took him far more seriously. They became aware of his charm and expertise. Only a very knowledgeable man could inject this sort of genuine enthusiasm into such a series, making it leap out from the screen to the viewers at home.

Yes, he was a male chauvinist at times – but so what? Attracting many new admirers as well as his long-time fans, he commanded great respect with his hands-on approach to the subject of our industrial past. His almost childlike wonder and love of all things dangerous, mechanical and long since gone was contagious and helped to revive people's interest in the industrial age. Indeed, the industries and working conditions experienced a generation or so ago now attracted many younger fans, some only eight or nine years old. They wanted to know more about the past and wrote to their flat-capped northern hero for autographs and any information he could give for their school projects.

Fred considered himself a throwback to the past. But for now, the *future* was indeed looking good.

Health and matrimonial troubles, which neither of us could anticipate, were still in the future. We were happy, in love and glad to be alive. He shone with well-being, had boundless energy and lived his life to the full. His positive energy attracted people to him and Fred felt, at long last, that his life was happy.

The *Industrial Age* series was highly successful. Public response and demand for Fred as a presenter was so great that the BBC gave the green light to David Hall for another series later in the year. Research would begin in June, with filming for six weeks in September. The new series would be called *Fred Dibnah's Magnificent Monuments*. This time the format would cover buildings and architecture, examining past engineering, building techniques and craftsmanship employed in building and later in restoring and maintaining them. It was set to be another winner.

In April, Fred was booked to do one of his after-dinner talks in Hull, North Humberside. Because of Fred's dislike of driving cars, I normally ferried him around to the functions and engagements he had to attend. On this occasion, we set off in my Rover Metro. The poor little thing had only known one owner before me and had been immaculate when I acquired it, proudly boasting its very low mileage. We'd stopped hiring cars some time ago and picked out the little Metro, not realising what hell it was in for. It had uncomplainingly trundled around the country many times loaded up with Fred, kids, videos and various other paraphernalia. We had done something like 20,000 miles in just over twelve months and that was now taking its toll.

The driver's seat was a bit askew and various whirrs, creaks and loud rumbles protested regularly during the long, tedious journeys, almost as much as Fred did if I dared stop off along the way at a motorway service station for lunch instead of a nice pub! The car was literally becoming a pain in the neck. My back ached from the deformed seat, and I kept getting pins and needles in my right arm because of the wheel tracking which kept going off to the left, no matter how many times it was fixed – making me constantly pull down hard on the steering wheel, sometimes for hours on end during the longer journeys

So, we embarked on another such trip...

It was a stormy day, raining and a bit blustery, yet quite warm for the time of year. As we climbed over the hills towards Yorkshire, I could hear the rumbling sound of distant thunder. The sky darkened and I put on the car headlamps for safety. We were just over the summit of the M62, when the front passenger side window – without warning – clanked sharply down into the door well, giving us all a shock. Fred tussled with it, trying to pull it back up, all to no avail. I dropped my speed from sixty to thirty, but the wind still howled uncomfortably and whistled around the interior like a typhoon as the rain swept in. Fred held on firmly to his cap as I slowed the little car down further to avoid him losing it altogether. 'Bloody hell, it's alright – we'll get there as long as me cap doesn't fly out the window – slow down a bit, baby!' he instructed.

Now, most people would panic about this situation and call the RAC. But never quite being able to do anything by the book, Fred reached in the back seat for my coat, wrapped it firmly around his head and shoulders, and announced: 'It's not so bad, love – carry on. It'll be alright when we get off the top of this bloody motorway and it stops raining. We'll get to Hull alright

... just pretend yer up a chimney or summat.'

After a few choice words where I called him eccentric, mad and just plain crazy, he was disgruntled by my intention to leave at the next exit to find a garage to do an emergency repair on the window. He made various remarks like: 'What are you worrying about, woman – it's not that far!' but Nathan and I outnumbered him two-to-one by protesting loudly about these travelling conditions. However, it was no use explaining to Fred that you were uncomfortable and freezing cold – all you got back was: 'You want to be at the top of a 250-foot chimney in winter, if you think this is bad, cock!'

So I took matters into my own hands and found a garage not too far from the slip-road exit. I also found out fame is indeed an asset at times – especially on occasions such as these, when you need something urgently. Finding the garage was open, I felt a lot better about the situation – but was crestfallen to discover that they didn't actually do repairs on the spot for the general public. It was a second-hand car outlet.

However, once the salesman copped sight of Fred's oily cap, engine driver's jacket and heard that familiar Boltonian twang announcing, 'Hey, mate! You couldn't tell us where we could get this window mended, could you? Damn thing's knackered, like,' it was a vastly different story!

The manager happened to be a keen Dibnah fan and we were quickly instructed to park up our tired car alongside the many shiny newer vehicles.

As the manager continued waving and excitedly gesticulating to the rest of the staff, 'It's Fred! It's Fred!' a small crowd gathered.

'Aye, I wouldn't care if it was a bloody horrible day or summat – we could have easily managed to get to Hull. Only a bit of bloody rain! Now take the weather when you are up a 200-foot chimney in a storm...'

I was grateful for the piping hot cup of coffee, and I wrapped both hands around it as I listened to Fred telling his tale.

'Lightning were bloody flashin' an all ... boom! boom!'

In the meantime, the mechanic had taken our humble car into the repair and maintenance bay. We sat amidst the fragrance of wax and the shiny, prized exhibits in the showroom listening to Fred 'holding court', the gang of men mesmerised, adding guffaws and asides when he made some particularly funny comment.

When Fred had finally finished his story, one of the sales team jocularly piped up: 'All the money you've made being on telly, Fred, and you're driving around in an old Metro! Why are you doing that, eh?'

'It's not mine, pal – it's the wife's car.'

'Well, buy her a new one, you tight bugger!'

'Have you seen this one over here – good car this – '

'She's after one of them Peugeot 406 things...'

'Oh yes ... but a bit more expensive than the Metro, Fred!'

'Eh, yer wot?'

'Yes ... I'd love one of *those*, Fred...'

'We have one coming next week, only £7,500...'

'Bloody hell, man, I'm not made of money you know. Don't give her any ideas!' Fred stood there, lifting his cap, scratching his bald head, looking nonplussed at where the conversation might lead. 'Me mam and dad would never have guessed one day a man would appear in front of me and say, "Go on, Fred – spend seven thousand quid on a motor car"! Jeez ... what a world we live in, an' all.'

Soon afterwards, we were ready to leave. They had graciously repaired the car for nothing except a few signed photos, a couple of handshakes and a promise from Fred to return for a pie and pint if ever he was in the area.

Realising it would only be a matter of time before it began regularly breaking down and causing an inconvenience or worse, I worried that my beloved little car might become dangerous. But Fred, not seeing any harm in it, said, 'If you think THIS bit of tackle is bad, you should have seen me first bloody Land Rover with the arse hanging out. Alison used to be scared stiff.'

But he *was* concerned about being late for appointments if the Metro broke down, so not long after the Hull trip we began to ponder the idea of a slightly better and more suitable vehicle ... maybe an estate car or something.

Fred looked flummoxed and rubbed his head again when I mentioned the kind of budget we should be thinking about spending and kept putting it off, but then fate intervened.

One day, a circular popped through the letterbox from the local Peugeot dealership. It seemed we were cordially invited to view the launch of the new-style Peugeot 406HDi. 'Refreshments will be available,' the leaflet informed us, and went on to say: 'Staff will be on hand to answer any questions you may have about our range of new and used Peugeots.'

I eventually dragged Fred along, under much protest. He decided he would simply turn up in his usual work clothes because he didn't see the event as being important. I worried about the possibility of damage to car interiors and had visions of a massive cleaning bill landing on our doormat, so I managed to persuade him to get changed into something more suitable.

We weren't really looking at buying a new car, but we could afford a reasonably decent used one – despite Fred's reservations about the whole affair manifested in his protest of going in dirty oily overalls. 'All me bloody women have had all me money anyway – so what does it matter?' he announced belligerently on the way there, worrying again about the cost.

'Yes but, Fred, do you not realise we need something better now – you're doing more travelling around the country than ever before!'

'I dunno ... too bloody much for me all this lark – I was happier when I was up me chimneys and looking forward to me cheese buttie and a pint at lunchtime before the man from the BBC came along. Humph!'

Then he announced he'd only *think* about buying a car.

Outside the dealership a lovely, used 406 model, not quite two years old, in Fred's favourite dark green, was parked up on the forecourt. 'How much!' he loudly declared, as another couple wandered past. He played to the gallery: 'Well, you can sod off, I'm not paying that kind of brass, baby, so there you are!' Then he shifted about a bit and mumbled something I didn't quite catch.

I dragged him through the doors into the showroom. Inside, on a long trestle table, there were bottles of wine, sandwiches and canapés.

'She's dragged me along here and I've had nowt for me lunch – nowt to do with me, all this car bother...' he explained, as one of the sales executives came over to shake his hand, enquiring as to why he'd come along.

'Good to see you, Fred – do you mind if we take a picture?'

'Naaah ... carry on, mate, yer alright. Might as well tuck into some of this splendid tackle yer've got laid on here, while me missus has a look round your posh shop an' all.'

We helped ourselves and Fred imbibed about half of the wine available on the launch day; the staff stood by worriedly as he tucked into the booze yet again, going from one end of the table to the other. 'Not bad this, mate – mind you, I like me Guinness better, but the wife likes this stuff...'

Eventually, after about an hour of talking and drinking, he looked a bit unfocused, telling his tales to the crowd that had gathered.

Time for some action.

I took advantage of the moment, putting forward my case about the green used Peugeot outside. By now Fred was ready for a quick test drive, without *too much* persuasion! The salesman went off to get the keys, telling us a little of the car's history as we clambered inside the spotless vehicle. At this point, Fred asked if he could pop back in and use the toilet, as he was bursting for a pee. Whilst he was away, I had one big question for the salesman – could he talk Fred into buying the car for us?

The immaculate Peugeot purred along the road, feeling comfortable and familiar, harking back to the days when we rented Linky.

I wanted it!

Incredibly – so did Fred!

'It's alright, this, mate – I like it ... better than our blue car... How much would you give us for that, then, like?' he enquired.

I thought we'd better get back to the dealership immediately, before the effects of the wine wore off; but I needn't have worried. Fred, never really a good businessman, continued, 'Tell us the damage, mate – don't worry, we've had a good year an' all, so we can afford one of these swanky things without going on't tick, like...'

We were in the showroom for most of the afternoon, and after a few swift kicks to the ankle when Fred started saying again what a good month or two we'd had on the after-dinner circuit, he remained unusually quiet whilst a solid deal was struck with the salesman.

Two days later, we took my beloved blue Metro along to the dealership and said our sad farewell, acquiring our very own green Linky 406 in its place.

Around that time, we received a telephone enquiry asking Fred if he'd like to visit Northern Ireland to give an after-dinner talk for the army stationed there.

I had never been to Northern Ireland before and the prospect worried me slightly. The Army sent a car with a driver to meet us at the airport, and it all felt a bit strange as we drove through the beautiful countryside and past all the familiar places I had only heard of and seen on the news. It took about an hour to reach Belfast where we were to stay overnight in a small house on the Army base, which was normally used for visiting relatives. As we arrived at the base, we were met by a group of officers and military personnel, who introduced themselves one by one and showed us to our digs.

It was a full afternoon, beginning with Fred and I being shown the weapons and guns currently used by the British Army. A sergeant asked if Fred wanted to try out a weapon and I was offered the chance to try my hand too. But I cast my mind back to earlier days working on the cruise liners;

during one occasion when I had participated in a clay pigeon shoot, I'd foolishly held the rifle away from my shoulder instead of tucking it in firmly as advised. It had kicked back with such alarming force that I thought I had broken my collar bone. Looking at the formidable weaponry on the table before me, I didn't feel like having a second shot, so to speak, and declined.

'Go on, you soft bugger,' said Fred and pointed to something that looked like an Uzi. 'I thought it would suit someone of your violent disposition,' he added cheekily.

Fred, by now donning ear-protectors, picked up one of the larger weapons, aimed – and fired several yards down the shooting range. He looked pleased with himself, saying he had always been interested in guns since he was a young chap. We trudged off, flanked by three soldiers, down to where three action targets in the shape of a man – who looked mysteriously like Clint Eastwood – were located at the bottom of the range. A collection of holes in the cardboard surrounded the place where the heart should be. So perfectly aimed was Fred's shot that the army lads joked they could do with him amongst their ranks. *So* perfect, that I imagined the targets had been rigged in Fred's honour to make him feel good about himself, but no – it was all his own skill! I was amazed at his deadly shot, as were the rest of the team, but Fred merely commented with a beaming grin that he was 'good with guns, and had always been interested in them'.

Afterwards, he spoke at length about a Luger pistol he once owned: 'Bloody beautiful piece of engineering that thing...'

We were taken to a square pad of tarmac where a helicopter awaited us. The blades suddenly whirred, rotated and whipped into action, taking us off in a diagonal lift, rather like being hauled up fast in a cage from the bottom of a mineshaft. We soared up over the centre of Omagh, the site of the previous year's bombing, and the terrible destruction was still clearly visible. On the promise of a guided tour of the area later by car, we stayed hovering in the air for about twenty minutes or so, wondering about the sheer nonsense of it all, the loss of so much life, and what it must be like for people living here. However, it was a thrilling experience in some ways, soaring round; the freedom made it seem that we were masters of the skies, if not the machine.

The car experience later was in some ways even better, but much sadder. The terrible scars on the buildings bore silent testimony to how we felt about the troubles, and I admitted to feeling a certain degree of menace as we drove through the area and were told details of the conflicts, which ultimately brought about the bombing. I was relieved to get back to the military base, away from this frightening but poignant experience.

But the day wasn't over yet; we were then shown around the different quarters on the Army base and met many of the Army Corps. One cheery young lad was from Bolton and was delighted to speak with someone from back home. His parents were Fred fans, and his dad wanted a model engine, he told us.

We eventually got back to the impersonal little house around 5.00 p.m., after a trip to the Officers' Mess for something to eat. We found a bottle of wine and some Guinness waiting for us and, as I opened the wine feeling a bit fazed by it all, Fred kept repeating how the lads over here were *real* men, and not like some of 'them wankers back home who never did owt'. I knew this was a huge mark of respect, meaning he could understand the very real danger they faced.

Later that evening, when Fred went off to do the talk in the Officers' Mess, I went off the base again, this time accompanying some of the officers' wives to a local restaurant for a girls' night out. A minibus was arranged for us and we had a superb time. I was struck by the true camaraderie that existed between the army wives and thought how great it must be to have that support. The wine and conversation flowed as the night wore on and, despite the stark differences in our lifestyles, I was warmly welcomed into the girls' lives.

Next day, after a hearty breakfast in the Officers' Mess, Fred and I went along to one of the numerous concrete buildings and were sorted out with some army surplus as a gift for Nathan. I got a smashing pair of army boots for steam rallies as well as a fine metal combat helmet as a souvenir – just the thing for when I was next in battle with Fred! He also came away weighted down with gifts and tried on various pairs of boots before finally settling, with an appreciative sniff of each boot, on a pair of shiny size eights with steel toe-caps that fit him perfectly.

As we left the base later that day, a cheer from the lads went up for Fred. He waved back at the crowd gathered there to see this brave man who earned the respect of these young soldiers by regularly facing danger himself.

CHAPTER 7
We're all going on a
summer holiday
'Them'll be the souls of the dead men below...'

Life was becoming much busier and far more complicated after the success of *Industrial Age*. The attention from fans and followers had increased more than two-fold and I was getting tougher in my attempts to protect Fred. Whereas before we could go into a pub or restaurant and sit in some quiet corner holding hands and having a laugh about something or other, it was now impossible to walk anywhere without drawing immediate attention.

I resented it at times. I hadn't learned to cope – and in some ways, I never did. The office work increased beyond all measure and I found it increasingly difficult to keep up with replying to fan mail, so lots of letters remained unanswered. It put a bit of a strain on things between us, because Fred was starting to accuse me of being 'stand-offish' with the public at times when we were out together and made reference to the fact that Alison had always replied promptly to the fan letters. But there was only one of me – and I seemed to be living all my life through Fred.

I daydreamed about times when we could walk hand in hand around some ancient industrial monument without being subjected to autograph hunters eagerly wanting to know all our business, or plonking themselves down at our table in some restaurant when we were enjoying an evening out.

The increased workload now meant constant calls, faxes and letters to discuss and sort out what was in Fred's best interests. Some things he was asked to do were unbelievable. One man wanted Fred to come to his daughter's wedding to 'give her away' in place of the father, as the bridegroom was a massive fan! Another wanted to know how much Fred would charge to take down the chimney on his house because he wanted to show off to the snobby neighbours how he'd managed to get a celebrity working on his house. The list went on, some bizarre requests, some ordinary but all unfeasible in the light of Fred's growing celebrity.

I had helped place Fred's professional life on a much better footing than ever before. In the past, due to his easy-going nature, many so-called friends and acquaintances had taken full advantage of him, sometimes blatantly exploiting him for their own ends.

When I eventually took over as his business manager, I was horrified to learn just how many times in the past Fred or his advisors had allowed the

Dibnah name to be used commercially, sometimes in the ambiguous name of 'friendship'. How could all this have happened? I found myself making waves as I did my level best to redress the balance. It seemed everywhere I looked into his business affairs there was someone trying to make money off his back. Nothing had been done to address this problem in the past; it was like a large garden choked with weeds, and I was the one with the sharp scythe.

I became very protective, endeavouring to get rid of the rot that had set in many years previously with bad management, a lackadaisical way of working, and various cash deals – or even worse: 'Here Fred, open-this-event-for-a-bag-of-nuts-and-bolts or whatever'!

But no one wants a bossy new interfering wife meddling in his affairs if it meant they would lose out. My actions were greatly resented by certain people but I persevered and tried to show Fred how much he'd been used by other people for their own ends. Meeting their disgruntled wrath head-on when I got on the phone stopped their little game. Fred shook his head in bewilderment and exclaimed: 'All I ever wanted was to be a steeplejack!'

Fred knew that this was going on – he wasn't stupid, but had a sort of flaw where he couldn't abide the thought of upsetting anyone by not being friendly and nice, or not helping out if they asked anything of him. He'd moan about things to me but when I'd say, 'Bloody hell, Fred, tell him he's out of order doing that, and tell him you want your fair cut!' he'd reply, 'Don't worry, cock, I'm not daft, I know what he's up to, like...'

But that would be that, and he would let people get away with anything!

The real problem, of course, lay in the fact that Fred never viewed himself as an entertainer or a commodity – especially in the early days. I was wary of accepting offers on Fred's behalf, especially any which at first seemed too good to be true. Before agreeing to anything, I would try to check it out. I am convinced that you needed mettle of a different kind to handle all the interest created from being in the public eye, and the darker side it sometimes generated. I didn't mind that the small faction of hangers-on didn't like me because I could see through their motives and I didn't like them either. Unfortunately for them, I wasn't some little woman whose middle name was subordination, afraid of opening her mouth, and I was going to sort it out!

For instance, a beer was once produced by Bank Top Brewery in Bolton bearing the name 'Fred's Cap', with a cartoon drawing of Fred in a flat cap on the label. As during his last marriage, permission was given on the basis of 'If it's a success, mate, send us some money'.

The beer *was* successful. We quite often saw it in pubs, at steam rallies, people talked about and regularly supped it ... and as far as I am aware, and according to Fred, he never got offered so much as a gallon or two of free ale every month! Certainly, I never saw him receive any in the years I was with him.

I later called time on that particular 'deal' as the brewery eventually came up with another beer alongside 'Fred's Cap' entitled 'Dr Dibnah', in commemoration of Fred's honorary doctorate from Aberdeen University.

This new brew was destined to be offered at a local beer festival to raise money for Bolton Boys and Girls Club. However, because they didn't ask if they could use the name 'Dibnah' and nothing was in writing – the same as with 'Fred's Cap' – I was gravely concerned about this set-up. It would have been no problem at all to use the name *solely* for the festival of course – if only we'd been consulted in the first place and got something down in writing that it was purely for charity. But the first we knew about the beer was reading about it in the local paper!

I contacted the owner of the brewery, saying he needed to clarify matters with Fred and that he simply couldn't use the Dibnah name without permission. We would need to discuss a royalty agreement if he continued to produce it – and while we were at it, were we ever going to get anything for 'Fred's Cap'?

It went down like a flat pint!

The resulting article about my 'interference' made the front page in the *Bolton Evening News*. The headline screamed in bold type: 'FRED'S BEER NAME FURY' and the opening paragraph stated: '*Bolton celebrity steeplejack*

Fred Dibnah has ordered his name to be removed from a beer specially brewed for a charity fund raising festival...'

I considered it a slightly unfair piece, which put a spin on things and made Fred out to be some temperamental star and me to be some kind of Cruella de Vil character, pushing matters along and spoiling the charity event by insisting the brewery had to withdraw the beer. We both wished the brewery no harm, just wanted to see Fred was remunerated for the future use of his name, that's all. Since there was no control agreed over the subsequent production and possible distribution of the beer after the festival, I felt justified in my actions. It was one of the first incidents where I realised I would make enemies and become known as 'being difficult' for trying to protect my husband's famous (and lucrative) name in business matters. The brewery later brought out two new beers called 'Old Slapper' and 'Gold Digger'. I think the mentality shown in those two names speaks for itself.

The main trouble with Fred was that although he was 100% sincere, forthright and outspoken at times, he could be unbelievably naïve. If someone was nice to his face, that's *exactly* how they appeared in his eyes: a nice, easy-going person. He belonged to a much simpler world where people were genuine through and through, and Fred never spoke badly of anyone he'd met (except later when he became ill). He gave them anything they asked for, or agreed to anything they might suggest or want of him. He believed everyone was as straightforward as he was; there was never any guile, any side, to them. Even if it was evident that an individual or company were trying to use their association with him to their own advantage and/or make money, he simply could not see it. If it became obvious later that someone had been taking advantage of him, he still said things like: 'Well, he never struck me as a bloke like that, cock – maybe he's having a hard time with the missus or summat, he's alright really, not a bad bloke really, you know, just a bit wild!'

One telling and rather bizarre instance of this was when he found that one of his 'close friends' had stolen some video merchandise on a few occasions. Fred merely shrugged and told me he knew about it. 'He's been at it years – he sells 'em down in't pub for his beer money; he's always skint – me last wife banned him from't house forrit!' But he didn't want to confront the person because he'd known him a long time and didn't want any trouble.

People who took advantage of his good nature deserved all they got, but because I caused flack, Fred often castigated me as 'being awkward' and dismissed my concerns with: 'What the bloody hell are you worrying about, woman – you've got a nice car in the drive, plenty of money in the bank, so what's up with you?'

 But that was hardly the point, was it?

I had long become used to his need to project his views emphatically on others at every opportunity, and populate 'Planet Dibnah' with new recruits. This sometimes took the form of talking 'at' people rather than 'with' them. Habitually given towards exaggeration for the sake of a good yarn, and having a rare talent for self-dramatisation, Fred would readily embellish a story to entertain the listener, rather than to boast or deceive. All that mattered was the common denominator: were they on a similar wavelength, relating to important matters in a 'man's world', or what? Women, expressing their mostly petty concerns (in his eyes), didn't interest Fred in the slightest; they were simply perceived as being from a different planet. He labelled them, at times: *just bloody women!*

To succeed with Fred, you either had to know about things he liked, or be willing to let him educate you, and that way he'd enjoy your company as he spoke about engines, mine shafts, old factories and such like. He would often reiterate the tale of Isambard Kingdom Brunel, whom Fred considered was not only one of the greatest men of all time, but had exactly the right idea when it came to affairs of the heart: 'His missus never saw him – he was working on his latest project all the time. Real men are always busy, you see, cock!'

To Fred a group of men, tough and lean as old chickens from years of long hard slog and sheer grind in blue-collar jobs, listening and sharing his interests in industry or the past, was all that counted. Old men, young men

– it didn't matter who so long as they were sympathetic towards the cause. They would gravitate towards him from all corners of Britain, seeking kinship, and sit around in the engine shed drinking tea, instant coffee, booze, smoking fags and eating pies with nicotine-stained fingers, their rheumy old eyes taking it all in – this slightly disgruntled generation so keen, like Fred, to compare the present unfavourably with the past. It was a far cry from the world of celebrity and was something you had to take on board if you loved him.

Not being in the least business-minded, Fred wasn't really interested in money; it was all a great burden to him. A common retort when faced with any dilemma where a business decision was concerned was: 'Yer know, I sometimes wish the bloody BBC had never come along into my life – I was a happy man then. If they never come back it wouldn't bother me a lot.'

His goal in life was to toil on his engines in his steam workshops and eventually recreate a coal mine in his garden, whereby he could relive the halcyon days of the industrial revolution where he considered he belonged, and which remained important to him throughout his entire life. As long as money was there without worry, then he was OK. Despite now being solvent, he didn't want to travel or see the world: 'I've not seen all of England yet!' He wanted to 'play' in his garden and enjoy digging his mock mine shaft with similar-minded friends, devising his 'endless rope haulage system' to complete the illusion that coal was being mined. The dream he had of being an industrialist in his own little world – the proud owner of his 'own pit'– helped pull him through some of the darkest days ahead.

I recently read and was intrigued by a George Formby biography, and was left wondering about the influence his wife Beryl had on him and his career. In the book she seemed callous at times, making poor defenceless George do all manner of daunting things he would otherwise never have done or got involved with. *She* chose his friends, dismissing those whom *he* thought were his friends, but whom she rightly considered 'hangers-on'. She got rid of others who came along with a view to exploiting him, handling business matters with a keen eye and attention to detail. Without a doubt, the vast wealth accruing from their dedication and hard work was her doing. I do not profess to be like Beryl Formby or have anything approaching her fantastic ability in business matters, but I do greatly admire what she did, protecting her husband from users and looking after his career. I can, therefore, identify with some of what she must have had to put up with on his behalf. George, like Fred, appeared to be a nice, genuine, simple soul who lived entirely for what he did best – in his case playing his ukulele and being loved by fans and the general public.

However, that said, Fred was a whole lot more of his own man than I suspect George was ever allowed to be. But as far as business was concerned, there were parallels and Fred could well have done with someone like Beryl Formby years ago. In some ways, Fred was a weak man, unable to say 'no' to anything he might be asked to do; on the other hand, he could be extremely stubborn, self-opinionated and self-centred at times, not realising others have feelings, wants and needs too. He didn't see this, so it didn't trouble him. He could still be himself, 'Mr Nice Guy', and not upset anyone. Everything was black and white, and he had no concept of abstract thought – it never occurred to him that things could be other than how they appeared.

The world was always a friend to be trusted.

When we first met in 1996, I was very embarrassed whenever he started to discuss how much he had in the bank, since we'd only seen each other a few times. One night, during a trip over to Bolton, he even showed me his bank statements to prove how broke he was! It wasn't only me he would tell this to; I heard him say it many times during my years with him, and some people would be embarrassed, not wanting all that personal information. At his wedding speech, for instance, he went off at a tangent telling everyone about the £600 he had before I came along. Who else would be that honest? But that was so typical of him; Fred saw no harm or any shame in telling anyone who would listen about his finances, or anything else for that matter. Nothing was private. It was his way of telling people he was just an ordinary bloke with no airs and graces. Fred didn't like or need money, power or fame to feel good about himself. He was simply 'Our Fred' and we all loved him.

There were some funny stories too, about how people had sometimes taken the Dibnah name to further their own ends. He laughed about how back in 1986, someone had systematically duped the public for two years by claiming to be his brother 'Frank Dibnah' (his father's name). The matter had come to light when the impostor set about conning a pub landlady in the Midlands out of £20. Detectives were looking for the man. He'd told a whole load of stories about dangerous jobs he and his famous 'brother' Fred had tackled, such as working together on York Minster after the fire. He even posed for a local newspaper after igniting the interest of the *Coventry Evening Telegraph* with his many valiant tales! The man, never named, had been living the high life, according to the papers, cashing in on his famous connection. He'd gone so far as arranging to have letterheads and business cards printed, and Fred said he obviously knew a lot about steeplejacking work.

A reporter overheard the man in a pub saying that he was in Coventry to do a big job on the Courtauld's chimney. Coincidence would have it that the reporter, who worked on the *Evening Telegraph*, was visiting the pub to cover a different story, but his ears pricked up when he heard the stranger mention the name 'Dibnah'. However, the reporter soon smelled a rat when he saw a notebook sticking out of the stranger's blue overalls with the words 'F. Dibner Steeplejack'. The name Dibnah was spelled wrongly! The reporter later checked with the management at Courtauld's and they had no plans to have work carried out on the chimney. The man was never found according to Fred – and we often wondered what had become of him after he was exposed in the paper as a fraud!

Life rolled – or rather zipped – by and I diligently toiled away in the office, placing us in a much better position than ever before. As I increasingly handled our business affairs, it placed our finances on a much better footing. I wish I could have met him years before, done a bit of a Beryl on him then...

I could see Fred needed professional guidance for his BBC programmes from someone practised in contractual law, and many other related matters which I simply couldn't handle. I contacted a professional agency called Arena Entertainments. It was Arena that had secured the Kellogg's Cornflakes commercial for Fred just before we met. They booked a few speaking engagements for him as well, but soon realised that it was an uphill battle due to his steeplejacking work. Arena needed to be certain Fred would turn up for gigs on time and not be stuck up some chimney, and also to liaise with someone who knew what they were doing.

Martin and Barry gradually took over the diary from me and I continued acting as office and business manager. I made telephone calls, arranged interviews, did bookkeeping, answered letters and generally acted as an interface between Fred and the public. It took many months for Arena and I to wend our way through the sheer maze of mistakes in the past, and finally get everything on a strictly professional footing. We seemed always to have some new issue to cope with, some problem to resolve, and it soon became apparent that Fred wasn't ever going to be like your average celebrity and behave in a predictable manner.

Martin and I had to try and work round some of the stuff Fred had already agreed verbally to do, such as turning up miles away with the traction engine for £100 and a bag or two of coal thrown in! None of this mattered to Fred: 'Oh, I don't bloody know, I just want to be out on me engine, like.' He simply wanted to go for the fun of it, and would have done so without any kind of payment except a few bags of coal and a pint or two of Guinness.

Fred was brilliantly gifted; he didn't want to be bothered with tedious things, preferring to apply his abilities to all things mechanical. I called it his 'mad professor syndrome'. But despite disagreeing with some of my tactics and strong-arm approach, I knew that Fred secretly valued the way Arena and I managed his affairs. It had taken away a lot of stress and worry from his shoulders. As the formula began to work and Fred's profile increased, sometimes, over a meal in a pub or a glass of wine or two later, he would shake his head in bewilderment and say things like: 'You know, cock, three good things have happened in life: meeting David Hall, as well as yon-mon in Leeds (meaning Martin at Arena) and you sorting everything out for me.'

Fred still liked to keep his hand in at that time, doing work as a steeple-jack. I tried to dissuade him in general, as he'd recently suffered from a few dizzy spells but he insisted he would never give up. So, we had this strange situation whereby one weekend he would be surrounded by thousands of people clamouring for photos and autographs on a steam rally and the following Wednesday he'd be swinging around some church steeple, looking forward to a pint or two later in a small family-run pub down the road with the local farmers and workers.

Despite being brave enough to earn his living 250 feet up in the sky and also being known as that famous 'chimney fella' – or 'chimney-feller' – he never got ideas above his station nor thought that he was better than the next man because he could now command a lot of money. His outspoken-ness and political incorrectness, delivered in simple, colloquial English, was as breezy and refreshing as it was informative, and the 'bloodies', 'buggers', 'sods' – and much worse – all added up to a complex mix of conversation you just couldn't help being fascinated and charmed by.

Early June came around and, wedged in between the seemingly endless routine of steam rallies, Fred went off for a couple of weeks with David to do some research on the intended new series *Magnificent Monuments*. At first, Fred didn't feel too sure about it, wanting instead to carry on with a series featuring steam engines like the last one. Returning from the trip, however, he felt more confident and began looking forward to the start of filming later in the year.

The weather was deliciously hot and a steam rally that should have taken us to Yorkshire had been cancelled. We had a few free days and it was the school holidays. As usual, Jack and Roger were over from the Isle of Man, so we decided we would take all three kids on holiday; since Fred had not taken me on honeymoon, he kept saying *this* was it instead! The delights of some far-off white sandy beach, drinking strange-sounding cocktails under a hot blazing sun whilst the kids frolicked happily in the azure sea were not for us. Not even the quintessential English seaside resort, faintly reminiscent of a bygone era, with cast-iron piers, funny hats, candy-floss and long promenades.

No. We decided instead to go to ... *Wigan Pier!* On a 12-ton steamroller, pulling the green living van behind us.

I had never slept in the timber living van before. Fred assured me it was very comfortable and, as we contemplated the trip, I viewed the cramped vehicle with great concern. I remembered Alison in one early programme, standing at the door while the rain poured down. 'It's raining in, Fred – the bed is getting wet!' she'd complained as her grubby hubby stood nearby. Fred merely replied, 'Gerra bucket then, luv!'

Shades of mouldy bus-seat beds from our first jaunt to Wales came back to haunt me – and how would I wash in front of these four males, I wondered? I watched as Jack helped to fettle the black oil lamps with paraffin; the other two boys, Nathan and Roger, loaded our sleeping bags amongst other stuff like packet food – and staple supplies such as beer – into the living van.

We needed plenty of coal to get to Wigan, which was about ten miles away, and this was always stored at the rear of the van in a little cubbyhole immediately under the bunks. It wasn't a problem, as you had ready access to the coal supply from outside through a little wooden door, kept locked by a six-inch key. We planned mostly to eat out during the trip and, as I reflected on the amount of Mars Bars and crisps going in the van, I supposed that meant that the usual fish and chips, pies and ale would be our staple diet for the next few days.

The weather was sultry and sweltering, so we made sure we also took lots of soft drinks with us. The atmosphere before we set off was one of anticipation. Excitement mounted as Fred and Jack got Betsy into steam and, a couple of hours later, expertly hooked her up to the van ready for our epic journey to distant Wigan.

I left my nice clothes and make-up behind, wearing instead a simple cream sun top and leggings. Finally, I clambered onto the step of the living van and took my place on Betsy's stepping board. It was time for the off. The engine rumbled and lurched forward noisily, immediately covering me with hot soot

from the chimney before we got to the end of our street. '*Whoof-whoof-whoof*'
the engine proudly chugged and off we went into the unknown ... or at least
to Wigan Pier.

I enjoyed the Trencherfield Mill Engine, located in the mill at the side of
Wigan Pier. That was the reason I had agreed to the trip initially. I had always
loved large mill rather than traction engines, and had visited Wigan Pier on
previous occasions. Built in 1906 by J. & E. Wood of Bolton, the horizontal
four-cylinder, triple-expansion, cross-compound steam engine was one of
Fred's great favourites – as well as mine. I had never seen anything so massive; the flywheel alone, at twenty-six feet diameter, weighs around seventy
tons. In its heyday, it ran some 60,000 ring and 24,000 mule spinners, and it
was capable of carrying fifty ropes, one and three quarter inches diameter.

Wigan Pier car park: the sight of Fred, naked from the waist up, swilling
off the oil and grime from the outward trip from his beer belly, using a small
white enamelled tin bowl containing murky hot water from the steaming
engine, in front of the steady gaze of the bemused public. That was enough
horror for me, and I most certainly wasn't going to attempt it too. I hadn't
bargained on an audience for my much-needed ablutions under a star-filled
moonlit night.

Then the business of the man and woman on the footplate – as Fred
opened the door and peered out to see what the noise was all about, I didn't

know who to throw a bucket of water over first. Fred was going 'Uh-uh-uh!' at the sight of the young, half-naked woman with her drawers around her ankles, who very nearly broke her neck jumping down whilst the randy bloke peppered the night with expletives only usually reserved for barrack-room talk.

And chip, chips, chips to eat...

Backache, headache...

'And how do I pee into this thing, Fred?'

He'd set up a large blue drum with a tube poking out the top. OK for men and boys...

'Well, yer'll 'ave to aim into tube, like, won't yer, cock,' he said

The Maypole Colliery on the way back. After showing us various mining books all depicting the scene, Fred's animated description of disaster and black, sulphurous smoke as he told us poignant tales of the 1908 disaster when sixty men were killed and trapped down below deep in the bowels of the earth. They had to flood the mine ... some of the mutilated dead bodies floated to the surface...

This resulted in young Roger screaming and begging for us to leave. The engine needed more steam and we were without coal, so we had to pick amidst the rubble for discarded bits of timber. I reluctantly wrapped a tartan travel rug around my head and shoulders to keep out the rain and, in the thunder and lightning of the bone-chilling day, picked about near the top of the mineshaft looking like a modern-day 'pit-brow lass'. I found two baby pigeons huddled together, and Jack ran back to tell Fred about my find. He made it worse by announcing to the wide-eyed little boys like John Laurie in *Dad's Army*: 'Them'll be the souls of the dead men below...'

It wasn't long before we hit the road again, thanks to Roger.

After enduring Fred steering and driving the difficult-to-handle vehicle during the long hours on a bumpy road, I was so glad when we finally returned home. As we approached our town along Derby Street, it looked like an oasis on the horizon must look to a person lost in the desert for days.

We reached home and I jumped off the engine, staggered indoors and scrambled upstairs looking forward to a good hot soak in a proper bathroom. I felt filthy and sticky. Unrecognisable, my long blonde plaited hair hung lankly down in a sooty great rope and, as I undressed, the smell of oil wafted up from my filthy clothes. I have never seen bath water so black; the soap would hardly lather, the shampoo was useless. As I cursed, scrubbing away the never-ending grime of the trip, I vowed never again. Sorry, you steam fans, but Fred was right – it *was* too much for me!

In truth I cannot really say I enjoyed the experience, although it did have its outstanding moments. The best part was the sense of a bohemian lifestyle, as we took to the road and later, sitting with Fred in the deserted car park at the side of the living van. The hot, close evening, sipping cool beer and enjoying total freedom from television, ticking clocks and ringing telephones and, as the balmy night closed in around us, feeling that we alone had created this world away from 'modern life' and all its trappings. Just as Fred wished, it was rather like going back in time. The worst part: oh, the grime, smoke, lack of proper food, toilet arrangements and general discomfort of travelling on the roller! I felt like a proverbial street urchin by the time we'd hit Bolton again.

During the return journey, one little boy tentatively approached us on his bike, mesmerised by the fiery iron monster before him, the likes of which he'd never seen before. He wanted to know if we all lived in the van all the time, like in a house. 'No!' I spluttered to the wide-eyed boy. 'Good heavens, NO!!!'

My next holiday would definitely be of the normal kind, where the only hot thing in sight would be the sun!

We were well into the rally season by now and, as always, time at home was precious. Fred got many requests to do charity work, but it was not always possible. One day, however, we received a telephone call from Justin Walker, the cousin of Nick Wilding, the cameraman who had taken the footage of the chimney at Barnoldswick. Justin was actively involved with the Macmillan Trust, raising funds to help fight cancer. Around this time the

Trust was promoting public awareness of cancer through a national coffee morning, sponsored by Nescafé, which would be held in a couple of months; Justin wanted to know if Fred would help to raise the profile. He explained that Jean Alexander, most famous for her role as Hilda Ogden in *Coronation Street*, was involved with the charity and had wondered about the possibility of meeting Fred and having her picture taken with him by the steamroller to help promote the event.

Arrangements were made, a date set, and Jean eventually arrived in our yard. She was very elegant and charming – not at all like Hilda Ogden, the brassy character she portrayed, and she showed great interest in the machinery and workshops – although I admit to her being a little worried about the effects on her neatly-pressed, cream linen trouser suit.

Fred said it wasn't the first time someone famous had been down to his back garden and told me about the veteran comedy actor Norman Rossington. He was appearing at the Manchester Palace Theatre in 1988 and, because he was into steam, had expressed an interest in meeting his hero, Fred Dibnah. Fred obliged and they spent an afternoon together discussing engines and playing about with various bits of tackle, as Fred put it.

Fred already had Betsy out in the yard by the time Jean arrived, steaming her up ready for the visit. I didn't think she might be keen to 'play' with his engines; however they both had a long conversation and posed in front of the hissing engine as photographs were taken by the press and Justin. It was a bit strange having Mrs Hilda Ogden in our yard – and I reckon if her henpecked husband Stan had still been around he would have found a great drinking mate and companion in 'Our Fred'.

The steam rally season continued until we visited the last one at Grand Henham, in Suffolk. We had to return to Bolton on the Sunday evening at the close of the rally. Fred needed to be up at 6.00 a.m. the next day, to be whisked off ready for the first set of shoot dates for *Magnificent Monuments*. It was to be filmed over the next six weeks, with only a break for weekends, two of which were taken up with personal appearance work. I don't know where Fred got his stamina from; we were exhausted from travelling during the summer and this weekend's rally (not to mention the effects of the corner bath in the hotel, this time!). Yet he was uncomplaining, and set off in good spirits early on the Monday morning.

When I think back to those early days of me actually staying away from home with my steeplejack business – how it was all very exciting and frightening...

By the time we were doing the Magnificent Monument *series, I had got quite used to all the posh and fancy hotels. I suppose I've even become a bit different like that. I like these fancy places! When I and Sheila went into a certain pub where we go to have something to eat when I'd got back, I made her laugh. I wasn't thinking; I said, 'It's alright this* bloody place, but there are no side plates or serviettes.' Me – I mean, all I was used to was a bag of chips at one time! I've got quite used to it now! Even sophisticated in some ways, I suppose. It's like food as well; my wife Sheila is a very good cook. At first, I was a bit wary of this vegetarian lark, but I must say, everything she's ever put down before me I've really enjoyed. I suppose I miss the odd bacon butty, but she knows I have the odd lapse or two now and then when I'm out and about, and I get it in the neck about that. I'm not too bothered about missing meat at home – I eat a lot of fish instead – and they say it's good for your brain! I've been introduced to the finer side of life: what with David Hall, who's a bit of a gourmet and wine connoisseur. The days of visits to the pie shop and the chippy still occasionally happen, but not as much as they used to. We've now got a round of nice country pubs, where we go out for lunch when it's raining and things like that. I take Sheila out every Saturday night for a meal when we are at home – I like eating out; I'd never had garlic bread I don't think, till I met Sheila – I really like that! Stilton mushroom, things like that... Wine's another thing – now I like that too – mind you, I won't ever give up a pint for it, though!

But all this travelling is a tougher game than you think. People have the idea that it's all wonderful, you know. You never stop; and it isn't like having a camcorder or summat like that, and pointing it at people, getting a continuous story. It's all spilt up into little bits: this is for programme one, and this is for programme six, programme three and all of that. You don't know where you are – especially if you are not a proper actor like me, but just a bum that climbs up chimneys! The thing is, not only do you have a fairly gruelling day racing about, at night – you've got your evening meal – then there's the usual race round the town or village you happen to be in, to see if you can find a good pub. Then the dangerous bit is getting locked in this good pub! That frequently happens; and then of course you have got to get up bright and early at seven the next morning, get on with it – pretty tough!

You meet some very nice people. When we were filming at the Victoria and Albert Museum in London, we met a young chap called Andre. He were an interesting man, and he showed us all round; we went up in the rooftops, all the original Victorian gold leaf, and the rivets. He showed as much enthusiasm for it all as I did; yet, it's his everyday job. The other one I can think of was 'Tam the Gun' at Edinburgh Castle. Tam actually resides in a little cubicle hidden in the castle walls! At one o'clock every day, he fires this cannon, which was quite exciting. It's all done with military precision, looking at his stopwatch and everything. They awarded him the MBE, or OBE or summat, for doing it over the many years he's actually done it. Every day, rain, snow, sunshine, he's there – all except Christmas Day. He's a real character! He actually gave me one of the shells.

The other side of the coin is when all the filming is over with. It isn't done by a long chalk. I think they call it post-production work or summat. I've got to go and sit in a soundproof box, and read aloud little bits from scripts, descriptions of where we've been called 'voice- overs'. I quite enjoy doing that; if you are interested in the subject, it's not really very difficult to do.

Then of course, for Magnificent Monuments they've had me doing drawings! I liked doing that; I spent about a fortnight doing drawings of things like exploded views

139

of St Paul's Cathedral, and Blackpool Tower – how it was built. All sorts of interesting stuff, like the principles of the Forth Railway Bridge, which were very interesting ... so there's more to it than acting daft in front of the camera. Mind you, I've always liked drawing, and it's come in dead handy a few times in the past too, with some of the jobs I've been asked to do.

There's also some funny things happen at times. I'd been over to Leeds to do one of these voice-over things, driving down the M62. Now it's got this V8 engine in it, it goes like the clappers – about sixty or seventy miles an hour! I were bombing along, and of course you get BEEP-BEEP behind you, and some guy who's seen the signwriting waving profusely as they overtake every few yards. It happens quite a lot, because literally thousands of people have seen the Land Rover on telly.

On this occasion, I heard this 'BEEP-BEEP-BEEP' and a hearse – complete with coffin with all the wreaths on top – passed me in the fast lane. It must have been doing about eighty miles an hour! The two undertakers inside, complete with wing collars and black overcoats, had the windows down, leaning out shouting 'Hiya FRED!' I couldn't believe it! What a laugh ... incredible!

CHAPTER 8
'Mr Frederick Dibnah, Famous Raconteur And Chimney Murderer!'

'Oh aye, I managed to get a cast-iron grid for Sheila,
she collects them'

There were one or two remaining scenes for *Magnificent Monuments* to be shot in our back yard. Fred had been telling everyone throughout the rally season that we were going to have a 'topping out' ceremony like in the old days on the finished chimney he had built for his boiler in the back garden: 'I'm getting me missus up there too – she's good at climbing chimneys; we're having a topping out ceremony, an all,' he'd say.

However, returning home from an afternoon shopping, I was astonished to find the scene had already been shot earlier that day with one of the usual crowd of men taking my place. I was annoyed, because Fred had spent the last few months telling everyone that I was going to do the topping out ceremony – some people later watching on television might assume I'd bottled out of the climb.

I asked David if he'd mind redoing the shot with me going up the chimney and he gladly obliged during a subsequent visit to the yard, with an impartial Fred wondering what all the fuss was about. The man who I had sidelined in my innocent request for a retake refused to speak to me ever again, and banded with a growing number of disgruntled men ever-present in the yard with their own axes to grind.

I never gave much thought to that man's attitude and, being very busy again, we had not given much thought to the Millennium celebrations either, which everyone was talking about. As usual, we received many invitations to parties, but instead decided to have a quiet family occasion at home. Jack and Roger were over so, really, Fred wanted to stay at home to be with his boys. Before the dawn of the new Millennium was on the horizon, however, Fred had yet another chimney to think about...

'We've got a chimney for you here, Fred...'

He told me which one it was, and of course, I know most of the chimney stacks now within a radius of about forty miles! Not many left. Anyway, I went up and had a look at it. I thought: well, if I am going to do it, I may as well have a fair price... I told them what I wanted, and they immediately said, 'Very acceptable, we'll do it.'

Then of course, life got very complicated with the new series, and time was of the essence. I tried to riddle out of this here job, because we'd set a date originally, and then the BBC wanted me.

I rang him up, and I said, 'Look, I can't possibly do this chimney stack on this date.'

He said, 'Oh-oh, you've GOT to do it, we've ordered the marquee!'

'Well, whadda you mean, you've ordered the marquee?'

He went: 'Well, the marquee is costing £5,000!'

'£5,000 for a marquee? I was only getting £2,000 for doing the bloody job! What is it for, any road, this marquee?'

He told me they were having a bit of a do afterwards. So I managed to get the date changed, and what a week we picked! It started raining and blowing, and never stopped all week. It is the worst sort of situation you can be in, when you are attempting to undermine a chimney stack and prop it up on sticks. Soon as the jackhammer hits the side of the chimney, the dust and grit start flying about and it goes in your eyes, and grinds your eyeballs away. By the end of the week, you look like you've been on the booze for a month — red all around your eyes and all of that! And to add insult to injury, the base of the chimney were made out of random rubble stone work. Brickwork of course, which is in layers, you can undermine even when the mortar is no good, because of the nice flat bed, you can get to it. But this random stone has not got a flat bed anywhere, it's all shapes. It's very difficult to prop up. Anyway, we struggled on, and we got it all propped up and everything were ready for the great day.

As usual, Fred wanted me to light the fire at the base of the chimney and in readiness I donned a fake-fur hat, black woollen coat, gloves and warm

boots, for it was a crisp, dry morning with a light dusting of frost and touch

of fog for atmosphere. Fred had been on site for two hours or so when I

arrived with Nathan. The weather was sharp and I was thankful for the *'fancy*

beer tent' as Fred called it, which was a large white marquee erected specially

for VIP guests.

I meandered around the muddy site for a while watching Fred and

the team preparing for the chimney drop, speaking occasionally to Eddie

Chattwood and the rest of the crew helping Fred to demolish the chimney.

Last minute preparations were afoot; Fred was in charge and everyone on the

team deferred to his expertise. He strutted around all sides of the chimney,

Victorian trammels in hand, examining the ancient brickwork from different

angles looking for tell-tale signs of cracks in its structure, and measuring the

distance between the tow holes drilled in its side at three-foot intervals to

detect signs of movement. I felt proud of him.

The excitement mounted as the time of the intended drop came closer.

None of the public was allowed on site by now and scores of people were

kept back by a sturdy chicken-wire fence.

Finally, stepping forward to seal the fate of the stack at 12.00 p.m., at

Fred's instruction I tentatively put forward the flaming, diesel-soaked torch

to the base of the chimney, igniting the parched wood. The fire sprang immediately to life, the colour of the crackling flames instantly burnishing the timber and greedily consuming it with a healthy roar. We waited by the ill-fated chimney at a safe distance and Fred, this larger than life iconic idol of steam, chimneys, television and engineering, stood close at hand as he always did, studying his gold pocket watch, adjusting his cap, and slightly letting go of the hooter for a moment or two to ponder the enormity of the scene that lay ahead.

It was his moment. People glanced in his direction as he stood at the side of the chimney, unmoving, unafraid; he knew his stuff, this expert steeple-jack. The telegraph poles burned slowly away in the fierce flames, and the chimney appeared to wilt slightly to one side as the fire gathered momentum, feeding on the creosote-soaked wood.

Seconds ticked slowly by, the tension increased and gradually a crack started to appear up the side of the chimney. Fred suddenly sounded the hooter and the chimney gracefully crashed down to earth in slow motion with a great rumbling 'thwack'. Plumes of ancient brick dust rose in protest and fogged the air. A collective cheer went up from the crowd. The 'drop' had gone according to plan. Fred grinned from ear to ear and waved at the crowd.

'Did you like that, Fred?' some bright spark shot out from near where I was standing.

'We're off to the fancy beer tent for some refreshment!' he informed the camera crew. I later found my group of friends inside the fancy tent – the busy marquee – entering into the fun of the proceedings. We approached and listened to what Fred was saying to those surrounding him. Standing by now in the middle of a dense crowd, he was telling one attentive listener, a retired British Telecom engineer as it turned out, that I called him a 'chimney murderer'. He enquired casually if the man wanted a Polo mint and, whilst the executioner nonchalantly fiddled with the silver foil on the pack to proffer it, he enquired if the man knew where he could locate some used telegraph poles because he wanted some to build a pit-winding engine shed in his back yard. The man's friend – another chap of a similar build to Fred – quickly shuffled forward, speaking about his nephew who worked down at the depot where they took all the old wooden poles when BT replaced them with the new plastic ones, and the possibility of getting some. Fred's attention was caught: his eyes lit up and, looking from side to side, he addressed this second man, and in mint-scented mellifluous tones enquired: 'Magic, cock! 'Ave you got his number, like?'

Fred half-tipped his oily cap and scratched his bald head. 'Bloody hell, if I could get some o' them sorted out I'd be a happy man – the last outfit I got 'em from used to charge me two quid each; that's nowt, that, is it? Built me pit head out of 'em. Trouble is, I haven't seen the bloke since, and they've buggered off somewhere. Used to have a slip of paper with a number on, but I've no idea where it went to.'

Pieces of paper were quickly exchanged and Fred expressed his gratitude with a Polo mint, saying that the man was welcome to come down to see his yard whenever he wanted.

Another man wearing a blue and red anorak stepped purposefully forward and asked if he could go up a chimney sometime with Fred when he was next working on one. It set Fred off into his long rhetoric about the health and safety blokes who nowadays, according to him, had stopped anyone doing anything exciting. 'Them guys have never done 'owt requiring any degree of real violence or toughness!' he shot out at the listening group, and carried on: 'You get some bloke coming up to you, you've got all the rain and wind to contend with, and he's standing there at the bottom of some chimney with his hard hat on – frightened to bloody death of coming up the ladder!'

A three-piece band played somewhere in a distant corner of the marquee, the music lending an air of grandeur to the occasion. To the strains of 'Smoke Gets in Your Eyes' executives from the developers of the site, Redrow Homes, all came forward to shake hands with the celebrity chimney murderer Fred Dibnah, and to compliment him on a job well done.

A tinny, disembodied voice with a fake Stateside accent piped up over the tannoy informing us that there would be a disco later, and went on in its annoying, light-hearted way to instruct the gathered crowd to 'enjoy themselves'. A young waiter came past with a silver tray bearing tall flutes of Bucks Fizz and other exotic concoctions; I reached up and removed a glass. I half expected someone in a white tuxedo to jump out asking if I wanted my drink shaken not stirred.

The poshest chimney drop I have ever done. People from companies such as Redrow and Wimpey arrived in helicopters! What it was really, was a public relations exercise in getting this piece of land ready to build prestigious houses on. That was the reason for the £5,000 beer tent, as you might say! It had a wooden floor, carpet and brass chandeliers, a band, hot and cold food, with a cookhouse attached. Then, in case it rained – a viewing pavilion! Free drinks for us; all in all, a great time was had by everybody. They even had a Tiger Moth doing loop-the-loops, to stop anybody getting bored while the fire burned before the chimney fell down! Anyway, down it went, and we all had a good time … a party afterwards. Oh aye, I managed to get a cast-iron grid for Sheila, she collects them. I spotted one, which was near the entrance to the works, and it had Horwich Urban District Council cast on it, so we brought that away with us as a memento of the job.

It will go like all the rest of the sites where I've knocked chimneys down. You will never know it was there, and there will be acres of brand-new houses, that everybody has a big mortgage for.

By 10.00 p.m., Nathan was stifling yawns and becoming restless, fidgeting with table decorations and cutlery. I was feeling fatigued by all the persistent attention, and Fred was becoming increasingly drunk. This was one of the true hallmarks of a chimney drop. It was a dirty, dangerous and very stressful job, and no one could ever blame Fred for wanting to relax in whatever way he chose when it was all over. From drilling that first hole in the brickwork with a jack-hammer he'd christened 'Big Bertha', to the 'drop' a week later, it was dangerous.

I approached the white linen-covered table, smudged now with many drink stains, where Fred was perched surrounded by a large group of attentive listeners. He was holding court and every inch a star – whether he wanted to be or not.

'I'm going home now, Fred,' I told him above the din of the music and racket of loud voices. Cigarette smoke wafted up my nostrils as I leaned over the shoulder of a seated man. Eddie Chattwood, Fred's good friend of many years and fellow steeplejack, sitting at his side equally drunk, looked at me with a dazed, unfocused expression. Eddie had been staying with us for the previous week, helping Fred for old time's sake with work on undermining the chimney as he usually did on these occasions.

'Shall we have to leave now, Sheila – or should we stay a little longer, what do you think?' he enquired politely, looking a bit concerned at this unexpected wifely intervention.

'No, Eddie, just make sure you both stumble into a taxi – or get a lift home afterwards ... and that you *don't* drive that damned Land Rover back to Bolton!'

Someone else pushed in and piped up, 'Do yer want another drink then Fred, or what?'

Fred tipped his head towards me and good-naturedly shouted, 'Yer what, cock, can't hear you, I'm DEAF – where're you off to then ... too much for you all this, is it!?'

I made my excuses and left to the blaring tune of 'The Only Way is Up'. Just as Fred waved me off with an exaggerated 'Ta-ta then' he was handed another pint of Guinness.

Around this time, Fred had been booked to appear in Stourbridge at the Town Hall for what they advertised as their 'Annual Guest Celebrity Lecture'.

We travelled down in Linky as usual on the day and arrived at the venue to be told by the organisers that all 750 seats had sold out within the first few hours of going on sale.

After a quick sound check on stage and a talk with a local reporter, Fred appeared blissfully unaware of the cavernous hall for the next two and a half hours, in the isolation of the spotlights, telling the cosy audience about his life and times.

As the night wore on, I cast an appreciative eye around this auditorium, noticing the rapt attention on the faces of the crowd, and realising that Fred had been sold 'too cheaply' if he could do this in a theatre. With his great stage presence, he was a natural speaker who commanded an audience large or small, old or young. It was obvious he could do theatre work as I'd tried to persuade him to in the past, and I hoped now he could see this for himself.

At the end of the show, the organisers approached me eagerly and, judging by the cost of the tickets on sale, it didn't take a mathematical genius to quickly work out that they'd made a heck of a lot of money from tonight's full house – even if they *had* provided us with dinner at the excellent restaurant in the rather nice quaint four-star hotel where we were staying.

Fred was signing autographs as the people filed out from the hall. The crowd couldn't get enough of him – and he still had more tales to tell the waiting queue. I had to keep jostling people forward and tapping his arm so that everyone would get a book or video signed.

'Come on Fred, you'd better get a move on – look at the size of the queue!' I exclaimed to him as he went off at a tangent about something or other. He peered at me with his owl-like stare and said to the next person: 'She's always telling me what to do. What's up with you? Christ, stop mithering, woman!'

It was all part of the show as far as they were concerned, and always got a bemused chuckle or two as people insisted good-naturedly that they didn't mind waiting.

The crowd would have stood there all night listening to him talk if they could have done. So, of course the organisers wanted another booking and who could blame them? Fred was full of glee and bounded around after everyone had left saying, 'A bloody good do that, cock, everyone laughed in the right place as well!'

The booking had been taken as a fifty-minute speech – and not as 'theatre format' two-and-a-half-hour-long show, which is how it had been presented thanks to Fred's enthusiasm in standing there on stage all evening.

I'd always wanted Fred to consider doing a theatre tour and constantly discussed it, expressing my eagerness for him to tour Britain in small provincial theatres replicating what he was doing in front of a sometimes boozy audience with his highly-successful after-dinner-talks. Because of my previous work in this sphere and in cabaret floor shows, I knew that theatre work was a lot easier because you have a captive audience paying a ticket price, rather than in a standard cabaret environment where the drinks are sometimes free-flowing and the crowd is not even sure who is on until you actually get up on stage. So far, Fred had steadfastly refused to consider my request stating, 'You can stuff that, cock – I'm a bloody steeplejack, not an actor!'

I knew instinctively that for theatre audiences, someone like Fred would go down a bomb with these anecdotes about his life, and he'd enjoy the medium. The second response was always, 'Why would anyone pay twelve quid a ticket to see a pillock like me on stage?'

I wisely let the subject drop for a while, but kept dropping hints. Then, a few months later (after a particularly rotten gig at a cricket club), he finally said 'What did you say about doing them theatres – y'know, that night in Stourbridge was a lot easier than talking to a bunch of drunken wankers I sometimes get at these sort of dos.'

From then on he was hooked on the idea, so as soon as I got the red light I contacted Martin, his agent at Arena, and together we began planning a tour around the country, advertising it as: 'An Evening with Fred Dibnah'. The format was a one-man stand-up show for two and a half hours, with a short interval. He would share his anecdotes about steeplejacking and his interest in steam to a paying audience like I'd originally intended him to do. In jest, he called himself, 'A proper professional actor, like some of them blokes you've been with before.'

Mind you, it brought about some difficulties. Fred wasn't accustomed to the more structured running order of a theatre show where you needed to be organised and take into account interval times and such like. As with everything else in life, he had his own unique way of going about things. On a few occasions, the theatre staff would be more than a little concerned to see all the drinks lined up on the bar, ready for thirsty patrons at the interval, getting warmer and warmer by the minute as Fred carried on regardless, going without the planned break an hour and a quarter into the show.

On one occasion, because of him being hard of hearing and unable to hear the stage manager from the left prompt corner, I had to go on stage and literally drag him off into the wings. I sallied forth and tugged at his sleeve mid-tale, and he said to the audience into the mike: 'What? Oh bloody hell, it's time I weren't here, I'll see you all after't interval like, ladies and gentlemen ... goodbye!' It got a great laugh from the audience, and Fred considered we should leave it in, but I didn't fancy standing around in the draughty wings, waiting for my five-second contrived stage appearance up and down the theatres of Britain for the next few months.

I tried gently to explain about 'running times', 'five minute calls' – the need to be mindful of the theatre staff, but he simply wouldn't have any of it.

'Why should I come off early? Ken Dodd never does, he goes on for hours. And the audience love him!' he would insist.

'Yeah, but you're not Ken Dodd!' I added, irritated by this flippancy.

'I bet he's never laddered a 200 foot chimney though.'

'I reckon we'd know about it if he had, Fred!'

'Hmmm... I might invite him to see me sheds sometime, he looks like a bloke who might show some real interest in my style. Wonder if he likes a pint or two?'

I was always amazed at just how many loyal fans Fred had gathered from various walks of life, all of whom respected and admired him. Some of them were internationally famous. Since seeing him in concert, I had been an ardent fan of the legendary keyboard wizard, Rick Wakeman. Being classically trained, his music is complex and full of variation and meaning. I'd been to a couple of his gigs in the past and noticed one day that Rick was doing a concert at the City Varieties Music Hall in Leeds. I decided to go. I mentioned it casually over tea one evening and was astounded when Fred announced he would like to go, too! Imagine my surprise on learning that because I played Rick's albums frequently on the CD player as I went about the housework, ironing or making tea, Fred was also developing a keen liking for his style of music.

If I missed a single day, the comment as he sat at the table supping red wine would be, 'Are you not puttin' Rick on that modern recording contraption you have there, then, cock?'

Another curiosity: Fred by now – and much to the displeasure of certain small-minded people – really enjoyed a glass or two of red to accompany the recital. In days gone by, wine was always met with much suspicion: 'Naaah, too fancy for me that stuff, cock!'

When I first met him, asking him to get a bottle from the local off-licence, he chirped out, 'Urrragh, yer what! How much is THAT gonna cost, then, eh, cock?' This unexpected wine-awareness started when I joined a famous wine club some time ago. At first, when various cases arrived, he was disparaging about the green bottles all bearing strange-sounding foreign names; but they sent some good stuff and Fred tentatively tried them. After a while he started drinking more of it than I did! I think David Hall introduced him to some of the joys of good wine when they were away filming together, as he too is a keen wine lover.

So, it was a daily dose of Rick Wakeman and a good red wine just before some vegetarian offering would be served up at teatime ... Fred didn't know what on earth it was or where it had come from, but seemed to like it. Mind you, his favourite dinner, fish and chips from the local chippy, didn't go amiss – and he drank wine with that, too!

I never tried to change Fred; he was extremely self-opinionated, and would soon tell you if he didn't like the stuff you were placing on the table in front of him. As his world became slightly bigger, and he started staying in smart hotels and getting invited to high-profile events, he sampled a wider variety of experiences. Why shouldn't he enjoy a few of the finer things of life – he'd worked long and hard enough for them? Why was it perceived as 'odd' by a minority of people that he liked spicy food like curry, for instance? One of the unlikeliest things was his keenness for smoked salmon.

In February I'd bought some to use with a pasta sauce, and everywhere we went from then on: ''Ave they got any of that smoked salmon, it's bloody lovely that stuff.'

He liked it so much that in later years his agent sent him a whole side of smoked salmon from Fortnum & Masons as a Christmas gift. We were eating it for weeks afterwards and even Fred got fed up of his beloved smoked salmon butties!

It was a funny experience to walk into some four-star hotel to be met with a rather snooty receptionist who didn't recognise him and of whom Fred immediately enquired: 'Do you 'ave any of them smoked salmon butties here, cock?'

Then there were freshly-squeezed juice concoctions. I'd originally arrived from Blackpool with a juicer which produced something akin to a lovely sweet, colourful milkshake from the humble carrot. Fred, gazing in wonder one day at the glass of orange liquid spewing forth from the nozzle, decided to try it. And from then on he was hooked. His favourite juice was carrot, celery and apple with fresh ginger added to give it bite. To anyone who would listen though, playing for effect – he was a bit of a romancer, and slightly embarrassed at being seen drinking healthy stuff – he'd say: 'Ahh, she's got me on them bloody vitamin pills as well, yer know.'

By stark contrast when we were alone: 'Thanks for looking after me, cock,

I dunno what I'd have done without you – could 'ave done with some of this tackle when I were up them chimneys and it were freezin' me bollocks off an' all!'

It was only a few people's misconception that I was trying to change him. From what little I heard, bizarrely, they considered that he shouldn't have any kind of foreign food or wine let alone healthy vegetarian stuff, in case he metamorphosed into some snobby, flat-capped, working-class gourmet, going about drinking pints of bubbly instead of beer.

Behind closed doors, he wasn't always 'Alf Garnett of the steam world'; we loved each other and had fun. To some of his male companions, the occasional croney and other casual retainers who lionised him, however, I was his nemesis, a veritable pest of the female kind set to wreak havoc and cause destruction, a hindrance – not to be trusted, not to be given any kind of regard. He often disparaged me and our marriage openly just to be 'blokey'. When we were alone, occasionally I saw in him the small, vulnerable, frightened soul that needed love like the next person. He was only human, my Fred; he was exceptional too – but ever wary and frightened of showing emotions to his mates in case it made him look less of a man.

I often wonder now if he was too worried about his 'image' with his peers – though he never struck me at the time as being 'image conscious' in the real sense. But it's true to say he steered a very lonely path as far as emotions and feelings went, for he inhabited an antiquated, blinkered, Dickensian world where men were always tough and impervious to such foibles as a woman's love – however badly they needed it.

The trouble is some of the simpler souls of the more ordinary kind readily believed anything he said, such as, 'She's got me on that bloody foreign stuff again ... naaah, where's me meat pie/bacon butty, then?' It was like a form of embarrassment on his part: if he sacrificed my values and sensibilities on the altar of the jaded observations of his male associates, then it wasn't he who could be perceived as weak or susceptible and ready to change at the mere whims of a woman. It was purely my fault in everyone's eyes for his reluctant enjoyment of garlicky spaghetti or whatever.

How many times have I heard the credo: 'You'll never change him, luv!' Well – I *did* change some of the things he'd usually expect to do with a wife, and so going to a live gig to see an international rock star in action would therefore not be well received in some quarters. Just like all the rest of the stuff he'd discovered and enjoyed with me. It was garlic bread all over again!

I booked the tickets for Rick Wakeman and on the night, after a meal in a Chinese restaurant, we were seated on the front row at the City Varieties Music Hall, leaving behind all thoughts of daft men with their sardonic remarks and parochial views. I warned him about the volume of music normally associated with rock concerts, but he was delighted: 'Bloody hell – at least I'll be able to hear it at full throttle then.' Being almost deaf in one ear, he was looking forward to appreciating the blaring music.

Amazingly, a couple of weeks after I had booked the tickets, I answered the telephone to a man called Frank Fellows. It turned out Mr Fellows had originally introduced Fred to David Hall. I handed over the phone to Fred and sat down in a nearby chair. Frank had once worked for Rick Wakeman, handling merchandising. After a lengthy chat, towards the end of the conversation, Fred piped up: 'Hey, we're off to see that mate of yours, Rick Wakeman. He's in concert soon at Leeds – bloody good music and all, isn't it, eh?'

I could hear the incredulity in Frank's voice. 'You're joking – you're joking, mate, you're JOKING!!!' As it turns out, Rick Wakeman, the big daddy of keyboards, was an avid Dibnah fan and well into watching his programmes on telly. Frank said he would ring Rick and tell him that a certain steeplejack whom he greatly admired would be out front wearing his flat cap, soaking up some serious sounds in Leeds on the night!

The question of it being a 'rock concert' came up on the way to the gig, and Fred said he'd never done 'owt daft' like this before. I assured him, as he adjusted his best flat cap, clean striped shirt and blue engine-driver's jacket ready for our night out, that it would not all be young teenyboppers. The audience would be mostly from an older age group, fully appreciative of the fine calibre of music, not merely some performer to scream at.

The quaint old theatre, with its lavish architectural features, was right up Fred's street. He said he remembered watching one of his favourite telly programmes, *The Good Old Days*, a Victorian music hall series which had been filmed there. He relished every single high-tech note that Rick played on keyboard and electric piano. During the interval, I went to purchase Rick's new album, whilst Fred, 'the rock-freak steeplejack' talked to burly, black-clad crew members, some bearing menacing tattoos, who were also keen Dibnah fans and asked about his new programmes on the BBC. It seemed a bit bizarre as these roadies crowded round trying to meet Fred, but he enjoyed their company and chatted away for some time.

At the end of the evening, as we were leaving our seats, a member of the stage crew – a large man with podgy features and a greying ponytail – darted over to speak to us. Rick, he announced rather gruffly, wanted to say hello and could we stay behind for a short while afterwards?

When the usual home-time dash had cleared, leaving the auditorium bereft of people save a few remaining fans, we were escorted by the burly roadie up the narrow central steps leading onto the empty, blacked-out stage. It had that same smell I recognised from theatres before: a dark, musty but exciting smell made up of theatregoers' expectations, grease paint and the hard work of the cast over many years. We passed Rick's revered and now silent Korg,

Kurtzweil and Yamaha synthesiser keyboards, stepping over the various thick black cables and leads which hooked up rack-mounted samplers and other 'midi' synthesisers which brought his music to life. Then we disappeared into the darkened wings of stage left and finally entered the dressing room where Rick waited patiently to meet Fred.

Rick was very approachable and friendly, casually dressed, always happy to come out to say hi to his fans; one of the boys, a gregarious 'muso' hanging loose after a gig – just an average bloke. Except for the incandescent musical talent: magical, breathtaking, hanging like a jewel in your memory as you chatted with him afterwards. It was hard to square this laid-back, unassuming guy with the mystical spell he'd cast which continued to haunt you well into the night.

He shook hands with us both and made much of the meeting; both men were getting on famously, swapping stories. Rick even asking Fred for *his* autograph at one point! But the highlight of the evening must surely be the incident as we left. Making our way back across the same stage, deserted except for a few busy stagehands, we were carefully descending the steep steps back into the auditorium when Rick suddenly grabbed out for Fred's arm and piped up, 'Go carefully on those steps, Fred, they're very, very steep, y'know!'

Immediately he realised, and was highly amused at, what he'd just said, bashfully proclaiming, 'I can't *believe* I've just said that! I've just told *Fred Dibnah* the famous steeplejack to be *careful* going down some steps, oh, oh my gawd; I can't believe I said that, sorry Fred!'

It was one of those daft situations where the more you laugh, the funnier it becomes, until finally you forget what you are actually laughing about. All three of us fell about as Fred doddered theatrically down the steps in an uncertain way, and Rick's statement just got funnier and funnier each time we repeated it.

Then Christmas was all around us in the shops, telly, magazines and newspapers, and it was time to decorate the festive tree once again. Shopping, queues, frustration and a few major credit-card bills later, and we were ready to have our own quiet family Millennium celebrations; nothing fancy, nothing grand – simply what we wanted.

I had invited my parents for New Year's Eve, and Jack and Roger were looking forward to our little family party. I decorated our kitchen, festooning it in the usual gaudy festive fashion, which complemented the hundreds of colourful cards pinned up on the wooden beams – jolly greetings from all over the country. I made up a small buffet for the evening whilst Jack blew up some balloons.

The boys were so excited, because the plan was to also steam up the boiler in the workshops, set up several more whistles, and let them all off together on the stroke of midnight. The whistles were part of Fred's large hoard rescued over many years from old spinning mills, weaving sheds and various long-gone steam locomotives. He handled each one lovingly, and explained to me where he'd originally found it. He was as excited as the boys at the prospect of hearing them all go off together.

Throughout the evening, all three boys were busy stoking the boiler, occasionally running into the house in search of food and soft drinks, crying, 'There's over 90 PSI on the boiler now, Sheila.'

My mum and dad let their hair down after a few drinks, dancing to the strains of Glenn Miller, which reminded them of when they first met at the Palais de Dance in Bolton during their salad days. Fred kept us all amused as he supped his Guinness by telling a collection of stories about places and people he had known throughout the years.

Towards the midnight hour, we brought out long champagne flutes, placing the bubbly on ice in a specially bought cooler for this auspicious occasion, and I took the whole lot out on a tray into the magical garden. I busied myself with the camera and we opened a big box of fireworks, ready to mark the New Year. Nathan was on firework duty, in charge of the intended display and stood by with a lighted taper ready for the countdown.

Not long to go now...

The final few moments of 1999...

Standing by, I was ready to pull the cord attached to a big bell rigged up over the shed. The bell would peal out in the cloak of darkness, giving Fred and the boys the signal to hoot the whistles at midnight. The countdown began: 10-9-8-7-6-5-4-3-2-1. I pulled the string and the bell rang out into the night. Nathan immediately lit two fireworks. The air gradually began to fill with an eerie steam symphony: loud whistles from days gone by, commissioned now to herald a new century, all vibrating and resonating at different pitches which made your eardrums quiver – the sound coming from somewhere above in the middle of your head – a fanfare you could actually feel as well as hear. The smell of sulphur too: the brilliance of crackling golden fire from the two fireworks showered the damp grass.

We all responded with a resounding, roaring cheer of approval. The strident sound of the whistles continued. The 100 PSI on the boiler pressure gauge dropped down to 5 PSI within a few minutes and it was indeed a truly magnificent moment; Fred's monument to the industrial age had heralded in this brave new Millennium.

Long live the Industrial Age.

Memories came back of New Year celebrations in the past.

Times as a kid, when I would ponder the enormity of the world. Being allowed to stay up way past bedtime and coming in through the front door, carrying a cob of coal with my mum for good luck – the exciting dawn of the next twelve months, uncharted, unknown. Times as an adult, jaded, when I no longer believed in Santa or that the world would somehow change for the better on the stroke of midnight, but knew without a shadow of a doubt that the forthcoming year might well change me instead.

But on this occasion, full of euphoria, we realised we had totally forgotten about the champagne. The bottle was cracked open at Fred's request, and all three boys vied for the first glass; Roger never having tasted it before wanted a full one, so I obliged. On the first sip, he wrinkled his nose, pulled a face and flatly declared he much preferred his dad's Guinness instead of Moët & Chandon!

CHAPTER 9
The height of bad manners...
'You need to be very tough being married to someone in the public eye — that is my opinion...'

After the plethora of after-dinner speaking engagements, and before the usual onset of the summer steam rally season, Fred had a rather interesting booking. It was Easter Monday, and the venue was The Hatworks in Stockport, for the opening of a new hat museum at the former hat factory. (I would later donate Fred's flat cap to them after his death.)

It is one of those unique industrial places which immediately fascinates you by introducing the processes of manufacture that go into producing something so familiar. Normally, you wouldn't even give them a second thought. It was also memorable because of the visually striking display of hats throughout the ages — all modes of fashion right up to the present day.

David Schilling, the grandson of the famous and celebrated Ascot hat designer Mrs Gertrude Schilling, was there to open the museum along with

Fred. Dapper, charismatic, quite charming (and rather dishy I thought) in his dark, well-cut pinstripe suit and jaunty, original headgear, he expressed great interest in Fred's climbing ability. And, since there was a large, red-brick chimney, which the museum was currently having mended, complete with steeplejacking ladders in situ, Fred didn't need much encouragement to get excited over a spot of climbing.

Fred wanted to go up the chimney as soon as he saw it, but I managed somehow to dissuade him in the face of much encouragement from the staff. He was wearing slippery-soled, military buffed, black brogues which were quite unsuitable for climbing 220 feet into the sky and there were too many health and safety issues. That, as usual, cut no ice with Fred who merely thought I was spoiling his fun. Somehow, I managed to keep my disgruntled man firmly on the ground and stick him in a corner most of the afternoon signing autographs and chatting to people instead of climbing chimneys. He wasn't happy. 'Bloody hell, woman, nowt wrong with me shoes.'

'Well, Fred, maybe if you'd have been wearing your boots ... but then there are the health and safety men to consider, too.'

'Christ! What do those blokes know? Half o' them have never laddered a 200 foot chimney in their lives!' he retorted in disgust.

You simply cannot keep a good man down, but we needed more than just army boots at the first rally of the season that year ... Fred ended up in wellies in Northamptonshire! This was our third annual visit to the Rushden Historical Transport Society Rally, at Lancaster Farm, Higham Ferrers. We liked, and looked forward to, this large rally; it was always very busy and well organised.

During this trip, however, the weather was a total let down. It had been raining for the best part of a week and the field was a veritable lake of deep, sticky mud. The wind and rain blustered continuously, conspiring to keep us mostly in the beer tent. We also spent a lot of time near the exhibitors' gate, at the side of Betsy which, like the other engines, could not be moved because of the mud. We sat under a tarpaulin cover, signing autographs.

Usually at a steam rally, the engines parade around the arena area at noon or 2.00 p.m., but on the first day there were no exhibits in the arena because of the bad weather. Bales of fresh straw had to be placed around the field in rows wherever possible, soaking up the soggy mess, to enable the public to gain access to sodden trade stall areas selling chips, burgers, tea, coffee, doughnuts, books, crockery, tools, army surplus and a host of other goods.

'Naaarr ... no damned good, this, cock – I'm off ter beer tent,' said Fred.

We were still busy with demands for autographs and videos, but it took the edge right off the event and finally we decided to make the best of a bad job by simply walking around talking to people. Fortunately on one of the stalls we managed to find Fred a pair of second-hand green wellies for a couple of quid, and he proudly trudged around the field looking like a character from a Disney film (all we needed now were the other six dwarves!), telling everyone he met that at one time you had to be posh to own a pair of green wellies where he came from.

Fellow steam man Peter Lidgett, a friend of Fred's for many years, was there with his big blue 1914 Fowler B6 Road locomotive called 'The Lion', its white Pickfords Heavy Haulage logo on the side of the massive dark-blue engine making it easily one of the most striking engines on display. It had been used in the First World War, and later belonged to Walter Denton Haulage Contractors in Hyde, and had been used to move boilers for Adamson Boiler Works. It now belonged to 'The Duke' (as I named him) who bore a handsome and striking resemblance to a younger version of the legendary screen idol John Wayne. I had casually remarked upon this to Fred a couple of years ago at the same rally, and to my horror Fred mentioned it to Peter right in front of me: 'Hey, mate – Sheila reckons you look like John Wayne.' I was relieved that he did not seem to mind and laughed about it later. As I got to know him better, as a joke whenever he rang our home to speak to Fred, he'd always introduce himself to me as John Wayne. He was a bit of a wild, exciting and unruly individual too, with a strong, charismatic personality and, like Fred, could hold many people in his thrall with his various anecdotes.

This steam version of a Hollywood double had invited us to a barbecue that evening on the sodden rally field. We didn't feel up to attending, however, because exhaustion had set in, so we went back to our digs in The Foxford Hotel, Rushden. After a long hot shower together and an undisturbed evening meal we retired early to our room – the bridal suite – for an early night. The hotel had some nice ale, Fred informed me, so it was no hardship for him to unwind, sipping beer as we lay there on the bed almost falling asleep after watching telly together, locked in each other's arms, looking forward to perhaps another kiss and a cuddle later on before lights out.

The hotel room phone rang and I reluctantly answered it. A voice at the other end announced, 'Hi Sheila, John Wayne here. I'm downstairs in the hotel with some friends. Is your man in?'

'Hi Peter! He's very tired, just a mo...'

In the warm room, I continued speaking for a while, discussing the bad weather. Fred was lying sprawled out naked on the four-poster bed, save for socks and flat cap, absent-mindedly fumbling with his various bits, casually glancing through a steam engine book, and doing his usual 'tuneless humming' to 'Don't Cry for Me Argentina'. He stopped and waited for me to finish the conversation. I covered the mouthpiece and said, 'Bloody hell, Freddie, its John Wayne, and he's downstairs *now* in the bar with some friends. He wants you to go down ... now what! Shall I get rid of him?'

'I don't want to go downstairs – I'm knackered, like.'

171

'Peter, listen, he doesn't want to come down, I think...'

'Put him on,' Peter asserted, sounding a bit miffed.

I obliged, and handed over the telephone.

'Hiya, mate! Dunno... I'm just 'avin' a bit of a bloody rest n' all...

aye... yeah, yeah...' Fred mumbled on. 'Mmmm... well, I dunno...'

The call continued as Fred listened and nodded his head.

'Yeah... yeah... yeah...' Fred wasn't speaking much, but was looking a bit lost, a bit uncertain.

I blurted out loudly, 'What does he want? Tell him we're having an evening together and an early night.'

I couldn't get the gist of what was being said at the other end, because Fred frantically shook his hand towards me in a dismissive way and kept going, 'Hmmm, hmmm...'

He ignored me and finally finished with, 'Oh all right, I'll be down in two minutes then...' groaning as he replaced the receiver. 'Bloody hell, like, I don't really feel like going downstairs, I'll only end up getting drunk.'

Slowly, he got up off the bed and padded around the room, sighing heavily, reluctantly starting to dress in his black jeans.

I wanted Fred to rest up for the night with me and so I picked up the receiver and rang the downstairs bar. I said, 'Listen Peter, he doesn't want to come downstairs, and as usual we've got a damned busy day tomorrow on the field, so he's not coming down to see you, sorry, but – no, NO!'

'Put him back on... I've got some friends here want to meet him.'

'*No*, Peter – we're having an early night!'

'Can I speak to him then?'

'No, he's in the bathroom, he's not available!'

'Can he not speak for himself these days, Sheila?'

'He's tired, Peter, he doesn't want to let you down, but he's so tired...'

'Put him on then.'

'No, Peter, he's not coming downstairs and he's not coming to the phone.'

The phone clicked down. The line had gone dead.

'Hippo, I think I'm in big trouble with Mr Wayne.'

'Well, never mind, cock, I didn't want to go down there anyway...'

That said, he started to undress again and gratefully flopped down on the bed just like a tired big hippo. We snuggled up in each other's arms and, after a cup of coffee from the kettle provided on a tray, cuddled up further and watched the small television set in the corner of the room. I caught a sigh of relief from Fred.

We had been given the four-poster bridal suite but, within twenty minutes, he was fast asleep.

The next day on the rally field Mr Lidgett avoided me and spoke only to Fred. No doubt like some others, he considered I was manipulating Fred and hindering his enjoyment by 'spoiling his fun'. As it turned out Mr Wayne, a highly astute man, was not very long sussing out that I only had Fred's best interests at heart and was looking after him whenever he needed it. So after that initial run-in, we gradually became firm pals, and eventually I considered him to be a true friend to my husband.

After Rushden, it was back to more routine personal appearances and after-dinner talks for Fred. Eventually came the trip down to Eastnor Castle for a Bank Holiday steam event. I always enjoyed our trips to see James Hervey-Bathurst and his wife, Sarah. We had the titillating thrill of sleeping in the same bed that Ronan Keating had slept in during his recent visit there – or at least I did; in fact, we were the next couple to use it, the night after Ronan! And for those who don't recognise the name, he's that fey, good-looking pop star with blond hair who used to be with a group called Boyzone. James remarked he would not have changed the sheets if only he'd known I liked him! The circular room, a beautifully designed and luxurious masterpiece in cream, yellow and gold which contained one of the most comfortable beds I'd ever slept in, was located in one of the turrets at the corner of the castle. As I gazed round, waiting for Fred to come upstairs from his chat and a few beers in the kitchen with James, I felt cosseted and privileged.

The future was looking good and we were happy together. Weepy, troubled rows were always over quickly; I knew that Fred was no ordinary man, so one had to suffer not only the media circus but some friction too. Fred was unique but human like the rest of us, and at times he was stressed out with pressure and the constant demands on his time.

We worked together as a team; the formula was good. My go-ahead modern outlook complemented his old-fashioned sensibilities; although neither of us was clever at fractions, we knew this situation equated to a whole. And on a practical level we thrived together; he needed me to look after him, run the home and business side of things, and I needed him to go out, increase his profile and get promoted to earn the money. We did have our differences and opposing views, often bickering over trite, silly things, but each took the consequent upbraiding with good humour, knowing where we belonged in the general plan of things. We needed the strength of each other and eventually settled our quarrels with dignity, until later when he became ill and the balance shifted and became distorted. Then I increasingly found that Fred and his crowd snubbed me in subtle and not so subtle ways, as his bitterness grew in line with the fatal tumour.

'You are a bloody awkward cow at times, but I do love you, you know,' he'd often say during the good times.

Around this time, a young man called Peter Carrier, from a college in Plymouth, wanted to interview us both for his dissertation. The topic:

examining how people's lives are affected by appearing in TV documentaries. At first he wanted merely to interview Fred, but later asked if he might include me as well, since our family life was affected by fame. He wanted to examine the side effects and impact of public intrusion on a relationship. Peter came along on one of our open days in the yard, which I often organised so that members of the public could come along on a designated day and meet 'Our Fred'. On this particular day, we had about fifty people present, and Peter learned firsthand simply by being there and observing visitors and their interaction with Fred.

He started the interview before people arrived and mentioned notices displayed in the window and on the front door with reference to 'not accepting casual callers'. Because our house is split into two levels, the door to the street is upstairs on the same level as the three bedrooms, but because of the heavy iron knocker the house literally reverberated each time someone used it. Peter asked how much of a problem this was for us; was all this constant knocking now considered an intrusion? I explained how Fred used to leave the gate open all day long at one time, and people would simply wander in. People turning up this way didn't bother Fred, but it constantly worried me because he was working in a potentially dangerous environment where much concentration was needed. The other worrying aspect was the way he constantly let strangers into the house. For example, one night around the time when we first met, a knock came at about 10.30 p.m. Three loud, clear thuds, straight out of the film *The Fog,* announced that there was someone or something on the other side of the heavy front door. The thuds at the door again rang out of the dark misty night...

'You're not going to answer it at this time of night, are you, Fred?'

'Aye! Why not?'

With that, he went upstairs and drew back the bar to see who was standing there. Footsteps sounded on the stairs and three burly, thick-set young men all aged about twenty-five, accompanied Fred into the middle downstairs room. Working in Bolton on a joinery job, they wanted to meet their hero, but were going back to Scotland in the morning. All three turned out to be really nice guys, but I was concerned at Fred's naïvety in letting the hefty-looking strangers indoors at that time of night. What would have happened if they'd been thugs? The danger of opening the door late at night like that was something I could never get him to consider.

And it made me think of all the other effects fame had on our life, too...

If, for instance, we happened to leave the driveway gate open for twenty minutes, somebody would immediately wander in expecting to be shown around, whether it was convenient to us or not. At my instigation, we had a sign put on the front door asking people not to call, but Fred later admonished me for this, saying it would encourage them to knock. Before this, people would rap on the door at least ten times a day to get a book signed, ask for an autograph or to be shown around the workshops.

It was like being under constant siege. No escape!

Towards the end of his life Fred didn't care much for my stand-offish approach in these matters, but as his profile increased he accepted the locked gates as a necessity if we were to have anything like a normal family life (which was now becoming non-existent). That is exactly what I missed most in my life with Fred: privacy!

These anecdotes are the two best examples I can think of to illustrate some of the more unsavoury aspects of being in the public eye, being at the mercy of some thoughtless individuals who thought fame equated with public ownership.

For a long while, Fred was always reluctant to have net curtains up at the windows, but was forced to give in due to a couple of unfortunate events.

One day, a chubby, middle-aged woman dressed in a blue twill coat arrived in a car together with another couple and a man who was presumably her husband. The other three were circling around outside the front railings, looking down the driveway, taking pictures, admiring the architecture of the building whilst the woman in blue was standing on the pavement directly outside our bedroom window. I was amazed to see her lean forward and start peering in through the panes, both hands held up to the leaded glass. The next moment, a white flash went off. I could see she was holding a camera directly against the windowpane and had taken a shot of our bed directly opposite the window!

Turning triumphantly and shouting loudly to the couple about her 'trophy', she looked very pleased indeed. Then the man I assumed to be her husband wandered over to where she was standing and peered in the window as well. I opened the front door and shot outside full of vitriol to tackle this extreme thoughtlessness; it took me ages to calm down afterwards.

Fred mumbled that something similar had once upset Alison.

The other incident again concerned people milling around outside our home. Fred was working on some scaffolding. It was near lunchtime and I called him indoors. Nipping out the back door, I quickly mentioned there were visitors lurking.

At the top of the oak-clad stone staircase indoors, there is a small oblong window. Fred set off upstairs to visit the bathroom before eating his lunch. Whilst on his way upstairs, the face of an elderly, whiskered man (who should have known better) suddenly appeared at the clear window at the top of the stairs. Shielding his eyes with both his hands, he peered close up to the glass and spotted Fred. His face lit up and he began banging loudly on the window, gesticulating to the others, 'He's here! He's here!' He continued banging, trying to attract attention, frustration making the banging harder as the glass rattled in its frame.

Fred lurched forward upstairs, out of sight. I stuck my face right up to the window and dare not repeat here what I shouted through the glass to this despicable, but now terrified, old man! He recoiled in horror, as though he'd been given an electric shock, but I had just about had enough of it. I could not comprehend the mentality of someone who would do such an ill-mannered and thoughtless thing at a person's home.

Then there were the many letters demanding Fred's oily cap or a line drawing done for the BBC programmes. They were almost always in the same mould: 'You must have an old cap you don't want' or 'My husband watches all your programmes, I'd like to surprise him with one of your drawings'. I used to give some of Fred's caps to charity, and they'd raise a bit of money. Dominic Brunt, perhaps better known as Paddy from *Emmerdale*, paid fifty quid for one once in an auction held at a celebrity fund-raising evening at Manchester Football Club!

Fred would never be left alone; there were always people wanting his attention. He didn't mind – nothing was too much trouble – but I couldn't be that gregarious and ended up feeling embittered about the whole thing. It didn't matter how patient or friendly you acted, it was never enough, and gradually you couldn't help but be turned into some kind of raging ogre, a viper angrily lashing out verbally whenever you needed peace and quiet. It is difficult to imagine if you've never had to deal with it. I guess it was the price to pay for loving him, putting up with people wanting to share every aspect of your life, and ultimately this played a much bigger part in events than I could ever imagine. But for now, I was blissfully unaware and didn't realise what powerful effects Fred had on people, and the remarkable way they needed to relate to him to make sense of their own lives.

Friends were important to Fred, but what is the true definition of a friend? How could you tell friend – or foe – if you didn't think badly of anyone at all, except your temperamental wife occasionally?

You could be sitting relaxing in a pub, or a restaurant. Someone spots him and decides they want to speak. They pull up a chair and plonk themselves down at your table without invitation. You, as the wife of this celebrity, do not exist from that moment on; they are blinded by the ray of the cathode tube, the living television personality before their very eyes. You may have been locked in some private conversation with your husband, enjoying an intimate moment together, but now it's 'him off the telly'. They demand to speak to 'Our Fred'. They will not take a hint and leave after a few moments. You then have to be quite blunt – or else you are stuck for the next half-hour, trying to enjoy your food, with some stranger taking your place in your husband's attention. These types think they are the only people ever to have approached you, and expect to be greeted like a long-lost friend. 'Hiya Fred.

You don't know me, but I feel like I've known you for ages... I like those new programmes on telly.' Then someone else appears: 'Hey! It's Fred, isn't it...!' They continue speaking, joining in with the other 'unwelcome' intruders, oblivious to the fact they've barged in on your personal time. Someone else appears – soon you have gathered a small crowd. It happened every time we went out together. But it was a one-sided battle, because Fred had time for everyone, and it was his genuine love of people they all wanted to make a connection with. I see that now. He made people feel good. It was his magic formula.

Whilst attending the open day for Twyfords Waterworks near Winchester, the organiser, Steve Wedge, had arranged for us all to have a quick lunch at a local pub. Steve had brought his son, Robert, along and we had Nathan with us. Robert was sitting opposite me, still finishing his lunch, when an unknown man sauntered casually up to our table. He leaned over Robert, who was struggling by now to eat as the man continued to hand pictures of a steam engine over to Fred. He never bothered to enquire if he might interrupt our lunch break for a moment, never realised one or more of us may resent this intrusion. All that mattered was his own gratification in speaking to Fred. I endured this thoughtlessness for about five minutes or so, witnessing poor Robert struggling to eat with a large, sweating man looming over him, and then I decided to speak my mind.

Later, his father, Steve, wondered about the blatant selfishness that results when people spot a celebrity. They seem to totally forget their manners; I wonder how they might feel and react in similar circumstances? No doubt some people will still shake their heads, bewildered by the frosty reception they once received from me as they recall their meeting with Fred. So if you ever got an ear-bashing from me, dear reader, so sorry – but you see, I only wanted to be with my hubby, and you were intruding on that day ... no matter *how* fascinating he was!

Of course, the majority of people are fine and respect your privacy. They are the ones with the shrewdness to realise that although a celebrity has been on television, it certainly doesn't mean they are public property. Fred was an icon. He got sacks full of mail from ex-engineers, ex-miners, and people interested in everything and anything that he had ever loved or been involved with. Fred respected most of his fans and always had time for a chat, even when he was feeling very poorly towards the end of his life.

The telephone calls were the most infuriating. Up to thirty a day and these were mostly from people who had managed to get our number from directory enquires. Invitations to stay with complete strangers, to weddings of people he had never met, people wanting him to point a chimney on their home, build things for them, look at a damp patch on their ceiling, meet a neighbour who was off work with flu, ring up Uncle Albert at his retirement party, send a letter to a relative in Australia, or perhaps chat to someone down the phone who considered themselves a friend because he'd once spoken to them at a rally many years ago. To Fred it didn't matter; if they were interesting to talk to, then that was fine by him. To me, it was tantamount to receiving nuisance calls.

Then there were the nutcases who would ring up at all hours with daft and sometimes insulting comments: 'Stuff the f***ing Industrial Revolution,' one idiot rang up to say at 11.00 p.m., then slammed down the phone. Even Fred, usually so easy-going, was getting fed-up with these calls, as people would sometimes ring up drunk, imitating his accent. It was worse still when the BBC programmes had been on television. The programmes would finish at 8.00 p.m., and we knew the telephone would ring straight away. It happened on every occasion without fail.

'You need to be very tough being married to someone in the public eye – that is my opinion...' Fred said when asked about his attitude to marriage and fame during an interview.

One woman rang on a Sunday, just as we sat down to dinner. I explained we were eating. She became quite irate as she could hear Fred's voice in the background, and because I would not put him on the line for a few minutes, she vented her full anger on me. In a huff, she icily declared: 'Huh – well, I'm surprised you are not ex-directory then, if you don't expect people to call you up!'

(Hey up, Missus! To be honest, so was I...)

The next day, I contacted the telephone company and arranged it. The calls diminished somewhat and life became slightly more bearable, but Fred sometimes had a grumble or two about not being able to speak to people who might have a steam engine which they wanted to pass on and give to a good home, or an enquiry for some interesting chimney felling job for him to tackle. They were the innocent casualties of our now ex-directory number.

I had many letters and requests to deal with. One photograph, which I considered to be the best one of all and has been extensively used, was taken by a man called Rod Smallman. We were at the Rushden Steam Rally again, in Northamptonshire on Spring Bank Holiday and the weather was much better than our previous visit. A man toting a camera came up to Fred as he stood by Betsy and casually took some shots, like so many others did. It was early and Fred was sipping a steaming mug of morning coffee.

'Do you mind, Fred?' the photographer enquired.

'Nahhh, you're alright, mate, go on!' said Fred, posing amiably for the shot.

A week later, we received one of the photographs from the gentleman, an amateur photographer who lived in Banbury. He wanted to know if Fred would sign it for his collection. The picture was marvellous: clear and sharp in every detail, and he had captured Fred's spirit exactly. It was obvious that the guy was a brilliant photographer and so I enquired about the possibility of making his picture into a publicity postcard. Mr Smallman kindly agreed. It became our best seller and Rod became our good friend. He went on to take many superb photographs of Fred, some of which you can see in this book.

CHAPTER 10
'Dr Dibnah, I presume?'

'Yeah ... well cock, I'm a mature student an' all!'

*T*he trip to Aberdeen to receive an Honorary Degree from the Robert Gordon University in 2000 was a true highlight in Fred's life, as indeed was receiving his second honorary doctorate from the University of Birmingham in 2004, then his MBE at Buckingham Palace later that same year.

We'd received the initial letter from Aberdeen University in early January 2000, and Fred immediately thought it was a bit of a wind-up. 'What do they want to give a degree to a daft bugger like me for, eh?' Fortunately, I took it seriously and responded to the university on his behalf.

A date was set for an afternoon ceremony on Wednesday, 5th July 2000, when Fred would become a Doctor of Technology. We soon received a second letter from the university informing us that Professor Norman Deans, the Head of the School of Electronic and Electrical Engineering, who would be presenting him for the award, wished to visit Fred in Bolton to get a bit of background for his laureate address on the day.

Neither of us being in any way academic, we were unsure as to what the good Professor Deans from the fusty halls of academia would think once he got here and was met with our '*eee bah gum*' attitude to life. He turned out to be a lovely, warm-hearted man; he obviously was a great fan, and was equally enthralled with the back garden workshops as he was with Fred.

The afternoon whizzed by. After a long day, Professor Deans eventually left for his evening flight back to Aberdeen, having had a taste of Fred's industrial northern way of life.

Before we were due to make the trip up to Scotland, however, we had to travel down to Kent for another steam rally at the Hop Farm near Paddock Wood. We had visited during the previous year's rally season. The event was far more successful on this trip than the weather, which seemed overcast and muggy for most of the weekend. But Fred did not misplace his reading glasses this time! We usually ended up searching for them at least five or six times during any rally, assuming someone had taken them as a personal souvenir. I once had to order a new pair for him after he swore someone had taken them as he signed autographs at one particular rally; later in the same month, he unexpectedly discovered them in a jacket pocket– just like some absent-minded professor. Being eccentric in every way, I presumed he would do well as 'Dr Dibnah'!

This would be the second time in less than two weeks we had made the trip to Scotland. We'd visited Mauchline in Ayrshire earlier that month for 'The Restoration of the Loudoun Spout Gala Day'. Mauchline is famous for its connections with Robert Burns, who lived just north of the village at East Mossgiel Farm from 1784 to 1788, and the Burns House Museum, dedicated to the great man and his works, attracts people from all over the globe each year. The other notable thing about Mauchline is the Loudoun Spout, situated on Loudoun Street, which dates from about 1763. It was placed there originally to provide water for passing cattle drovers and their stock. It also provided people of the village with drinking water long before it was piped directly into their homes, and one of the main reasons for visiting the village at that time was the purity and availability of the spring water, which comes up from the sandstone rock beneath the village. Our friend Jimmy Davidson, who came to our wedding, was the secretary on the local committee responsible for the restoration of the Spout, which had ceased to flow in 1997. Much dedication, support and hard work had gone into the Spout's restoration and Jimmy suggested it would make the day a red-letter one if the committee had Fred and his engine Betsy along for this important occasion.

Everyone greeted us warmly when we arrived in Mauchline, and Fred looked forward to the parade of vintage transport through the village.

Nothing was too much bother to make us feel welcome. On the day of the event, horses and carts, vintage tractors, lorries, cars, military vehicles, motorcycles – and another steam traction engine as well as Fred's – gathered for the procession. We gradually progressed through the village, waving at the growing crowds, proceeding down Loudoun Street, to where a small platform and PA system had been erected for the day at the side of the Spout.

A woman with local connections, called Stroma Hamilton-Campbell, had travelled up from London and conducted the official opening ceremony with 'Our Fred'. After a few words from both of them, the crowd cheered loudly and cameras clicked as everyone posed for photos. Finally, we clambered up on Betsy again, smiled and waved at the crowds, eventually rumbling along the road in a chuff of black soot to where the gala was being held in a nearby field.

Once I had got over the initial shock of learning I had to officially open the gala and hand out prize cups to the Rose Queen and her assistants in front of the waiting crowds, I began to relax and enjoy myself – until I was approached over lunch in the pub to judge the 'Bonny Baby' contest. I left a highly amused Fred in mid-sentence during a conversation with a fan, and went back onto the field for the ordeal...

'Sole judge, Mrs Sheila Dibnah,' someone announced as I walked onto the makeshift stage. Apparently, no one from the village wanted to be responsible for any bad feeling, as there had been an altercation in the past when two feuding mothers had nearly come to blows over the judge's decision – so they'd asked me to stand in, instead. (Gulp!)

I looked at each angelic little cherub and furtively glanced at his or her doting mum as well. Once I had ascertained that there were no 'bruisers' present, who would not take kindly to their little darlings being snubbed, I breathed a sigh of relief and gave what I considered to be a fair judgement without fear of grievous bodily harm. The prizes were presented and, since I'd suffered no ill effects such as a black eye, the afternoon seemed to sail by happily. I returned to Fred, who was enjoying talking with the driver of the other steamroller.

Fred was also booked to appear later that evening at the local community centre for 'An Evening with Fred Dibnah'. We arrived at the packed hall about five minutes early. People cheered as Fred waltzed up to the front and immediately launched into his fascinating stories. He stood there and held the audience mesmerised for more than two hours. It was only when he'd finished, one of the organisers strolled forward, smiling, holding up a sheet of paper, waving it about saying, 'It was very good indeed, thank you, Fred, but *this* was supposed to be your introduction!' Fred had gone straight into his talk without even bothering to be introduced to the audience first! That was so typical of him.

'Oh heck – sorry mate, 'n' all...' said a bashful Fred, turning and laughing with the audience. It brought the roof down.

The next day, Sunday, I wanted to return quickly to Bolton as it was Nathan's fifteenth birthday. He had not wanted to come along on this trip preferring, like all teenage boys, to spend time with his mates on his special day. Fred had to load Betsy onto the low-loader at 5.00 p.m., so I left him in the good company of some local folk who owned a farm where the engine was stored and waiting to be steamed up. As I sped south along the M6 in Linky, I was glad to be heading home and wondered how long it would take Fred to travel from Ayrshire with the haulage man and a low-loader. Later, about 7.00 p.m., I got a call from Fred: 'Hiya, flower – it's me! I can't get back tonight, luv, the low-loader guy isn't setting off 'til five in the morning, his tachograph is up or summat, so I'll see you tomorrow instead, cock!'

I replaced the receiver and felt a bit guilty for dashing off and leaving him stranded there on his own. I knew for sure he would not have any problems, but then suddenly I remembered he did not have any money on him...

Aye ... eventually five o'clock came round, and the bloke with the low-loader arrived bang on time. The engine was being particularly awkward, couldn't get any steam pressure up. It were getting on towards quarter to six when it had enough steam in its belly to get it on the low-loader. By this time, a great crowd had gathered, all the neighbours had come to see this performance of Mr Dibnah putting his engine on a low-loader! It's as though there's some kind of ritual, you know, as though it might fall off when it's being put on. Having done this operation many times in the past, if it isn't raining, it's easy. When it's rainy, you sometimes get a bit of wheel spin, as you might say, and it's a bit dodgy.

But the weather was kind and good, so on to the low-loader it went. Then we proceeded to strap it on. I said to the low-loader man, 'I'm going to come back with you tonight,' and he looked at me with great surprise on his face and said, 'Well... I'm not going back tonight!' which leaves me marooned in Ayrshire, without any money, two hundred miles from home. I knew somebody would find me some digs for the night, but the problem was the haulier's HQ was twenty miles nearer to England, which would have meant him coming back for me at five o'clock in the morning, which was his intended setting-off time!

Anyway, we all had a meeting, and it was decided that I should go and spend the night at the wagon driver's house with his missus and his kid and get an early start at five o'clock.

We set off on the twenty miles with the wagon and steamroller on the back, parked it up and went to his house. I found out that it had all been arranged for me to stay with his mother-in-law and his father-in-law at their house. All the relations ended up coming round, so it was a big night talking about chimneys and steam engines; having 'wee drams' of whiskey, which went on till about quarter to three in the morning! Then we had to get up at five o'clock ... and we were back in Lancashire for about dinnertime...

Again, this was so typical of Fred – turning a drama into a fun time.

However, our next trip up to Scotland for Fred's honorary degree was a little more organised. We set off the day before the event, knowing it was a long, tiring journey to Aberdeen, looking forward to our planned stay in Dundee for the night. We would arrive in Aberdeen refreshed and ready for the ceremony.

The journey to Scotland seemed to take much longer than our last visit to Aberdeen two years before mainly because Fred decided (being chief navigator as usual) that we would take the 'short cut'. Anyone who has ever travelled in a car with him will know exactly what this entails. The general idea seemed to be that smaller roads are somehow quicker, and I suppose when you were used to travelling at 5m.p.h. wielding the iron steering wheel of twelve-tons of steam engine – then yes, this would be the case.

However, we ended up stuck behind slow-moving traffic with Fred busily eying the local beauty spots declaring, 'Oh! look at that, luv,' as I tried my best to keep calm, whipping around tractors and caravans as he carried on admiring the architecture and scenery, or leisurely reading his old book on mining techniques.

We soldiered on next morning to Aberdeen, dressed in our finery for the occasion. Approaching the outskirts of the city, we found the Music Hall, where the graduation ceremony was to be held later that day.

It all became very real and meaningful whilst sitting in the car reading a pamphlet about the history of the university. Its roots can be traced back to Robert Gordon himself, a very successful and eminent Aberdeen merchant who willed his estate to build a hospital to educate scholars in the mid-eighteenth century. Throughout the past 250 years the institute continued to strive for excellence, and in the latter part of the twentieth century was accorded university status in recognition of the academic standing of its courses. It was indeed an honour to be considered for an award.

After killing some time in a local bookshop, we headed back towards the venue on foot to find Professor Deans standing outside the university building, surrounded by students, proud parents, professors and academic staff who had attended the morning's ceremony. In awe of the fresh-faced young graduates spilling out from the building, their black-and-white ensemble testifying to their endeavours over the past few years, we walked towards Professor Deans.

'They're all very young, aren't they, Fred?' I mused.

'Yeah ... well, cock, I'm a mature student an' all!'

The professor led us inside the building, through impressive double doors, into the robing rooms and through into the main auditorium where about 300 seats were waiting to be filled during the afternoon ceremony. Fred was instructed on the protocol of how to accept the award, and after a small rehearsal we were shown to the Round Room in time for an elegant buffet lunch and a glass or two of wine. I told Fred not to have too much but people kept filling his glass, although thankfully it didn't seem to have any effect on him whatsoever.

In due course I took my seat on an ornate cast-iron balcony in the main hall. I was placed between Sheila Stevely, the Principal and Vice-Chancellor's wife, and Mrs Macdonald, whose husband Donald, the Chief Executive of Macdonald Hotels, was to receive one of the two honorary Doctor of Business Administration awards that afternoon. The other award was going to Bryan Keith, a businessman with seven companies based in Aberdeen.

I waited, clutching my little zoom-lens Pentax, chatting to the others and glancing through the booklet that accompanied the event. The ceremony would include the many graduates seated in the auditorium below who were also waiting eagerly for their awards. The air fairly tingled with expectation, and I looked at the happy families of the clever and gifted young people who surrounded us. The organ music began, the pipes demanding everyone's attention with their regal sounds.

We stood up as a procession entered the hall consisting of staff, governors, academic council, Chancellor, Vice-Chancellor, and Fred with the two other honorary graduands, Bryan and Donald. Well, I had often wondered what it would take to get Fred into colourful garments (his favourite colour being dark blue), and I certainly wasn't disappointed on this occasion. Attired in a vivid red robe, trimmed with white, and a black hat complete with a red tassel, Fred made his way up onto the platform with the two others. I reflected on how deserving he was of this award – as indeed all three were – and felt touched by the moment.

He was first on and Professor Deans read out a glowing testimonial for five minutes about a life amidst black smoke and sturdy steaming engines. There can't have been one person present who didn't feel this was a very timely award, as Fred's achievements were read out. Sir Bob Reid, Chancellor of the university, conferred the honorary degree of Doctor of Technology on Fred, who then returned to his seat on the platform, grinning and proudly clutching his red tube containing a certificate.

Dr Frederick Dibnah!

Although the ceremony lasted well over two hours, it seemed to pass very quickly and before long it was time to rise again as the platform party and the graduates below left the hall. Soon afterwards, I was with Fred and the others in the robing room where a professional photographer was setting up to take pictures of the trio, preserving their big day for posterity. Fred was beaming and very talkative, and posed for his pictures quite happily.

The occasion was a formal one, but not at all stuffy. I could not resist the urge to share my views that Fred resembled a cross between Henry VIII and the Widow Twanky in his voluminous red robes and jaunty tasselled hat, which brought a hearty laugh from all the people gathered around us. Fortunately, I was able to talk him out of wearing his own flat cap for the ceremony – the university didn't seem to object strongly to his request to wear it but prudently it was decided it might be more appropriate to wear the traditional one with a tassel instead. I'd seen him wearing his flat cap over a 'hard hat' on demolition sites many times in the past, so I was not surprised it managed to creep back into the official and unofficial photographs at some point. With a gruff 'Humph', he firmly secured it back in place over his bald pate. I had worried slightly when he joked he was going to wear it on top of the mortarboard!

Members of the press were waiting outside and one leapt forward, bearing a small aluminium ladder, requesting Fred climb up for a few photographs. Good-natured as ever he gladly obliged after signing a few autographs, robes flapping gently in the breeze as people circled around to watch the spectacle and produce their own cameras.

After all the fuss, we came back down to earth and headed off to an opulent five-star hotel where there was a celebratory dinner for the honorary graduates that evening. There had been two ceremonies the previous day and two more were due to be held next day, and the honorary graduates from each day were present at the dinner. Like Fred, they all received a token gift of a silver 'Quaich' from the University. This is a small shallow drinking vessel for whisky or brandy, the name being derived from the Gaelic word CUACH. The inscription read 'Fred Dibnah Hon D Tech'. However, we certainly did not continually fill it with whisky or brandy during the evening, mindful of our last trip up to Aberdeen and the resulting unforgettable hangover!

It turned out to be a lovely occasion for us both; I could see how proud he was. Fred said, 'I wish me mam were here to see it an' all...'

On the return to Bolton next day, he was unusually quiet, and I knew he was thinking about his humble beginnings, as he kept mentioning his lack of education. He said how strange it was that he had ended up at a university, honoured with a degree.

Life was never dull or boring; however, it could be fatiguing at times, such as during that week when we covered over 1,500 miles by car.

A day later Fred had a booking at the Black Country Living Museum, in the West Midlands, for the launch of the steam narrow boat *The President*. The event was organised to raise funds for the restoration of the coal-fired narrowboat which was built in 1909 at a cost of £600. The idea was to have a 'Midsummer Steam Evening' at the museum, with an appearance and book-signing event by Fred. We set off in usual midsummer weather – grey, overcast skies and lashing rain – which meant for the best part of the journey the screen wipers beat a frantic battle against the relentless blustery M6 downpour. When we arrived at the museum, it was apparent that the evening would be a huge success despite the weather. The doors opened ten minutes early due to a large crowd waiting outside, and I took my place alongside Fred to sell merchandise. Soon we were in full swing, and our photographer friend Rod Smallman was inundated with requests from people for pictures of themselves standing alongside their hero.

The evening's schedule involved Fred being shown around the various locations for public demonstrations and exhibitions at previously arranged intervals. I needed to assist the organisers to 'jostle' Fred along to the next attraction on time. It wasn't easy because he got carried away talking, so it was always me they came to when they found it difficult to drag him away from some fellow steam buff or retired engineer, as one of the organisers discovered this particular evening.

'Fred, could we please ask you to come this way?'

(No response – oops! Someone had picked his deaf side.)

Fred studied the elderly man standing in front of him, with whom he was discussing various bits of engineering paraphernalia.

'Hmmm... I've got some of them in me shed, like,' said Fred, stroking his chin, deep in thought. 'Some bugger just turned up one day and asked if I wanted them – get given all sorts of stuff, I do an' all.'

An organiser stepped into view and piped up, 'Come on, Fred, plenty time for chatting later, got to move on now, we need you down at...'

CENTRAL CHANCERY OF THE ORDERS OF KNIGHTHOOD
ST JAMES'S PALACE, SW1A 1BH
TELEPHONE 020 7930 4832
FAX 020 7839 2983

From: Miss Rachel Wells, LVO

24th February 2004

Dear Mr Dibnah,

On 26th January an invitation to the Investiture to be held at Buckingham Palace on Wednesday, 10th March next was sent to you at the address below.

We do not appear to have received a reply, and I am wondering whether our original letter went astray   I wonder if you would be kind enough to let me know as soon as possible whether you will be able to attend the Ceremony on that date.

Perhaps you would telephone me on the above number (Extension 4322) or on my direct line 0207 024 5764.

I will look forward to hearing from you.

Yours sincerely,

Assistant Secretary

Frederick Dibnah Esq., MBE,
Park Cottage,
121 Radcliffe Road,
Bolton,
Greater Manchester
BL2 1NU

The letter arrives from St James Palace, informing us of Fred's Investiture Ceremony at Buckingham Palace. By this time, things were very strained between us, and I learned of his intention not to take me.

My ticket to what should have been one of the happiest days of my life. Fred's MBE award from The Queen at Buckingham Palace.

Fred wore this shirt as a dare after buying it for £40.00 when he was drunk. It is now a popular item on the national speaker's circuit whenever it accompanies me on my talks!

A proud man. Fred was awarded an honorary degree of Doctor of Technology for his achievement in engineering by Robert Gordon University in Aberdeen in the summer of 2001.

Fred felt better posing for pictures wearing his trademark flat cap after being made Doctor of Technology in 2001 at Robert Gordon University, Aberdeen. He would go on to receive another honorary degree in 2004 from the University of Birmingham.

Always a cheery smile for everyone who wanted his autograph in beautiful copper-plate handwriting. He would sit all day long doing this, without complaint, at the height of his fame when more than 6.5 million people watched his programmes.

© Rod Smallman

Fred loved a pint while out on the rallies with his engine.

© Rod Smallman

That cheeky smile that melted the nation's heart.

© *Rod Smallman*

Fred on one of the engines at a steam open day at Eastnor Castle in Herefordshire. This beautiful country house estate is owned by Fred's close friend and steam enthusiast James Hervey-Bathurst.

Fred ready for one of his black-tie after-dinner speaking engagements. He never felt comfortable in this 'get up' (as he called it). I suggested doing the talks in his trademark engine drivers jacket, waistcoat and gold watch chain. The posh audiences loved it just as much as Fred!

© Sheila Dibnah Collection

Fred stands at the side of our bed in Eastnor Castle. I went around telling everyone I'd slept in the same bed as pop star Ronan Keating (who had used it the night before)!

© Sheila Dibnah Collection

An early photograph of Fred taken when he first hit our television screens in the late 1970s.

Fred interrupted the speaker by absent-mindedly waving his right hand. 'Aye mate – I won't keep you a minute ... this bloke used to work at a nut and bolt factory...' and carried on to the man in front of him. 'Now then! Let me tell you about me troubles with them rivets...'

A few more minutes dragged by as Fred described his current wish list. 'I dunno, can't get these bloody things now. In't old days like... '

'Yes, Fred, I have about fifty of those left – you can have them if you like, I'm retired now – we'll have to get together sometime,' said the elderly man.

The organiser moved forward again and, with an extended arm, politely enquired, 'Please can we move on now, Fred, the press are waiting...'

Fred quickly glanced in his direction, but continued in conspiratorial tones to the man he was speaking with. 'Ne'r mind these lot fer't minute, mate – do you wanna come up and see me garden like? Here's me number if ever you fancy a trip up ter see me sheds an' all!' Fred handed a well-thumbed receipt with our telephone number written on the back in his copperplate handwriting. 'Ring up and check I'm in first though, never a minute to myself these days...' Then he firmly shook the hand of the delighted man.

Worried, the organiser darted a slightly irritated look in my direction but by now the engineer in Fred had taken over the celebrity side as he continued: 'Bloody hell, man! Whitworth nuts in them sizes, eh? Now, I reckon there's only one other place that still makes 'em that size as I can think of, and that's in Atherton, near where I live ... used some for me pit-head gear from there ... they're still bloody human in Atherton, and that's a fact!'

Another member of staff stepped forward. 'Erm, Fred – there are members of the press waiting, and the local radio is here doing a live broadcast in ten minutes...' He looked worriedly at his errant charge and tapped his watch in mild annoyance.

Fred chuckled slightly and continued to the man he was talking to: 'Aye ... well, if you have any half-inch threaded bar available, like...'

Minutes passed by slowly and, as I pushed my way forward, he was still talking. 'Yeah, yeah ... country's knackered an all...'

'Come on Freddie, time to go.' I grabbed his sleeve and yanked hard.

'Bloody hell ... five-sixteenths of an inch, eh?' Fred carried on regardless to the man, who by now was looking a bit uncomfortable with all the fuss. 'Yeah, yeah, just a minute, cock, this bloke worked at...'

'Come on *right now* – I mean *right now!*' I insisted.

'Oh bloody hell. Women! Me life's never me own these days ... stop going on at me! Yes, alright, yes ... see you later mate, aye – goodbye.' He nodded his head, winked, did a mock salute, grinning and shuffling forward like a naughty schoolboy, with me firmly guiding his arm. We were moving again.

Then an autograph hunter appeared in front of us and blocked the way. 'Please can you sign my book, Fred? Are you still climbing up chimneys and steeples, by the way?' the friendly middle-aged woman enquired of her hero.

His face softened: 'Yeah! Too bloody right I am. I'm not dead yet!'

A member of the harassed staff countered: 'Sorry, we're just on our way to the rolling mill, madam, and then we're expected at the narrowboat. Mr Dibnah will be signing in the shop later about nine-thirty, he'll be very happy to do it for you then.'

Undeterred, Fred carried on. 'Ahhh, yer alright, love – give it here, won't take a minute. Yeah, I'm just doing the second biggest steeple in England, at Preston. I've got me ladders up ... top's knackered though. Did a chimney once in Canvey Island ... bloody thing fell down a day early ... concrete base only three foot thick.' He was away again – steeplejack now taking over from engineer.

Five more people appeared with autograph books and various scraps of paper, cameras flashed, and still Fred carried on embellishing his story. Even more people gathered round, all asking interesting questions, which the evening's star attraction was more than happy to answer at great length. The organisers looked fretfully at their watches and then at me as we all stepped forward through the swelling crowd, trying to get him on the move again.

'Bloody hell – I could murder a pint...'

'Come on, Fred, this way,' I replied and gave him a gentle push forward.

Another man goes, 'Fred! Just a minute – can you stand with the wife...?'

'Aye, 'course I can!'

'Smile please, Mr Dibnah! Oops! Try again – flash didn't go off...'

'Did you see that bloody beautiful pit-head gear just over there as you came in – got one in me garden like that ... planning department won't let me dig me mine shaft though...'

He was off again. I had to smile.

Not easy! The people's hero, you see...

The President was waiting, and we were to sample the pleasure of a short trip on the canal. Just enough time to eat the promised supper of fish and chips. The rain bedraggled my hair and diluted my enjoyment as I stood drenched on deck with three others, eating the steaming chips. Meanwhile Fred enjoyed his – someone had brought him a pint as well – down in the engine room with the steam boys!

Back on dry land, I had no desire to stay outdoors; even my own childhood wonder, the smoky black, cast-iron 'keck lamps' (or old-fashioned road menders' lamps) strategically placed on each side of the footpaths around the site to light the way, failed to invigorate me and lift the gloom of the soggy dusk. We managed somehow to get Fred to the various rendezvous points and, after a quick drink in the pub, we headed back towards the shop at the museum entrance for more signing, where a large crowd patiently waited, armed with books, pens, smiles and cameras. Fred shuffled forward with the same cheeky grin as before, and raised his hand in a friendly gesture to the waiting crowds, happy to speak and spend time with every last one of them.

Despite the utterly rotten weather, it had been great fun, and there was a happy atmosphere among the fans and admirers who patiently waited their turn to speak with Fred. Again, I greatly admired the pleasure and enjoyment he gave to ordinary folk. As elsewhere in the country, people in the Black Country just loved 'Our Fred'.

'Well, it's been a busy week, love. We'll take it easy on the way home, and stop for a nice lunch somewhere, eh?' he said next day as we got in the car, strapping on our seatbelts and heading for home.

We stopped off at Buxton where we happened upon a book fair in the Pavilion Hall. Fred was excited to discover four old volumes of *The Practice and Technique of Coal Mining* and within five minutes he was in engineering heaven, quiet for once as he studied the thick volumes. Crowds gathered around him, nudging each other as he perched on the stall-owner's chair, deeply engrossed in the books. He ended up buying them and we had to lug them back to the car, parked about a mile away, stopping on the way to speak to people and sign more autographs, with me holding the heavy volumes as Fred got round again to Whitworth nuts, threaded bar and the state of the country now that National Service had been abolished...

I was hungry after my busy morning hauling mining books around

Buxton. On the journey back to Bolton we came across a pub in Disley, near Manchester, and ordered lunch. It looked impressive from outside, a large establishment that seemed to be run by no one over the age of twenty, including the chef who, judging by the quality of both our meals, had only recently acquired some basic cooking skills. Fred wanted a pint of draught bitter as usual. Halfway through watery pasta and stone-baked fish and chips, a female member of staff suddenly ran past the table shouting, 'OK every-one – I am going to have to ask you all to evacuate the building, we have a fire in the kitchen.'

Fred and I glanced at each other in dismay. At first we thought it was a bit of a joke, until the truth dawned on us – this was for real, the kitchen *was* on fire! 'Bloody hell, cock, we'd better leg it – but watch it, don't knock me pint over!' and with that he grabbed hold of his glass.

An acrid smell assaulted our noses as we left our seats.

Fred picked up his plate too and I followed clutching mine, quickly leav-ing the pub and heading out into the fresh air towards Linky. We arranged ourselves inside the car, spreading out a newspaper as a makeshift tablecloth, and carried on eating our food with the knives and forks we had pinched as we left. Shortly after we'd settled in the car with our impromptu picnic, a fire engine arrived on the scene, and screeched to a noisy halt, followed by another one soon after that. Then a paramedics' van swept into view ...

thankfully, no one seemed to be hurt. Finally the police arrived and rushed into the building, just as clouds of thick smoke started to pour through a side window.

It certainly added some spice to a very mundane meal, and we had to see the funny side as we both sat there eating, with smoke billowing out from the roof of the doomed building. The only regret Fred had was that he couldn't have another pint with his dinner – he said he didn't like warm ale!

Around this time, Fred was discussing with David Hall the concept of filming a one-off programme later in the year focusing on the great engineers of the Victorian Age, such as Brunel, Stephenson, Scott-Russell and Armstrong. This hour-long documentary, earmarked as *Fred Dibnah's Victorian Heroes*, was a great source of inspiration to both David and Fred, and they were very excited about the project. Eventually, filming began in October after the endless round of steam rallies and public appearance work finally drew to a close and before the busy run-up to Christmas with after-dinner talks. There was more travelling to places such as Portsmouth, London, Bristol, Telford, Newcastle and York, but to Fred seeing the work of the greatest engineers was like a holiday.

After the Bristol location, Fred returned home and cried as he told me how he'd handled Brunel's personal diaries and letters at Bristol University Library, where he'd read the thoughts of his hero about his wonderful feats of engineering written in his own handwriting. Clifton Suspension Bridge and Great Western Railway, for which Brunel had designed everything himself, appealed to Fred, and he could identify with Brunel's enthusiasm for everything he did. I could see Fred was very emotional about being involved in this programme. When it was eventually aired, it was another success and Fred said it was one of his particular favourites.

Life seemed good, money was flowing in and Fred was happy doing what he loved best when time permitted. We had everything organised by now; Fred was eating sensibly and drinking moderately and it was a good, if slightly eccentric, lifestyle. Basically, we were very happy and very much in love.

Life continued after Christmas and New Year in an endless round of rallies, organised events, after-dinner speaking engagements and filming dates. It was a busy, sometimes frustrating, but ultimately fulfilling time. We toured the country clocking up more than 25,000 miles in a year. We were exhausted but secure in the knowledge we would never have to worry again about paying bills, and there was always money available for treats. Fred intended to start renovating his Aveling and Porter Colonial Steam tractor again, on which he'd been working sporadically for many years. It was only now that he was in a financial position to do so.

But I was getting fed-up with the increasing number of visitors to the back-garden workshops; this was becoming a major issue and sometimes a source of conflict between us. It was impossible to have anything like a normal home life, and it was worse than ever before. I couldn't cope with all this constant attention. Unlike Fred I wasn't eager to 'play to the gallery' as I called it, and took no prisoners. 'Why can't you be nice to people?' he'd angrily shoot off after anyone had happened to fall foul of my anger.

In April, I felt I needed a break and expressed interest in a foreign holiday but Fred didn't want to go. He exclaimed: 'I've not seen all of England yet!' whenever I tried to force the issue.

We'd been to the Isle of Wight a couple of times during the past two summers but the hot sun and (in his eyes) lack of anything constructive to do on the island had made Fred very bored and irritable at times. He was glad to get back home. I could not picture him in some hot, arid climate. I recalled the image of him at the height of summer in one of the most expensive hotels on the Isle of Wight, all decked out in his engine driver's jacket and flat cap, perched on a white plastic sun lounger, moaning aloud: 'Bah! Why the bloody hell don't thi' make proper chairs these days, eh?' There he was sitting uncomfortably by the outdoor swimming pool, amidst all the well-tanned bodies and skimpy bikinis, attempting to read one of his coal mining or engineering books in the blistering heat.

I decided that Nathan and I would go and I thought I might ask Roger if he wanted to come too. Jack showed no interest at all, being a chip off the old block, so arrangements were made for the three of us to go to southern Spain. I booked a two-week trip to Puerto Banus, near Marbella, staying in a five-star hotel. We were due to fly out in mid-May.

I returned from shopping to find Fred in the driveway, tugging and pulling at a telegraph pole on his own. These would normally take two or three men to shift any distance. He had moved it several yards down the driveway but, when he saw me, stopped what he was doing for a moment or two. Still panting heavily, he expressed his dissatisfaction that no-one had been available when he needed help. I nitpicked, only to be met by, 'Stop moaning and going on at me, woman!'

Later that evening, rubbing his lower tummy and complaining of a dull ache, Fred drank Guinness in front of the telly. I knew he must have been experiencing a lot of pain even to mention it. This was so unlike him; I thought back to when his hand had been caught in the steam hammer and how resilient he'd been. I expressed my concern that he may have caused a hernia; again came the response: 'Stop mithering me, woman – it's nowt!'

Next day the pain was still there, perhaps slightly worse if anything, and I suggested the doctor but he refused, again saying it was 'nowt'. This went on for three days until finally, after being doubled up on the floor in agony for more than two hours, I bullied him into the car and drove him to the Accident & Emergency department at our local hospital.

Some rudimentary examinations and an x-ray later, he was informed he was badly constipated, and sent home with laxatives. He felt marginally better after the laxatives and life carried on the same as always, but the pain niggled from time to time. Of course, I would only learn of this recurring pain after a day or two, because he would say things like, 'Nahhh! I didn't want to worry you or owt, cock.'

Not long before we were due to go on holiday, however, he started to feel the sharp pain again and was called into hospital for some further tests. It seemed he was not passing water as he should and the consultants thought this might be worth looking into. It was all very vague as to what exactly the problem was, and they needed to investigate further. Fred insisted Nathan, Roger and I still went away on our holiday, and Peter Lidgett – or 'John Wayne' – stepped forward, offering to take over the task of driving Fred around for his appointments during the two weeks we were away.

So we headed off to Manchester Airport knowing Fred was in capable hands, but I still felt concerned.

I got a telephone update each evening and it seemed Fred was enjoying the break too – as 'The Duke' was just as wild as Fred, and therefore on the steam rallies they visited there were no restrictions of the female kind in force in the beer tent afterwards!

We returned home after two weeks, tanned, relaxed and ready for anything.

I had enjoyed the holiday so much that I thought about selling my property in Blackpool and buying a small apartment in Spain with the proceeds, but ended up buying a large flat to renovate in Blackpool instead. Fred liked that idea better and said he would help me do it up; he was delighted I'd got a project of my own, which he said would keep me out of his hair whilst he got on with the time-consuming business of doing up his traction engine, which was still in a million bits in the back garden.

Jack and Roger returned to the Isle of Man after our holiday, and Fred and I got on with the endless round of filming dates, steam rallies, personal appearances and other demands on Fred's time. He now seemed fully recovered; the only problem was that he had do something called self-catheterization because his bladder seemed to be still retaining water, and he would eventually need a prostate operation. He explained with mischievous glee just what this dreadful practice entailed to everyone who would listen, and I could see men's eyes watering as he went on about the length of the plastic pipe and what he did with it. Fred and I made light of it and we nicknamed the process his 'crenulating'.

'Hey up, cock, is't bathroom free yet, like? 'Av got t'do me crenulating, before that bloke turns up with them bearings 'n' all!'

As usual, being very tough, Fred did not mollycoddle himself in the slightest, putting his ordeal down as 'nowt'. He seemed to be a hundred per cent better with the 'crenulations', suffered no further pain, and worked long hours in the shed on his Aveling & Porter steam tractor whenever he could.

Several months later, however, the pain in his belly returned with greater force. Fred had to visit hospital for several outpatient appointments and, after a series of biopsies, x-rays and scans, it was decided that his right kidney was unhealthily bloated and not working properly so it would have to be removed. It was a blow but we were quite sure that this would resolve the problem, as it was generally considered that the kidney had been damaged by 'urine retention'.

Fred was admitted to hospital for surgery. He sailed through his operation with no complications, making a wonderful recovery whilst keeping all the patients and nursing staff on the urology ward amused with his never-ending tales of 'crenulations', liking it to mechanical engineering pumps and steam valves.

I visited the ward one day to find Fred propped up in bed, talking to another man around the same age sitting at the side in his pyjamas and dressing gown. 'Hey up, love,' said Fred, as I approached the bed. 'We're just talking about me Weir water pump!'

I thought for a minute he was going on about 'crenulating' again, but it soon became clear that this was something else. The man next to him had once worked as an engineer in a local firm much respected by Fred: 'Aye!

Well... this 'ere boiler feed pump, like,' he leaned a bit closer to the man, 'I'd be jiggered without it...'

The man smiled and nodded knowingly, listening to Fred who ended with the tale about once getting his hand caught under the mechanical steam hammer in the shed. As usual, before turning his attention to me, Fred winked confidently at the man and said, 'When you and I are better and out of this bloody place, mate – you'll have to come down and see me garden when I've got steam up...'

Sadly, the man never did.

CHAPTER 11
'It's bad news, I'm afraid...'

'Oh, she's probably too busy and wants to tell me to give up the booze, or summat!'

T hen a day dawned which meant life would never be the same again, changing us and our basically happy marriage beyond all recognition: Monday 29th October 2001.

The day started like any other. Fred sat chatting away on the telephone in the middle room, whilst I busied myself at the kitchen sink absent-mindedly washing a small glass chandelier I'd recently bought for the new flat in Blackpool. Fred ended his conversation after about half an hour, and sauntered into the kitchen. The phone rang again, and I groaned inwardly as he went to answer it, glancing at the clock. I had hoped for a pub lunch with him.

I could tell this call was different. Fred wasn't doing most of the talking and, as I glanced across through the doorway, I noticed he looked oddly uncomfortable. Unsmiling, squirming about in the chair, he was nodding his head in a fast, quirky manner most unlike him, with his blue eyes wide and staring. I walked into the room, and stood before him. He said weakly into the receiver. 'OK, we'll both be there, thanks for calling then...'

He replaced the receiver and at once became flustered. He told me that the consultant urologist who had carried out his kidney operation, Miss Gillian Mobb, had asked that he come in and 'bring the wife along' on Wednesday afternoon at 2.00 p.m. That was two whole days away.

With a sense of dread, we discussed the implications. Warning bells were ringing as the 'big C' word flitted through my mind for the first time but I kept these alarming feelings to myself. I simply said we should not have to wait with this hanging over us, and insisted Fred ring back if it was so important and tell them he wanted to know what was going on. At first he was reluctant to face what Miss Mobb had to say, making excuses like, 'Oh, she's probably too busy and wants to tell me to give up the booze, or summat!' But he rang back eventually and Miss Mobb told him he could come in that same morning, and to bring me along.

We left for the hospital around 11.30 a.m. and went straight into the urology department. A man asked what we were doing there and requested an autograph, before I silenced him by saying this wasn't the appropriate time. My nerves were on edge; Fred was unusually quiet and ignored the silly man who carried on regardless about how he'd seen Fred on telly, and what did he think of being famous?

Miss Mobb eventually came into the stuffy waiting room, and guided us into a small side room containing the usual examination couch, cheery blue fabric curtain, and sink with chrome lever taps, stark overhead light and orange Formica chairs. A staff nurse, whom we'd seen during Fred's time on A4 Ward after the kidney operation, was also present and looked glum.

Cancer: the news hit us like a sledgehammer. We were informed that the removed kidney had contained a tumour and after tests the tumour was found to be malignant. Fred had cancer. It was official.

I held his hand. We looked at each other first in silence and then voiced our shock as the implications of what we'd just been told sank in. I started to cry and someone handed me a tissue as tears continued to well up uncontrollably. The dreaded word hung in the air like icicles, and the room – so hot a minute or two ago – turned into the coldest place on earth.

Fred took the news well, fair and square on the chin like the brave man he was. I continued to stare at Miss Mobb, as she bandied around words that only a few short moments ago had belonged in a particular time warp when my Uncle Norman on my dad's side had died of cancer many years ago. Subsequently my best friend, a fire-eater named Judy Allen, suffered the same fate in the mid-eighties.

'Cancer, chemotherapy, Christie Hospital, radiotherapy, oncologists, survival rates' and other horrors that up until now we'd never really thought about, were real – happening to us. I recalled reading the renowned jockey Bob Champion's story about his own fight with cancer back in the eighties, and the cocktail of drugs with strange-sounding names he'd had to endure and which made him very sick. Suddenly we were making arrangements to come back to the hospital later that afternoon to see a Dr Wylie, a senior consultant from the leading cancer hospital, the Christie, in Manchester.

It all seemed unreal.

Shortly afterwards we left the hospital, returning home to let the shock sink in. We were both shaking during the short car journey, reeling from the news. We would go back there at 2.00 p.m. to meet Dr Wylie, to discuss what happened next, as it looked like Fred would need chemotherapy treatment at the Christie Hospital.

Just as I opened the back door, the telephone was ringing again. I felt a quick flash of pure annoyance – good God Almighty, would we never get any bloody peace from that damned thing? Even now, with mind-blowing stuff like this to face, you couldn't even have a single moment to yourself.

I felt like ripping it from the wall.

Fred instructed me to answer it – it might just be the hospital, he said.

It was.

Irritated, I picked up the handset and my mum's voice came on loud and clear at the other end, sounding very distracted and urgent: 'Sheila, your dad's had a bit of an accident.'

'What's happened, where are you – is he OK?'

'I'm at the hospital with him now.'

'Hospital? We've just come from there! What's happened, Mum, what's he done, has he hurt himself bad, or what?'

'You'd better get yourself down here now... he's had a fall...'

'A fall? Has he broken his leg or something?'

'No, but he fell of a ladde ... banged his head.'

'What's he doing up a ladder? Is he badly hurt or what?'

'Just come to A&E as soon as you can,' she said, sounding very strange.

I replaced the receiver and turned to Fred, shaking my head in puzzlement, explaining what mum had said. We turned and went straight out of the door. By now, I was feeling sick with worry and fuzzy, like I was in some kind of dream world. Nothing seemed real this morning. Fred was talking constantly about cancer, and I kept thinking about my dad as we drove back up to the hospital, not knowing quite what lay ahead.

At A&E we were met by my mum, who explained that my dad had fallen twenty-one feet from the top of an aluminium ladder whilst examining some shoddy work carried out by dodgy workmen at their home. He'd given cash to some cowboy builders and the job didn't get finished properly. My dad decided, at the age of seventy-one, to get the ladders from the garage and go up on the roof to see what these idiots had done, despite having had a hip replacement operation and serious rheumatoid arthritis, which made him very unsteady on his legs.

He was now undergoing tests; they were sending a scan image of his brain to Hope Hospital to see the damage he had sustained to his head. Mum tearfully explained that the doctor said he could be badly brain-damaged, or might even die. I simply couldn't take it in and sat there, numb and in shock.

We waited and waited, then someone came to speak to Fred to see if he wanted to postpone his meeting with Dr Wylie so he could be with me in A&E. I said there was no point in Fred missing his meeting; we needed to know what would happen with his treatment and get it started as soon as possible. So, when the time came, he reluctantly left my mum and I and went to another part of the hospital to see Dr Wylie.

At last, my mum and I were shown into the cubicle where Dad now was being attended by two doctors. I don't know what I expected, but not this, no ... not this. Nothing could have prepared me and, as I stood at the foot of the bed reeling from the sight in front of me, a loud wail left my lips. For there, under the harsh fluorescent lights, lay my father covered in a green draped garment from the waist down, arms by his sides on the trolley, with tubes, pipes, monitors attached at the wrists and forearms. Machines at either side of him steadily made bleeping noises, whilst one above showed a thin green line on a dark background; it was an electrocardiogram machine, measuring brain activity, and now lay ominously redundant. On his chest, small paper circles about three inches across with shiny metal centres, which looked bizarrely like robot nipples, were stuck to his skin in places where he had been quickly shaved in preparation. His face was half covered with a thin plastic mask and another thick transparent pipe entered his mouth at the side, distorting his features. This in turn led to a machine which made a kind of mechanical breathing noise in co-ordination with the rise and fall of his chest. It was a ventilator. His ailing head was bandaged in a snow-white gauzy fabric, and there were patches of bright red blood here and there around the damaged area above his closed eyes.

I had a strange feeling like I might either laugh or cry. Nausea rose as I dry-retched time and time again. Someone gave me a drink of water and I was grateful for it. My mum and I took a seat on either side of him and I grabbed hold of his hand. It had a strange, clammy coolness about it and his pallor was waxen and almost grey, like that of a dead person. When I stroked his arm it felt slightly warmer, but was still cool under my touch.

I spoke to him, pleaded with him to wake up, cried, whimpered and at last asked the doctors: 'Can he hear us?' The doctors glanced guardedly at each other, and simply said he'd suffered a severe injury, and they weren't too sure yet, but were awaiting the results of some tests.

We would know soon what the situation was.

We sat like that for the longest time, and eventually another doctor came into the cubicle. He said they had now received the results of the tests back from Hope Hospital. There was no hope for my dad. All brain activity had ceased, he told us, and he was only being kept alive by the ventilator. The horrific moment came – they intended to turn off the ventilator because he could never recover. We sat there, my mum and I, solemn and mindful as the room became gradually silent. Then we held Dad's hand, said our good-byes and watched him slip quietly away from us as the machine stopped its robotic, impersonal progress.

He was dead, my dad was gone...

Meanwhile, elsewhere in the hospital Fred was talking to Dr Wylie and being informed that his chemotherapy would have to start immediately. He was to have a cycle of six sessions. I cannot remember the exact sequence of events that happened next but, somehow, Fred and I caught up with each other in the hospital and we returned home with Mum, all of us in shock from the day's events.

I later had to go to the morgue with my son, Nathan, because he was very close to his granddad, and his immediate response was 'I want to see him'. It was awful.

The night was long, dark and lonely. Leaving Fred tossing and turning restlessly in bed but nevertheless still sleeping, I crept downstairs in the middle of the night and got into the makeshift camp bed where my mum was fitfully trying to sleep. We hugged each other and cried all night, waiting for the dawn to break through the curtains and hopefully make some sense of the day.

Fred got up at 6.00 a.m., made us strong cups of coffee, and the three of us sat talking, locked together in misery, our lives turned topsy-turvy, until the demands of the day took over at 9.00 a.m. With a cold, heavy heart I went into overdrive immediately, sorting out funeral affairs, attempting to bolster up a shell-shocked Fred and blotting out some of the pain for my mum's sake.

The day of my dad's funeral arrived, and my mum was hysterical. They'd known each other since she was twelve. We had to get through this as best we could, then Fred and I would have to go to the Christie the following morning to discuss his care plan, have some tests done on his remaining kidney and see if it would stand up to the gruelling course of chemotherapy.

We arrived at the Christie. I found it very hard to enter the hospital. I became giddy and Fred was slightly cross with me. Once inside, matters got worse. Everyone kept coming up to us, wanting to know what Fred was doing there. I was amazed at their audacity – *how dare they*? Were we not entitled to some privacy like everyone else? I found it intrusive and couldn't be sociable under these circumstances. I was very curt with the nosiest of them, but then started giggling like a fool through sheer exhaustion and fear.

We took a seat, and waited for Dr Wylie. For about twenty minutes we sat in this glass fishbowl with people staring at us from all directions and pointing fingers, watching a sad procession of white, ghost-like, hairless people go by in wheelchairs. They reminded me of pale, fleeting shadows.

Finally the doctor was ready to see us. We followed him into a room. He studiously examined his papers on a clipboard in front of him, and told us exactly what the treatment entailed. Fred, as always not wanting to have it softened, piped up: 'What are me chances, mate, with me having this cancer an' all? Am I likely to die with it, or what – how long will I last do you reckon...?'

Dr Wylie looked a bit taken aback. He replied, 'Do you want to know, Fred, are you sure... we can only give you a guide?'

Well, he had asked – and we got the stark reply: 'Well, Fred, this is a particularly aggressive form of cancer. Are you certain you want to know... we don't usually...'

Fred spat out like a curse, 'Aye! Let's get it over with and then I can fight the bloody thing. I've a lot to do before I die!'

Dr Wylie explained, 'The form of cancer you have is quite a rare one,

Fred. It's quite difficult to treat and, as I say, it's quite aggressive. We would expect you to survive for about twelve months without treatment. It could be slightly less – it could be slightly more – but it will be around that mark. But as I say – it is very difficult to treat and it's spread into your lymph glands and invaded some of the surrounding fatty tissues of the kidney, but we'll give the chemotherapy a go, and it might be successful if we are lucky.'

Twelve months! I immediately burst into tears again, and Fred just sat there, wringing his hands and talking nineteen to the dozen. I couldn't hear him by then. It wasn't real... please God, no... it can't be! Presently, the doctor left the room and we remained rooted to the spot, hoping somehow it was all a bad mistake and that he'd come back in and say he'd got hold of the wrong notes and told us the wrong prognosis.

We finally walked back along the corridor, clinging onto each other. As everyone knows, cancer is not contagious, but suddenly I became giddy again, looked at all the sick people surrounding me, and felt like running away screeching at the top of my voice, 'Get away from us! Get away! Get away!'

I had to get out of there immediately so I speeded up, dragging poor Fred along roughly by the arm, bolting out of the front door, taking long deep breaths of cool air outside. My eyes burned; everything was too hot, too close and too awful. It felt like a leper colony and I couldn't cope.

Fred went in for his first overnight chemotherapy session, smiling and cheerful as only he could be in the face of gloom. No doubt the people on the same ward at the Christie enjoyed his tales and enthusiasm as the strong chemicals pumped into his bloodstream.

I picked him up next day and said he should lie down a while. 'Bugger that!' he retorted. 'If I'm bloody dying, I'm bloody dying my way! Pour me a glass of that wine, luv.'

I stood there transfixed as I watched him down two anti-sickness tablets with half a bottle of red wine. And then later: 'Nip up to the off-licence, and get me Guinness for me, will you, cock?'

'Fred, you can't drink – you've just had chemotherapy!'

'Who sez! Are you going, or shall I...?' he demanded. He wasn't normally like this, but I knew the first tell-tale signs if there was going to be a drink-fuelled row: the glittering eyes, sneering put-downs, sarcastic comments. It was a more and more common occurrence since he'd first become ill. I dreaded him getting drunk. With this new, increased level of alcohol consumption on a regular basis sometimes came a drunkard's thirst for rage, and it wasn't worth it – we were both far too exhausted and upset tonight for a row.

So, against my better judgement, I went for the Guinness and he drained all four cans that evening, on top of the half bottle of wine he'd already had. 'What is this guy made of?' I wondered to myself, as he sat at the kitchen table, drinking and reading his book on coal mining, showing no ill-effects from the booze, chemotherapy and cocktail of anti-sickness drugs. Next day he felt slightly muzzy but set about working on his Aveling & Porter tractor with renewed gusto.

Nothing stopped him in his tracks and we continued to travel around the country over the next few weeks. Fred, as ever, seemed to be strong and resilient through the entire six cycles of chemotherapy.

I was trying to come to terms with my bereavement, but Fred didn't seem supportive because of the shock of discovering he had terminal cancer. At times he appeared uncharacteristically cruel towards me, saying I seemed more preoccupied with my mother, unsupportive of his plight. He kept saying, 'I'm dying, woman, don't you bloody understand?' This aggression was usually a result of heavy drinking sessions and the unfamiliar terror of serious illness which he now faced.

For the first time in his dangerous life, Fred knew real fear.

The die was cast for what would later become an increasingly regular pattern, whereby one minute he was fine and then he'd turn into some kind of Jekyll and Hyde character where everything was my fault. He didn't mind telling those around who would listen, or he would pick a public opportunity to show his growing discontent with me.

Towards the back end of the summer, we were travelling around doing the usual after-dinner stuff, and he had a booking in Shrewsbury for a Rotary Club ladies' night at a swanky hotel. I'd happened across a lovely, expensive dress for only £5 whilst buying some work shirts from Oxfam. I wore it on this particular occasion. After the meal, as fifteen or so people sat around in the lounge area talking to Fred, a jocular man winked and commented, 'You have a lovely wife, Fred – how do you do it, you lucky old bugger?'

'She's stunning!' another commented, good-naturedly joining in.

'What beautiful hair!' from elsewhere.

'I love your dress too, you look lovely.'

At one time, Fred would have squeezed my hand, eyes shining with pride, joining in the fun and basking in the open admiration of his wife, but now he merely came back with the caustic quip: 'Aye, and she's not expensive to run, either ... tell 'em where you got yer dress from, cock...'

I could see it coming as he went on, 'Go on, tell 'em how much you paid for it an all ... go on, tell 'em'. He fixed me with a strange defiant stare, waiting for me to say something, challenging me to speak out.

The other Fred was back, the new cruel one.

'It's nothing,' I stuttered, to the sea of expectant faces. 'It was bought in a sale... it's nothing special...'

'Aye, she's not expensive to run. Her last bloke wouldn't buy her owt, run off with another woman, didn't he, cock, but she's not short of money now.' He lashed out, waiting for my response. 'She has all me money ... all me women have.'

'Well, dear, you look really lovely this evening,' another lady countered

'No ... tell 'em where you got it, tell 'em cock.'

By now aware of the simmering tension, the whole group awaited my response: 'It's not important, Fred – I got it in a sale is all he means.'

But he was getting into his stride, enjoying the moment. 'She never buys owt new, wears second-hand stuff from jumble sales or Oxfam, gets all me shirts from there too – only gave a fiver for that thing she's got up in tonight. Doesn't look too bad though... got it from a charity shop, didn't you, cock?' Adding for good measure, 'She was driving a car with the arse hanging out when she met me, but she's bloody all right now... Ha-ha, bloody women; never trust em, the lot of em. Bollocks!'

Fred winked and nodded knowingly, drawing deeply at his pint, giving me a long, slow, meaningful look over the top of his beer glass, and made a snorting noise like a muffled laugh. I flushed bright red, made an excuse and immediately left the group, hearing his gleeful retort as I walked away: 'Bloody women! Can never understand them – they're off a different planet – ignore her, she's a funny bugger at times.'

He later apologised, saying he'd had a bit too much to drink and he was only having a bit of fun. That was the first time Fred had been so cruel to me in public. Sadly, however, it would not be the last...

CHAPTER 12
Fred and the steam mafia

'No, not bloody tomatoes again – are you trying to kill me, or what?!'

*A*nd yet, before matters became much worse, we still had our fun together. For instance, during a trip out once, to Southport, we stopped off at a pub for our lunch. As ever, Fred had an eye for a pretty face. Each time one especially lovely young waitress sauntered by our table, he'd go: 'Hmmm!' This happened about five or six times, and eventually she brought our plates, setting them down before us. 'Hmmm!' went Fred, in full approval of not only the piping hot food.

After the meal, she eventually came to clear away. Rubbing his tummy appreciatively, Fred said: 'Thanks for that, love, it was smashing, and the boiler's now indeed fully stoked!'

Saucily, she replied, 'Yes sir, but is it *still* fully functional though?'

'Hmmmm!' went Fred.

After she'd walked away I decided to have some fun. 'God, Fred, you dirty old sod! I simply cannot believe you just said that to a pretty young girl! Do you know what it means if you tell some lass that "your boiler is fully stoked"?' I enquired, full of mischief.

He looked puzzled. 'Eh? No, why, what do you mean? What's matter with that?'

I smiled at him. 'Well, its youth-speak, you know, Fred – modern lingo for "I've got a raging great hard-on". It's like saying to her you are up for it, ready for sexual conquests, in a state of arousal... you'd say that to someone these days as a euphemism for showing you want sex!'

'Eh?'

'Yes, you've just told her you're sexually aroused!'

'Gawd, Christ... No... It doesn't, does it?' He looked astonished, slapped the top of his cap several times and pulled a Harold Steptoe face. Grimacing he continued, 'Naahh – bloody modern world – I never know where I'm up to with this lot... Christ almighty, why is life so complicated these days? When I were a lad there were none of this caper, you just asked girls owt for a sup at local boozer or summat.'

'Oh nooo – these days if you see someone you fancy, you just tell them straight out you are up for it. "The boiler is fully stoked", she could see you fancied her so it's like telling her you're ready for action. You made out you wanted to shag her!' I pressed on by now full of devilment. 'So you see, Fred, that's why she asked if it was still *fully* functional – probably thought you couldn't get a stiffy or something after all that beer, or your age, eh?'

'You're bloody having me on, woman!'

'No, Fred, this is how it is these days.'

'Eh?'

'Yeah, it's true – ask Nathan!'

'Aye, it's all that American telly rubbish like what he watches.'

'Fancy you telling the waitress you had a big hard-on, eh?'

'Christ! I can't believe I said that...'

He looked genuinely shocked because Fred was never crude to women. The pretty girl soon returned enquiring if we wanted to see a sweet menu. Fred had the good grace to noticeably redden, and say, 'Hey, listen, cock, I didn't mean owt by what I just said. Gawd, I'm reet sorry like, I didn't mean it you know – I just didn't know what I was saying.'

'Sorry?' She eyed him, then glanced at me as if to say 'What's he going on about?' and added in a distant, impersonal voice: 'That's all right, sir, no problem. Can I get you anything else?'

Fred pressed on: 'It's this modern world you see – I can't keep up with it, it's like them computers where everybody pushes plastic mice around all day or them daft telly adverts for selling cars, I can't understand them either. Her lad's the same –I don't know what the bloody hell he's on about half the time. I hope it didn't upset you or owt ... I didn't mean to embarrass you, love. I'm reet sorry an' all.'

She looked a bit flustered. 'No problem, that's OK, sir, that's quite all right.' She decided she must be dealing with someone suffering from a kind of mental instability and, picking up the sweet menus, beat a hasty retreat to the safety of the next table, furtively glancing across at us from a safe distance.

On the way out, as I settled the bill, Fred leant over the bar, and confided to the guy on the till: 'Tell the young lass over there I didn't mean owt funny, like.'

It was ages before I finally confessed, and I had much secret amusement as Fred solemnly declared over the phone to several mates during the days after the event, 'Eh, you'll never guess what – I told some young lass in a pub t'other day that I had a big hard-on!'

I thought it was so funny. Fred eventually saw the joke and said, 'Yer rotten sod!' when I told him what I'd done.

'Fred, is your boiler fully stoked, or what?' I would ask whenever a pretty young waitress served us during our future frequent forays into pubs.

'Bugger off, you daft bitch!' he'd laugh, and we'd enjoy a chuckle or two about it. Lovely, treasured days with a very special man before it all went increasingly wrong...

Fred continued filming with friend and producer David Hall, and the next offering was entitled *Fred Dibnah's Building of Britain*. Both previous series, *Industrial Age* and *Magnificent Monuments* had been well-received, depicting Fred in a new light as a historian and television presenter. There was no reason to suggest this new series would not be met with the same enthusiasm.

David and Fred had chemistry and worked extremely well together, gradually becoming firm friends. Fred trusted David's guidance to get the best from each location, and studied his scripts with a determination to succeed. By now, David had dissuaded Fred from punctuating sentences with '*yeah-yeah-yeah-yeah-yeah...*' It was a big improvement; however, it had been replaced by '*Um-u-m-um-um-um*' instead!

The *Building of Britain* series brought an even higher profile and with it came letters from a different sector of the population such as academics and people who could complete *The Times* crossword in one morning. Fred would often chuckle about this, and as well, say, 'I wish me mam could see me now, like...'

He was inundated with requests to be honorary president of various historical and preservation societies or organisations the length and breadth of England. It became obvious Fred was by now a far cry from the caricature days of Don Howarth. It was impossible to cope with the number of letters or to single out causes more worthy than the last, so we had to refuse genuine requests in fairness not only to all those who had made them, but also to Fred, who was exhausted at times and seemed to find no rest from being under the spotlight.

The *Evening with Fred Dibnah* theatre tour was set up in selected small regional theatres throughout Britain. It was obvious we were on to a winner as the shows got under way, and his casual way of working was an immediate hit with the public.

Where most entertainers would relax backstage before a show, trying to steady their nerves and stage fright, Fred's idea of a pre-show build-up was to sit in the bar and sign countless autographs for his fans. This was most unconventional. So was the sound check and run-through with the stage crew, where Fred took all of five minutes as he shuffled on to the stage and addressed the crew: 'I'm alright, cock, just stick them bright lights up so I can see the faces, that's all what matters, mate. Now where's tha thunder box, eh?'

I tried to dissuade him from doing pre-show signing sessions to preserve not only his stamina, but also the air of mystery and kudos attached to any theatre show, but he was so eager to meet fans he simply wanted to be out there as soon as possible to have a chat. He had a big heart and the public loved him for it.

It was the same at the end of the show: he refused to leave the theatre until every last person waiting to meet him had enjoyed a reasonable chat and had their leaflet, poster, book or photograph or whatever signed with his large, flourishing, Victorian style, copperplate signature. He went on regardless of time and made many people happy with his unselfishness. It was never a question of number-crunching with Fred when it came to box-office returns, but how many people he could attract to speak to that night. He wanted passionately to share his wondrous tales and adventures with fans, all of whom he had the greatest respect for.

In more than seven years together, I never once saw Fred be anything less than genuine and nice to the people he met, not even towards the end when he was very poorly and often needed to rest. Not many men would have the mental and emotional stamina for this – especially if they'd been diagnosed with terminal cancer. But Fred was different, and everyone was potentially a friend. He was a natural for the stage environment.

About the time of the cancer diagnosis, Fred became acquainted with Alf Molyneux. He met Alf, a very genuine man, in a traditional pub a few miles away from Bolton in a small coal mining community called Tyldsely, near Atherton. Fred would visit the pub frequently when we were not travelling somewhere, usually on Thursday nights with his friend Harry Foreshaw, whose family owned a local demolition company. Harry would pick Fred up in his Range Rover around 9.00 p.m., and drop him home just after midnight. Other friends would also be at the pub that evening, such as Alan Davies, who was at the time curator of the Salford Mining Museum. Set in a mining community, many ex-miners would use the pub as a favourite watering hole; one of these was Alf, who would go there with another genuine guy, his old mining pal Jimmy Crookes.

Alf Molyneux: strong, capable and, as a retired miner, not afraid of danger or hard slog was just the kind of man Fred related to. Before meeting Fred, Alf had never been particularly interested in steam engines or watched Fred's programmes on T.V., but soon Alf found himself mesmerized by the animated and enthusiastic way the steeplejack described his passion about building a replica coal mine and restoring his Aveling & Porter Steam Tractor. It was not long before the usual 'Why don't you come and have a look at me garden, like?' was suggested to Alf, who readily took up the offer. Of course, once he had enticed Alf down several times, Fred was soon enquiring if he'd like to give a hand around the place, which Alf gladly agreed to do.

Fred already had Ian Thompson as his right-hand man. Ian helped with riveting work on the new engine and had been a visitor for a great number of years, but ever mindful that more hands equalled more work done, it was not long before Fred asked Alf if he'd fancy making his visits a regular occurrence. Soon, Alf was visiting three or four times a week and, because he had an allotment, I didn't complain when he turned up with all manner of delicious, organic, home-grown vegetables.

Before long, Alf started bringing his pal to lend a hand with one of the many tasks in the yard. Jimmy, like Alf, had worked hard all his life in the coal industry, having been a 'boss down't pit – a clever bloke' as Fred later put it. But on most days, only Alf and Ian worked in the garden. However, after more and more exposure on television, Fred's day became increasingly punctuated by a steady stream of other casual visitors all wanting to lend a hand on and off – and now, whenever Fred opened the top gates from early morning there seemed a growing band of ever-present men, some of whom seemed cool towards me, resenting me right from the word go for reasons best known to themselves.

I initially called this band of men, 'Dad's Army' and for some of its members, I later refer to them in this book as the 'Steam Mafia'.

Saturdays were always the busiest for Dad's Army. It was a veritable open house, where steam machinery would be running all day. This gathering of men, now mostly the regular visitors, some not – some merely strangers wanting to get involved in the action and be a part of 'Fred's world', were always turning up around 11.00 a.m., staying until around teatime, was a great source of free labour to Fred. They would congregate, drink tea, coffee, eat meat pies and meet up each weekend whilst we were at home. I found it intrusive and difficult to get a moment alone with my husband. I was also worried about the affects of the work they were doing. The hospital told Fred to avoid anything which may compromise his immune system. He'd gone through a cycle of chemotherapy and wasn't supposed to handle anything dirty which could cause massive infection. Here he was, working in unthinkable conditions covered in muck. But he carried on regardless and more people started to arrive once they'd heard the news about Fred's health problems, either to help in the yard or just to sit and have a brew with him.

As Alf Molyneux said during an interview with film producer Paul Donoghue: 'It was open house, it got pretty hectic at times, he'd get up (Fred), have his boiled egg, open the top gate and people would flood in all day long. We got snowed under at times.'

There were other casual visitors too, so-called good 'friends' or close acquaintances who said they knew Fred well over a lifetime, but really only contacted him when they wanted something or he could be useful to them in some way. To me, these were the real users and hangers-on but Fred didn't see it like that and didn't refuse to help when asked, no matter how busy or exhausted he was.

He never saw people in a bad light and I tried to protect him from their interference whenever I could. Fred didn't like this attitude, and the trouble was he told these men about my complaints. It started to foster more resentment amongst certain individuals, who now viewed me as 'interfering', especially when Fred was always down at the pub paying for their frequent dinners and numerous pints of ale.

One of them even stole money and video merchandise from him, but Fred merely called him 'a loveable rogue', saying he was a known scrounger, who spent all his own money on booze, and was well-known for occasionally selling the stolen videos in the pub to earn a bit of pin money as a sideline. I was amazed Fred knew about it and did nothing. But that was Fred – he was a very generous person, and all he would say whenever I mentioned it was: 'We're doing well now, that poor bugger is skint most of the time these days, so what yer mitherin' about, woman?'

The end of the year arrived again, but Christmas didn't seem to be such a magical time as usual. Fred kept pronouncing it might be his last. I was coping with my mum and her grief and, of course, my own grief about losing my dad, which seemed magnified by the forthcoming festive season. I was so worried about Mum, as both my parents had always made a big fuss of Christmas, and this time it was going to be hard for her being alone. Nathan missed his granddad too. All three of us went through the festive period under a dark, black cloud and nothing seemed to lift it.

Jack and Roger came over for the New Year, and that helped Fred to cope somewhat, but I think we were all glad when it was finally over and we could put away the decorations, which served as a terrible reminder of better times. The most heartbreaking thing I remember is on New Year's Eve just after the stroke of midnight Fred said to me, 'I might not be here this time next year, cock.'

The three months after Christmas were spent in a whirl of chemotherapy treatment, hospital visits, theatre dates around the country, personal appearances, filming dates and after-dinner talks. I nursed him, bore the abusive drinking episodes, but I still loved my Hippo deeply and tried to deny what was happening. I just don't know how he kept it up; on the dates he wasn't having chemotherapy, being poorly or travelling, he was working flat out renovating his Aveling & Porter steam tractor with the better members of Dad's Army, as well as helping me to do up the flat which I'd bought in Blackpool. He would sometimes bring along Alf, Jimmy and Ian to help. The gruelling workload would have been enough to floor most men in perfect health, but not Fred – he worked with superhuman strength, even designing and building his own hydraulic riveter to rivet the boiler to perfection.

'Yeah, about fourteen or fifteen years ago, I bought a steam tractor for about £2,500...'

Nothing was going to stop him now. He was determined that this engine would be in steam before he became too weak to work and this thought must have been one of the things that kept him going for as long as he did.

241

Another amazing feat of strength was that Fred, whilst undergoing chemotherapy, readily undertook another chimney-felling operation. He was contracted by a local company called Woodford Industries Limited to clear a 180 feet factory chimney located on the Kirklees Valley Industrial Estate in Brandlesholme, near Bury. The chimney was to be dropped on Sunday 28th April 2002. I couldn't believe it when he told me about it and was angry with him, labelling him 'stupid' to attempt it, but was met with the usual: 'What are you mithering about, woman!'

Later, when things became bad and his mind distorted, he remembered me calling him 'stupid' around this time, and he dwelled on the fact I'd called him a 'pillock' and amplified the meaning out of context, making it sound like I thought he was generally stupid. He never forgot it.

The job of preparing a chimney for felling usually takes a week, and the team started on the 15th April. The group of men had been working away at the chimney whilst we were travelling to speaking engagements, and Fred's good pal, fellow steeplejack Eddie Chattwood, was amongst the men as usual.

I liked Eddie and his wife Margaret. They were always very friendly and sociable to me. Eddy had known and worked with Fred for a great many years, and seemed totally at ease within himself; he wasn't interested in the limelight. The chimney drop at Bury went without event, ending in the usual style – as Fred would say – in the pub afterwards, and he had a great time with his friends, telling his stories.

Fred's health seemed to be bearing up remarkably well on the face of it, but I was becoming increasingly worried about this growing capacity for drink, especially the effect it might be having on his single remaining kidney. When we met, he'd be content with two bottles of Guinness a night from the local off-licence, but when the supplier stopped getting Guinness in glass bottles from a particular source and put the price up slightly he went elsewhere, and it soon increased to four cans per night instead. Now, since the illness, it was routinely a bottle of wine a night as well as the four cans of Guinness, and sometimes Scotch too. I didn't like Fred drinking too much because it made him moody, self-absorbed, depressed and argumentative. He'd sit in the parlour repeatedly watching his BBC programmes on video, drowning his sorrows for a few hours and complain bitterly if I tried to turn over whenever I wanted to watch *Coronation Street* or something else, adding, 'Without these films, cock, you'd be penniless.' It wasn't like him to be this self-absorbed; I think he wanted to relive a time when he was well and trouble free.

There was simply no arguing with him when he became belligerent; he could always shoot you down in flames in the most articulate way, and knew exactly what to say to needle you. He was becoming difficult to live with and, because I was fiery by nature, we would have the most spectacular rows, only to make up again within a few hours unless it was about something more serious, and then it could go on for days.

It is no secret that by now I disliked his eldest son, Jack. I found him surly and difficult. Roger, by contrast, was sunny by nature and always got on extremely well with Nathan and me. I also liked Fred's middle daughter, Lorna. But it was only after Fred was diagnosed with cancer that her visits became more frequent than the usual yearly one at Christmas when we got to know each other well. Fred's eldest daughter, Jayne, and his youngest, Caroline, hadn't seen their dad for around sixteen years, so I didn't really get to know them until Fred was dying.

The biggest trigger of any argument was my dislike of Jack, whom Fred naturally adored. Unlike my own son's upbringing, discipline seemed to be very lax in the Dibnah household. I considered his manners atrocious and told Fred so on many occasions, which always sparked off another big row. I knew he wanted me and Jack to get on, but we gradually got to the point where we couldn't stand the sight of each other, and this would cause difficulties whenever he came to visit, staying with us sometimes during school holidays.

It seemed to me that the illness was affecting Fred's personality in many ways; it was certainly affecting our marriage and our love for each other. I loved him with all my heart but nothing I could do or say seemed to help.

People reassured me that when someone is ill, they sometimes take it out on their nearest and dearest. One particular time he'd not spoken to me for two days and there had been rows over silly little things; then something happened which I'd never known happen before. It was unheard of for Fred to speak badly of *anyone* who was trying to help in the garden workshops, but this day he was particularly angry and broke the silence between us, barging in at teatime, telling me about the 'mithering bastards' who had been working on the steam tractor and had caused the new throat plate to warp.

He grumbled that it was about £500 worth of work ruined, as it would need a new one. Surprisingly, he suddenly buried his head in both hands and started to sob about it. He said he was very sorry for having been so horrid to me of late, but being a perfectionist he was upset about the ruined throat plate and I didn't know what it meant to him when it went wrong. It cost him time and he hadn't got much of that left.

But I was amazed that he was annoyed with his Dad's Army. I didn't particularly care for the way they seemed to know all our personal business. By now a few of them were trying to treat me as though I didn't exist by tramping through the house whenever they felt like it, using it like a café.

I gave Fred a big hug and he continued sobbing about having to do the 'crenulating' with a catheter as well. It was understandably getting him down and I suspected was the kernel of what was bugging him. I insisted we should see the urologist Miss Mobb about an operation on his prostate gland to see if it would relieve the need for this awful self-catheterisation procedure. Soon after that, we received some news: we had to go to the Christie Hospital to get the results of the extensive tests Fred had been subjected to when he'd finished the course of chemotherapy.

We sat there together on the designated day, frightened and apprehensive, dimly aware of some distant voices outside the door in this small antiseptic-smelling room, waiting for his specialist, Dr Wylie, to come in and discuss the findings. We'd know in about twenty minutes whether there was any hope or not.

Dr Wylie entered the room and Fred fearlessly piped up: 'Tell me straight, mate, am I a gonner or what?'

'Well, Fred, congratulations – you've done remarkably well with the chemotherapy, much better than we all expected. Given the tests you've had, we can find no trace of the cancer remaining in your tissue surrounding the affected area. The chemotherapy seems to have worked.'

It didn't sink in at first; Fred was convinced he'd be going back there for 'the death sentence', as he put it. The good news was only slightly marred by the next bit: 'But unfortunately, Fred, we cannot say you are "cured". You've gone into what we call remission and it can only be deemed that you are all clear and not at risk once you've been clear for four years. But we'll have you in for regular tests.'

It was time for joyous celebration, and I felt as though a boulder had been lifted from our shoulders. I hugged Fred, hugged Dr Wylie and thanked God – but still Fred wasn't sure.

'What if the bloody thing comes back – he told me I'd be dead in twelve months anyway at first!' he reflected later over a celebratory meal. I tried to reassure him as best I could, but indeed there was an element of fear, a faint whiff of uncertainty in the air, and despite the warming effects of the red wine, we could feel a slight chill deep within our bones. But for now at least, life seemed good again.

I continued giving Fred a diet containing lots of fresh fruit juice, plenty of vegetables. I made him eat wholemeal bread and mountains of tomatoes containing a natural chemical substance called lycopene, which supposedly helps to inhibit free radicals and prevents cancer cells from growing.

'Get these down yer, Fred!'

'No, not bloody tomatoes again – are you trying to kill me, or what?!'

Around this time, Fred was discussing the making of another series with David Hall, entitled *Fred Dibnah's Age of Steam*. This would be closer to Fred's heart as a steam enthusiast, and he looked forward eagerly to the locations David Hall had earmarked for them to visit. I hoped that would cheer him up; as well as the good news from Dr Wylie it gave him something else to look forward to.

Fred also threw himself full tilt into working on his Aveling & Porter tractor out in the back garden whenever he could. Dad's Army had, by now, grown into a solid bunch of daily regulars. As well as helping on the steam tractor, they also set about digging the pit at Fred's direction – or the proposed mock mineshaft as it was known.

The idea was to eventually recreate a working example of how coal was once mined. It would consist of a 1.5m brick-lined mineshaft 21.64m deep, a 1.65m diameter arched tunnel, a wooden winding house complete with steam-driven winding gear, an endless rope hauling system and a narrow-gauge incline railway, which would relay pit tubs containing coal. The idea was to 'mine' the coal and pull it up the shaft in tubs, which would travel along the railway track, past the winding shed, and down to the steep banking towards the river (at the bottom of the garden), and along a tunnel 'outcropping' from the banking up to the bottom of the mineshaft again, where it would be put in 'the cage' and hauled by the steam winding mechanism to the top of the mineshaft to complete the circuit, thus giving the impression of a working mine.

Much to Fred's annoyance, I let the side down and said I didn't like the idea at all, condemning it as 'too near the house'. I was worried about Fred and the sheer hard graft it would take to complete this fanciful idea. It was a massive feat of engineering; projects of this size mean hard work and he'd been poorly. We still had the rest of the summer steam rally circuit to get through, as well as filming and personal appearance dates, so the pit tended to take second place to the exhausting schedule ahead. I hoped he might lose some interest in the pit as he saw his engine nearing completion.

It was the run-up to Christmas again and the flat in Blackpool was almost fully renovated. Since Fred's boys were not coming over for the festivities this year, I decided we would spend Christmas in Blackpool. Fred came with me to finish off bits and pieces and I got the Christmas tree and decorations out. I'd worked diligently in my spare time to get the final touches to the flat completed in time, and on Christmas Eve all four of us set off in the car; Fred, Mum, Nathan and me.

We arrived in Blackpool around 2.00 p.m. I lit the Christmas tree, put on some festive music, opened a pack of mince pies and looked forward to some of my friends coming around later that evening for a drink with us.

Fred, unsmiling, unspeaking, obviously fed-up, flopped down on the sofa and stuck his head belligerently in a steam book. I asked if anyone wanted a drink, meaning a coffee. Fred, in a black mood, demanded a straight whisky. My mum had recently been on holiday with my uncle and had brought back a litre bottle of Courvoisier, which she'd saved for Christmas. I didn't really want Fred to have a strong drink so early on, so asked if he wanted Guinness instead, as I had no whisky. But he'd already spotted the Courvoisier: 'Bollocks! I'll have that there instead.'

Mum and I had a glass of sherry each, and Fred asked for a top-up long before we'd finished ours. I shuddered as I caught the look in his eyes.

'Leave the bottle,' he said as I put the stopper back in. I could see it was one of those days when I'd do nothing right, so I kept out of his way for the afternoon, attending to preparations for the evening meal.

By teatime, Fred was obviously quite drunk, stamping his feet and expressing, in language frowned upon by elderly ladies, exactly what he thought of Blackpool: 'They are all f***ing slot machine playing pillocks who come here, Mavis ... never done 'owt proper with their lives,' he said to my shocked mother.

Having supped about a third of the bottle of Courvoisier, two glasses of Harvey's Bristol Cream, four cans of Guinness, two large glasses of red wine and a Bailey's Irish Cream, he turned on my mum – the verbal results of all this heavy drinking. 'F***ng hell, Mavis – what am I f***ng doing in this dump, when I should be at home in mi' bloody shed?'

He refused any offer of food and sat on the sofa, repeatedly moaning about the rooftop view out of the front bay window. My friends arrived about 7.00 p.m., discovering Fred sprawled out on the sofa still declaring hatred of the terracotta rooftops in an Alf Garnett politically-incorrect style.

It quickly became apparent that he was less than happy with the 'yuppie' company as he saw it and, after a few embarrassing exchanges, they all left within the hour.

The night wore on tediously to its conclusion around midnight as Fred became increasingly moody, insulting, coarse and very, very drunk. We watched in amazement as he finished off three-quarters of the litre bottle of Courvoisier, becoming even more abusive when we tried to take it from him. There was a near disastrous attempt when he slid off the sofa, banged his head hard on a side table, proclaiming 'F***ing bastards,' and 'They say I'm supposed to be cured, in good order now but they don't know how me belly feels inside. I'm a dead man... I've had it.'

All three of us had to drag him to bed like a rag doll and get him undressed whilst he kept dribbling and trying to half-heartedly lunge at us, proclaiming he was dying and only wanted his two little lads there instead of us. Why had they been stolen away from their home and their dad? It was awful to see the devastating reason behind his deep unhappiness – like catching someone unexpectedly naked – but there was nothing we could do, only let him rant and rave on, keeping up the pretence he was all right emotionally and physically until finally he fell asleep. He had been through such a lot recently and was in bad shape on both counts. He told my mum he wanted to go to see Jesus – it was heartbreaking.

Next day I cooked Christmas lunch for 3.00 p.m., but Fred was still in bed. I went through to see if he wanted to get up. Understandably, he said he felt very unwell with his resulting hangover, and didn't want any dinner. We'd held it off for nearly an hour but it was getting dried up and unpalatable. We'd all lost interest in eating when he finally came through into the dining room, asking for his dinner. He ate very little, merely saying he wanted to go home, and now felt very sick indeed.

After a tense meal, he went back to bed and fell asleep. My mum and I went out for a short stroll along the nearby beach to clear our minds. On our return we all packed our things and planned to travel home the next day, so that Fred could be back in his own surroundings.

But ultimately we didn't hold it against him. It was my mistake taking Fred away from his beloved home and his engines when he considered it might be his last Christmas. The emotional and physical pain he felt must have been profound and disturbing, resulting in a black mood where he needed to drown himself in drink. Of course, he would want to spend what he considered his last Christmas on earth in his own little world in Bolton.

CHAPTER 13
News of a gong ... and the final chimney drop

'As long as I can finish me engine off, cock, it doesn't overly worry me about owt else though'

The New Year brought the usual amount of celebrity work, and Fred worked in the garden whenever he could. Filming dates for *Age of Steam* had been pencilled in the diary to begin in February, March, May and June. Family life continued as normal with Nathan learning to drive, and me seeing Peter Kay in his *Mum Wants a Bungalow* theatre tour at the Opera House in Blackpool. Going to the gym in my spare time, I felt physically in top peak – but emotionally I was stressed out. Fred seemed a little more settled, things got back on an even keel, and apart from him complaining about feeling a little 'bloated' and constipated, he continued with his gruelling schedule.

However, when spring came round again it was obvious there was something badly wrong. He was now getting quite a lot of pain. At first I put this down to effects of drinking, but for Fred to express discomfort, you knew it had to be awful. Arrangements were made for more tests at the hospital to see what the problem was.

We still did a lot of travelling and I lost count of all the places Fred was to visit with the *Evening with Fred Dibnah* theatre tour: Wakefield, Shrewsbury, Cambridge, Buxton, Accrington, York, Middlesbrough, Hornchurch, Leeds, Reading, Kempston, Felixstowe and Hastings. And this was just up to the end of March! What makes this especially outstanding, and shows the true extent of his determination and grit, is that between the theatre date in Hornchurch on the 16th of March and the one in Felixstowe on the 29th March, Fred had an operation in Royal Bolton Hospital on the 17th March to remove polyps in his bladder. No-one watching that two-and-a-half-hour, one-man show in Felixstowe, where he stood for the duration on stage, would have guessed that he was recuperating from surgery and in anything less than perfect health. Of course Fred would tell anyone who would listen about his health problems, but he looked no different from usual: full of vim, vitality and vigour.

In fact, he always brought an element of surreal humour to an otherwise grim situation, and I recall becoming exasperated with him as he lay in the hospital bed recovering from the surgery. Over the bed was one of those 'patient line' screens, the kind which you can activate with a pre-paid card to watch television, or use the telephone. I'd asked the previous day if he wanted me to set it up but he pulled a face and waved his hand, 'Naaah, bloody thing – I don't want to watch that ... got some mining books to read ... better than all that crap they show these days!'

However, when I returned at visiting time next day, he discovered one of his programmes was to be shown on the BBC that evening and wanted to see it. As I listened to the operator at the other end of the line informing me of the right sequence for getting it all working, in the background I could hear: 'Is that bloody thing on yet, or what? I can't see owt yet ... how do you use this bloody remote effort? What the hell does *this* mean, "press enter" ... is the damned thing on yet? I can't see owt ... bloody modern world – you can't even be ill in peace ... naaah.' It was Fred playing to the small audience of elderly men toting wee-bags at their bedsides, most of whom were enjoying the impromptu show from their local hero after their own operations!

'Shhhh ... I can't hear a thing, Fred,' I said as I fiddled with the instructions. He examined the flimsy piece of plastic in his hand, pulled a face and asked, 'Well, what are you supposed to press here then? Is it wired up proper or what?'

He turned and asked the bloke in the next bed, asking how he'd got his on. His three visitors started to explain how to work it. There was much mumbling and grumbling so I shot out, 'Just a minute, Fred – I can't hear what the woman at the other end is saying.'

'EH? YOU WHAT, COCK?' he shouted so loud that no doubt the next ward could hear. 'Is it working now, or what?' Thankfully the screen burst into action and I was able to carry on with the visit.

As time went by, we discovered the cancer had returned in the surrounding fatty tissue of the right kidney that had been removed, and with it came the growing worm in the apple of our marriage, eventually turning it rotten to the core. The news came as no great shock to Fred, who took it in his usual stride, and said he'd never believed that it had truly gone away in the first place. We were told that he would need to undergo another cycle of chemotherapy, as more surgery would not cure it. There were secondary cancers in his lymph glands too. There were more filming dates to complete, and more theatre dates in the diary, but Fred steadfastly refused to cancel any of them, claiming he wouldn't let down fans that'd paid good money to see him.

So we carried on ... London, Hertford, Folkestone, Haynes, Swindon, Yarm in Cleveland, Telford, Lowestoft, Dorking, Reading, Derby, Kent and Aberdeen... All interspersed with worrying hospital dates and tests, gruelling chemotherapy sessions, sickness, stress, rows, renovating the steam tractor and, in addition, ceaselessly digging the pit in the back yard.

Fred's sense of humour prevailed. One day a man whom he had met in the Christie turned up to see him at Radcliffe Road. He'd been undergoing chemotherapy the same as Fred. As he came down the path, Fred brightened and chirped out, ' 'Ave they given you a date yet, mate, or what?'

Puzzled, the man said, 'What for?'

'Fer bloody dying, that's what!' said Fred. 'They've given me twelve months, the bastards!'

Fans and followers had always been of paramount importance to Fred – especially youngsters who expressed interest in what he was doing. For example, in May 2002 after a local chimney drop in Tottington, near Bury (a town not far from Bolton), Fred received a letter from a lady whose little boy, Alex, had stood peering patiently out of his bedroom window waiting for the chimney to fall on the day at the designated time. Unfortunately, he had gotten fed-up of the long delay due to the adverse weather conditions. At the very moment he left the window, the chimney suddenly crashed to the ground – and he missed it. It broke his little heart and he cried for hours afterwards, according to his mum's letter. As soon as Fred learned of this, busy as he was, he got in his Land Rover and headed to Bury to deliver a signed copy of *The Ups and Downs of Chimneys* to the little boy. The family were away at the time, but Fred later received a second letter saying that Alex was thrilled to find the video waiting for him, and was already driving his mum and dad nuts with it!

That was so typical of Fred's kindness and generosity; he would do anything for anybody, no matter how well-known he became. People mattered and that's what endeared him to complete strangers, this caring thoughtfulness towards them without a hint of arrogance. Despite being a genius in certain respects, he was still just an average bloke trying to earn a crust like the rest of us.

Fred was now at the very zenith of his career as a television personality and, despite his very serious health problems, had no intention of stepping down or retiring. It seemed so unfair; he had worked remarkably hard all his life, had enjoyed some of the trappings of success – and now this. But far more important to Fred, and one of the things he most wanted to do – along with getting the engine finished – was to see the pit project completed in the back garden. So once again he started to lay courses of brickwork down the shaft, with a view to getting it completed if planning permission could be obtained. I showed remorse and said I now supported the project. I could see it would keep him going as he poured his remaining stamina into making it happen, but secretly I considered it would never come to fruition; without Fred to oversee and direct the sinking of the shaft, the others lacked the skills to complete the project.

Fred had been speaking with David Hall about the mineshaft. David was intrigued by the concept and fully supported Fred in his quest. After the successful showing of *Age of Steam* on BBC2, Fred and David began talking about making a programme entitled *Dig with Dibnah*, which would be a one-off, hour-long documentary focusing on the problems Fred faced in engineering a mock mineshaft. Being a 'human interest' tale, it would concentrate on Fred's relationship with 'the men', particularly Alf Molyneux and Jimmy Crookes, who would feature going about their daily activities, assisting Fred with the pit and other projects in the yard.

The chemotherapy hit Fred harder this time round. During the first lot of treatment he seemed invincible and apart from bouts of sickness sailed through it relatively unscathed. It was easy to forget the enormity of what he was going through because he never complained. Now, however, he complained constantly of 'pins and needles' in his feet and I noticed he looked pale and wan. He tired easily, constantly felt sick, and had to take medication to counteract this. He was constipated all the time with the drugs, and this made him feel bloated. It hadn't stopped his heavy drinking, though, and I was still annoyed to see him swilling down anti-sickness tablets with large glasses of wine when he returned home after chemotherapy. He suffered from recurring bladder infections, and would do the same with prescribed antibiotics. But I was always met with the usual resistance whenever I complained: 'Stop your mithering, woman!'

Fred considered himself invincible, but by now he knew there was slim chance of the cancer going away. He was determined to enjoy what was left of his life in his own way. So we carried on, still more dates in the diary: Bristol, Dartford, Croydon, Llandudno, Exeter, Plymouth, Torquay, Barnstaple, Salisbury, Birmingham, Southport, Southend-on-Sea and Yeovil.

The list went on and on and so, valiantly, did Fred without missing one single date. The long hours travelling, frustrating journeys trying to navigate around strange towns (before SAT-NAV), two hours standing up on stage, endless queues of fans and people vying to speak to him late into the night, tedious hours of signing autographs, posing for pictures, interviews, phone calls –'*Fred do this/Fred do that*' and night after night in a different hotel... I just don't know how he did it. There was some kind of unhealthy, weird fascination in watching not only how he managed to move great pieces of iron and timber back home, and wielded heavy sledgehammers for an hour or two at a time, but also coped with the steady flow of people turning up to see him and asking all sorts of questions. Plus there was the usual plethora of like-minded engineering types to deal with as well. It was quite simply superhuman; I still don't know how he found the time and patience for everyone. It was an incredible tribute to his steely determination not to be beaten by the cancer and his diminishing strength.

He was pleased with progress on the tractor, saying to David that if he could only get a series depicting travelling around Britain on his nearly completed engine, it would have been worth all the hassle – or twenty-two years and two divorces.

By now, Fred and I had started to talk about the workshops and steam paraphernalia if anything happened to him. I was reluctant to discuss this at first; it was like admitting defeat. We'd already had similar discussions about my welfare if I was widowed when he first learned he had cancer; this time round it seemed far more real and frightening, because we could see the physical symptoms of what was happening to him. First time round, he was so strong, so fit – it didn't really sink in. To me, and to others, Fred was super-human. But now we were living with the sort of grief usually experienced after a bereavement, which mainly consisted of anger, denial, injustice, sense of loss and total fear – and it put a tremendous strain on our marriage. We knew the outcome, a one-way ticket for me to being a young widow; it was just a question of when.

I was scared about everything, I was crying all the time – what was happening to Fred brought back the loss of my father. I felt I was on the edge of a cliff and so, with Fred's encouragement during his better periods, I bought a buy-to-let property in Blackpool, with a mortgage, using £13,000 of our funds as a deposit.

To add to the problems, Fred was telling anyone he met, 'Aye, wife's spending me money on property so she'll be OK when I kick t' bucket, like.' I couldn't make him see how inappropriate this was and tried to prevent him from telling people everything that happened in our lives. He said he was only joking ... but it didn't seem that way; people tended to take everything he said at face value.

'As long as I can finish me engine off, cock, it doesn't overly worry me about owt else though ... but I wanna do me engine up and finish me pit if I can before I die,' he said.

Money or the things it could buy never interested Fred. He wanted enough to spend on his engines without worrying, and enough so that he hadn't got to bother about household bills landing on the doormat. 'If the BBC bugger off tomorrow and never come back, it doesn't worry me a lot ... I've done the work of two men in my life, and that's a fact,' he would often say – and he meant it too.

It was becoming a bizarre, topsy-turvy life. One day we'd be off to the Christie, having more tests, being prescribed more medication and I would look after him whenever he felt poorly; next day he'd be fine and have the strength of ten men, bounding around buying rounds of drinks in a local pub at some 'lock in' after a theatre date. You'd think there was nothing at all wrong with him as you watched him in conversation. I joked that he had a clone that did all the public appearances whilst he hid away in his shed and merrily played with his steam engines.

Towards the end of the year a letter came from St James' Palace in London, informing Fred that he'd been nominated to receive an award in the

New Year's Honour's List. *An MBE no less*! I always remember that particular morning; he tentatively opened the official, expensive-looking cream envelope bearing the fancy dark-pink crest in one corner and, after reading the contents, casually chucked the letter across the table to me, nearly knocking over my boiled egg.

'Naaah,' he said. 'Some daft bugger's having me on here. An MBE? Who the bloody hell would want to give a pillock like me a gong, eh!'

I studied the letter carefully. 'Wow! It's true, Fred; you're going to be mentioned in the New Year's Honours' List!'

'Yer what?'

'It's true – you're going to be known as Dr Fred Dibnah MBE.'

'Eh? Bugger off, you daft bat.'

'No ... you'll have to meet the Queen, and get dressed up in a suit...'

'Give over, I don't believe you ... who's sent it, they're taking the p...'

'You're off to London to Buckingham Palace to meet the Queen.'

'Eh? Where? WHEN?'

'Have a look...'

Thought someone was 'avin me on. Well, bloody hell, but I'm wearing me cap to meet Her Majesty. Anyroad, her Charlie likes me programmes I've heard tell... I was at Eastnor Castle visiting me mate James Hervey-Bathurst once like, and this posh lady comes up to me and says, 'Oooh, we are friends of Charles, you know, and he always makes a particular point of watching your programmes on the television, Mr Dibnah'. Gawd, I thought to myself — this is royalty watching you on telly, Fred! Your mam would have been reet proud. She was a proper Royalist me mam, like. Had some fancy frilly cups with a picture of the Queen and Prince Phillip on the side or summat, and she had a nice colour picture which I've now got hanging up in me shed, bit battered now, like. Always called me 'our Freddie' my mam did — 'Our Freddie's on the box tonight you know,' she'd say in a posh voice to Mr Tranter who lived round t'corner or to the woman in the pie shop at the end of our street.

He pretended he was not bothered at first, but inside he was secretly delighted and also told everyone he met about his honorary degree in 'back-street mechanicing' as he called it, which he'd received from Aberdeen University. Now he was getting a 'gong' for services to British broadcasting as well. It could not have gone to a more deserving candidate and I was delighted for him. I can still see how his beaming face lit up.

The chemotherapy sessions seemed to be going well and we had high hopes, as Fred heard stories that it was 'new stuff from America' which had a good success rating. We spoke in more depth, and I sold my property in Blackpool and looked around for another renovation project to secure my future. Fred gave me several thousand pounds towards this and said I could have more if I needed it. He willingly wrote out two cheques: 'It'll be yours when I've gone anyway, cock.'

I had some deep concerns, but mostly I was worried about his increasing emotional dependence on drink to cope with his awful plight. The split personality after he imbibed a lot of booze was never far under the surface. Whilst sober he was fine, saying how much he worried that I would be well looked after if anything should happen, but drink seemed to bring out a dark, nasty side. If he'd been more depressed and cantankerous towards me than usual, he would say later, 'Ahhh, I'm just a bit pissed off, cock. I didn't mean anything by it really...' By contrast, other days, he would constantly blame me for causing problems and nit-pick at everything, which resulted in rows between us. Perhaps on reflection, I should have kept my mouth shut and not responded. I still loved him deeply, but my own fears meant, irrationally, I was angry that he was dying and going to leave me on my own.

Ordinarily, Fred could easily handle very large quantities of alcohol but with powerful medication, at times it seemed to despatch him into some kind of madness which tipped the balance of his anxious mind, sometimes making him frighteningly aggressive with little or no provocation.

Towards the end of January, we visited the Christie Hospital for a CT scan appointment. We waited in a crowded reception area for a couple of hours, only to be told that the machine was not working properly so we would have to return the following Tuesday. During the long wait our eyes darted round the stuffy room noticing the pale, waif-like appearance and despairing looks on the faces of the worst-affected cancer patients. Fred would occasionally whisper in his none-too-muted tones: 'Bloody hell, cock, look at that poor bugger there. He's barely alive poor sod...' As the minutes ticked by we fidgeted in the moulded plastic chairs; I could tell he was growing more and more spooked by the surroundings. People were even asking for an autograph – it was surreal, awful. Understandably, this long wait and the subsequent outcome put us both in a black mood and as we returned home in the car, we began bickering about trivialities, scoring points off each other as usual. We arrived back home in Bolton feeling very stressed out and now a very real row had developed.

Once indoors, Fred got the booze out and plonked down at the kitchen table with a gruff comment about the place being 'filthy'. It was. I had grown fed up with his constant criticism of my housekeeping abilities. He had simple ideas and expectations of an old-fashioned wife who would cook, clean, fetch, carry, obediently following her master's voice. It had escaped his notice that I was also running all the celebrity side of things, acting as business manager, running my own business affairs in Blackpool, running the home, running him up and down the country and looking after my elderly mother who had almost suffered a mental breakdown after the loss of my father, her childhood sweetheart. It all took a great deal of time and effort, leaving very little for myself. I didn't intend trying to keep dirty, industrial living conditions spick and span and resented the streams of men trudging in and out of the house to make coffee, or the various friends, visitors and occasional television crew using the bathroom, making it feel like a public lavatory with the rank pong they often left behind.

I had had enough, so I left the housework and downed tools. The house was indeed mucky, and it got worse the more the visitors used it. We were making a lot of money by now and I wanted to get a cleaner twice a week, but Fred simply would not hear of it. He said: 'Susie Woo had one of those, but she'd got two kids and a job to do, so she needed one.' This trite quip annoyed me and, coupled with the stress of putting up with his illness, this is why I 'went on strike'. If I could not have any domestic help, then the house would just have to do the way it was! I did all the food shopping, provided wholesome, healthy meals, did the washing, ironing and washed the car, so that was me done!

By teatime after the Christie trip, Fred was still seated at the kitchen table. He'd already drunk four cans of Guinness and a half bottle of red wine. I was fired up too, frustrated by the day's events. He started on a bottle of Scotch, saying he did not want any food as he could not eat 'in a pigsty' which, he bizarrely added, had probably given him the cancer in the first place!

As usual, as he became more inebriated he also got more boorish, maudlin and pensive, criticising everything I stood for. When I argued back he got angrier. He declared with a knowing nod and a wink in my direction, 'Aye! They all warned me – don't get bloody wed again, Fred, whatever you do ... shoulda listened to 'em, bloody women, all the same an' all. Me mates were right – should of GOT RID when I had chance. None of 'em out there like you, woman!'

Choked at this, I decided not to say anything further, keeping calm for now, seeing the danger signs. I left the room to watch television in the front parlour. No bonding tonight, no discussing what would happen to his engines and his workshops – just pure loathing, and I knew there would be trouble at some stage that evening.

About two hours later, he staggered into the parlour and stood in front of where I sitting, challenging me with an unfocused look, and again started criticising everything. He kept telling me he was going to get a gun and shoot himself because he had suffered long enough and wanted to end it, since he was not in charge of his life any more (the significance of this statement later became relevant).

I had not heard him talk like this before. I became fretful, leapt up and tried to take the bottle of whisky from him, but he backed off and started snarling like some cornered wild animal, '*Leave me alone!*'

Then he flopped down in his green leather chair. I left him sitting on his own, mumbling about how he had had it, and went to bed. 'My belly is sore, why don't you leave me alone...' he groaned as he sat there rubbing his right side, in deep misery by now.

Around 2.00 a.m., I was awakened by a loud crash downstairs. I sat bolt upright in bed and listened. I could hear Fred stumbling around trying to get upstairs. I got up to help him, but stopped at the top of the stairs. He had not seen me but was making odd comments, saying he wished we had never met and women in general were all the same. I waited and listened, wondering what to do next. He was obviously very drunk, perhaps needing help to get upstairs, but I decided to stay clear of him. I did not fancy another row. Gradually, he managed to get himself upstairs but he kept saying, 'Not much longer now, not much longer...'

Eventually, he stumbled into the bathroom and I heard him fall down. Alarmed, I rushed to open the door but when I tried entering the bathroom, he screeched at the top of his voice for me to leave him alone; he didn't want me near him. Not knowing what to do, I felt helpless and just stood there listening to him ranting and trying to get up. I wondered how much he had had to drink and went downstairs to look for the bottle of whisky. It was in the kitchen and no more than an inch was left in the bottom of it. Disturbingly, at the side of the bottle was a brown plastic phial of tablets, lying open on its side. Only three tablets remained. When I read the label, they were prescribed to someone else. I thought of his words: 'Not much longer now...' and immediately panicked, not knowing what to do. I rang 999 for the ambulance, as I thought he might have taken tablets with the booze.

The paramedics arrived shortly afterwards and burst into the bathroom. Fred was uncoordinated, drunk, lying in the empty bathtub, unable to get out. They had to lift him, and as they held him upright his knees turned to jelly. I was frantic, but we gradually ascertained that he had not taken many of the tablets, which were painkillers. The paramedics stayed for a while to keep their eye on him once they finally got him to bed. Then they left and, exhausted, I retired uneasily to my own bed. It was now after 3.00 a.m. Finally, Fred was quiet.

There were other concerns too. He seemed to be confiding all our personal and financial business to Dad's Army or anyone who would listen to his distorted views about me. We would argue fiercely and then two days later he would show such remorse, telling me that he still loved me, turning up with a nice bottle of wine as a peace offering. But it was like walking on thin ice, and at times he spat out that 'all *his men* knew what I was like' and that they had actually suggested he '*get rid*' of the problem by asking for a divorce. I saw the glazed look, the way he'd sneer during these periods. It wasn't my husband, just some stranger I now lived with.

It was only after he died that I came to realise the full implications of Fred telling everything to this band of men and sharing his illness with them.

It fuelled their twisted views on all my shortcomings. I should have taken this more seriously and watched my back, but what could I do – how could I ever know that the situation between myself and Fred had developed into something of a blood sport, a witch-hunt by malicious people to see how far they could goad him?

I was subject to various actions and prejudices from those who considered they were doing him a service by making me an outsider. Some of it was no doubt later fuelled by jealousy and resentment from other quarters too, but mostly it was because of what Fred had said about me. The more he shared this with people outside the marriage, the more they seemed to have direct influence on him. No clearer was this demonstrated than when an incident occurred right out of the blue.

He announced he was not going to take me to Buckingham Palace when he collected the MBE. I didn't take any notice at first, thinking he was cross; he was having a particularly bad day as work on his tractor was not going to plan. It was so typical of Fred to blurt out something in frustration if things were not going well in the garden; I was used to this and no doubt his other wives had been too. However, the day after he made the comment, we visited the Christie Hospital for more chemotherapy and he repeated what he had said in a more relaxed, casual manner over our evening meal. Worried and anxious, I enquired what he meant, and he simply replied, 'You'll see, you'll find out...'

I tried to stop him as he washed down antibiotics with a bottle of wine, followed by a third of a bottle of brandy and two cans of Guinness. Again, I asked what he meant, but he said I should mind my own business, as I was not the one dying and he would do as he liked about his MBE.

Shocked, I changed the subject; he was becoming loud and highly animated, and this was sometimes a sign of a row. But he turned aggressive and said he supported the views of 'those who had shown an unbelievable interest in his life's work' and not some 'f***ing woman who had only been here five minutes'. He added that he was not inviting me to the MBE ceremony at Buckingham Palace because I was 'a disgrace with my unsupportive attitude', and that all the men who respected him would consider him a 'f***ing pillock' if he took me along with him. He said he had spoken with 'his men' and they backed him a hundred per cent in his decision not to take me.

Amazingly, this was simply because I had grumbled about them digging the mineshaft and being ever-present in the back garden! Many a time, I would go out after 9.00 p.m., and shout: 'Why don't you all bugger off home, eh? Fred and I need a bit of time for us.'

I tried to leave the room but he blocked me and said, 'Why don't you just f**k off to Blackpool, then we can all get on with our work in peace? Leave us alone.'

It was awful; his eyes were distant, glazed, he looked like a stranger but there was nothing I could do, only vent my own anger as all the pent-up bitterness of the past months came to the fore. I was also surprised at his using the swear word towards me, since Fred loathed men who swore in front of women. The unjustness of his decision not to take me to London meant I snapped back. I lost my temper and slapped him hard across the face, then stormed off upstairs, shouting and threatening to have it out with these men about their evil interference.

Fuelled by my own temper, I stormed back downstairs to confront him. Incensed by the decision to exclude me from his special day, I grabbed his favourite antique oil lamp from the table and deliberately dropped it onto the tiled kitchen floor. The clear glass gallery immediately shattered like a thousand teardrops.

He made a guttural noise and staggered unsteadily to his feet, shouting loudly at me. Enraged, red in the face, he squared up and lurched forward ready to hit out. I could see he meant it too, so I backed off and ran upstairs again, only this time he followed me, bellowing he was 'going to show me something else, baby – you've bloody had it now...'

I shot into the master bedroom and kicked the door shut but, surprisingly fast and agile, he quickly blocked it with his foot. He made another odd noise and rushed at me, swinging his arm back and catching me on the right-hand side of my head with his fist. Colours exploded at the back of my eyes, everything went blurred and I went down, cowering on the floor like some wounded animal. But he was not done, bellowing out he would kill me. I was stunned as several hard blows rained down and I thought I might eventually pass out through shock and fear. Finally, I managed to crawl away, and he flopped down wearily on his brass bed, groaning, 'Oh mother – what the f**k have I done to deserve this? Please God let it all be over soon ... let me shuffle off this mortal coil... I wanna DIE!'

Stunned, terrified and hurting – it was the first time he had lashed out – I stumbled as fast as I could downstairs and out of the back door, trembling and not sure what to do next. My head felt like I'd been hit with a jackhammer and my legs wouldn't bear the weight under my shaky body. I sat outside in the dark for the longest time, worried about my right eye. Then I went back indoors for the car keys on the kitchen table, wanting to be anywhere but here.

By now, Fred had come back downstairs and was sitting hunched up in the kitchen. He did not look at me, but croaked, 'Why don't you bugger off back to Blackpool. Leave me alone to die, please let me die in peace!' He buried his head in his hands, sobbing, 'Oh God, mother, PLEASE let me die!' His shoulders heaved as misery took over at the end of this ugly scene and he sobbed into his hands.

Next day, and for about a week afterwards, there was one of those pressure-cooker atmospheres at home, whereby nothing you do can take away the harsh words said in anger. Because he had also hit out on this occasion, I felt humiliated and bitter. Fred shuffled past me, looking down whenever he entered the house. I kept out of the way. Dad's Army, observing from a safe distance, said nothing.

Fred spent time with his men, and went to the pub for his tea with some of them or often ate fish and chips alone in the shed. This went on for just over a week. Then one evening he came indoors to make himself a brew and looked so tired, old, dishevelled and poorly. His belly was enormous on the side where the tumour was, and he was rubbing the spot. I felt a keen stab of guilt, knowing he should be eating proper food instead of pies and chips all the time, so I gently asked if he wanted some tea. He welcomed the chance to speak. Coming across to hug me tenderly, he broke the ice by saying, 'You and I shouldn't argue, cock – we've enough on our plates at present. I'm sorry, I know I've been a bit of a bastard to live with an' all, but you don't know what it's like to have some bloke with letters after his name sit in front of you and tell you you're done for.'

'Well, the chemo might work...' I offered.

'Aaahh... I'm half the man I used to be, woman – do you understand that? I'm knackered – you don't know how my belly feels inside. I'm dying, woman, do you understand that? I'm dying. Look at me hands, they're dead ... they look like bloody claws.'

Not knowing how to respond, I smiled slightly. 'Bony claws, Fred?' I said to lighten the mood. One of our private jokes during the happier times was the state of his hands after a lifetime of sheer hard graft, which I had always referred to as 'bony claws'. Much to his amusement I maintained that we should have named our company 'Bony Claw Productions'.

Fred relaxed a bit and shook his head saying, 'Oh, baby, what will become of me? I am so sorry, love, so sorry. I shouldn't have hit you. I've never hit a woman before. I'm frightened though, bloody scared stiff.'

'You know I love you, Hippo, I do,' I went on, warily testing the water. 'But why do you always have to side with them lot out there – why should Dad's Army have any say in what happens between us or in our life? Why should it matter to them if I go to the Palace or not?'

Wearily shaking his head, he raised a hand as if to say 'you don't under-stand' and flopped down at the table. He said that because I didn't like his mates, they didn't like me either. He said I should be nice to them and things would get better. That is why we argued, he continued, because I didn't like his friends and it would be better if I did. I stood looking at him silently, pondering on what to say next to avoid another row. Did he not realise it was sometimes the drink causing rows, too?

I hated these men by now, hated their power, their knowledge, and their presence – but mostly hated their place in the heart of our marriage which should have been mine.

Fred went on to tell me he had always experienced problems relating to women, because they were from a different planet. Maybe that was why his other wives had buggered off, because he couldn't understand them. However, men were different, he said, more stable, you knew where you were with them. He felt easy with men, could talk to them, share things.

I kept my own thoughts to myself. Why should I have to humour a bunch of grown men, some of whom were always ready to step in and take my husband's attention, and were downright intrusive on a daily basis whenever we were home? These ever-present men, mostly living their lives through Fred instead of doing their own thing, I thought they were a pathetic lot!

However, there was a darker side to it; I was amazed to learn from Fred that, whenever the latest row was mentioned, one of the more forceful ones kept suggesting to Fred that he get a divorce. It was bizarre, he was dying, and he had less than ten months to live.

'Do you want a divorce then?' I asked. 'After all we've gone through, do you want a divorce at this late stage?' It was incredible; hot tears stung my eyes and my tummy felt like it was in freefall. What was going on here? I felt out of my depth, like I'd wandered into alien territory. I didn't know my husband by now and, apart from the illness, didn't understand what was happening with the dynamics of the marriage.

'Do I bollocks!' he retorted.

'Then why the comments all the time, Fred?'

'Because you think you're so bloody smart.'

'What? Why? I don't understand what you're getting at?'

He continued: 'These blokes aren't bloody daft. They see you giving me a hard time so they think I should get rid of you, all that skriking you do and falling out ... they see it all and tell me I should get shut of you ... and to be honest I have to agree at times, but I don't want a bloody divorce from you. I've told them no, I wouldn't go that far.'

I was angry again now, and spat out, 'What are you on about? What has it got to do with a bunch of f***ing old men all trying their best to be a "Fred Dibnah"?'

Fred pulled a face and said, 'Well, for instance, you stopped Jack coming this Christmas, and I was upset and they all saw that.'

'But, Fred,' I countered. 'You *know* he wanted to stay in the Isle of Man because he was attending his friend's birthday party. Roger came over, didn't he, so why are you blaming me because of Jack not coming over?'

'Yeah, but Jack knows he's not welcome here – all my men know that. They all tell me what I should do and shouldn't do, because you don't always get on with him,' he replied, watching me carefully for a response.

'What? I don't understand,' I said, flustered. 'Why, Fred, why are you *listening* to these men?'

'Well, Jack doesn't like you,' he countered. It was pointless by now trying to justify with Fred how I felt about his eldest son.

We began to go round in circles. Jack did not like me and I did not like him. We knew this. However, what did *this* have to do with Fred's *men?*

We had invited the boys to spend Christmas with us but Jack changed his mind nearer the time. However, it had become a real issue for Fred; he was not very well emotionally or physically by now and thought it would be his last Christmas. He was livid for what he saw as me spoiling everything.

These comments proved just how far matters had gone. I recall him once threatening me with the solicitors in late December 2003, saying he wanted a divorce. But he calmed down later and said he loved me, despite me *'being an awkward bitch at times...'*. However, Fred blamed me totally for Jack's inability to fit in whenever he came over to stay with us. Spurred on by some of the men, Fred had been to see a solicitor about a divorce and the resulting paperwork (I learned later) had gone to the address of the main ringleader. This man had been outwardly friendly with me, going out of his way to be nice by chatting to me frequently, buying me flowers and little gifts to cheer me up; but at the same time he was spurring Fred on behind my back to try for a divorce. That's how involved these men were in our married life.

Fred calmed down after several days, saying something like: 'I'm bloody dying, woman – what the bloody hell do I want a divorce for, you daft sod!' But he explained that he had the respect of '*his men*' with whom he would discuss his problems. However, Fred stressed again that he did not want a divorce, and said the episode was a reaction to all the arguing. He actually said he felt pressured by a certain individual to take the matter further, but would not name the man despite me begging for a name. 'It will only cause trouble, cock, and I've enough of that already.' But then he added spitefully, 'I thought you should know where you stand, baby, when you act like you do. Them lot out there know what you are like and stick by me. None of 'em like you.'

'Why are you telling me all this now, Fred'? I challenged, confused.

'Because you don't know everything that goes on, you just think you do; you're not as clever as you think. Why should some bloody woman think she can come here, and stop us all doing our work? You've only been here two minutes.'

Why was he treating me like this? I was his wife.

I couldn't make sense of what he was trying to tell me and handled it all wrong by getting defensive, carrying on at him. 'What's it got to do with them lot out there, then?'

I hadn't a clue what to make of this and was confused and frightened. I also knew how erratic Fred's behaviour had become by this time and, aware of his duplicity, knew that he'd been grumbling about me to anyone who would happen to be around at the time – even complete strangers. Later, genuine people I now have reason to trust, such as Alf Molyneux, David Hall and Alan McEwen told me that Fred would often stand in a pub or someone's kitchen systematically going through all the things I was supposed to have said and done, embellishing it, calling me names just as he'd done about his other two wives in the past. The damaging thing now of course was that he was ill and it sounded terrible to the observer. Later, he would be sorry and say he hadn't really meant it, that '*I wasn't so bad after all*'. The complexity of his nature bore no malice; but he was articulate and able to voice his opinion and, like the rest of us, could be naturally prone to change that opinion even though some people considered his spoken word was 'gospel' and hung on his every statement.

Fred returned to the shed and when he came back into the house later I felt deflated, ganged up on and totally at a loss what to say next. He merely added that '*the men*' would help him if he needed it and that was all that mattered to him. He added unkindly that if I didn't like it then I could just bugger off to Blackpool with my mother and let him get on with what was left of the rest of his life in peace. I looked at him and saw a stranger.

However, as the night progressed things relaxed between us a little. I still could not be entirely sure if he wanted me to remain or go, so next morning I reluctantly broached the subject again over breakfast.

'Did you mean that last night when you said you wanted me to leave, Fred?'

'You're a daft bugger at times, no ... who would look after me then? I love you in a funny kind of way, and I need you as well. Look, it's just, well, my friends don't like you, and I feel a bit of a dickhead at times when we fall out about stuff.'

'Then why don't you keep your trap shut about our private life, instead of telling them everything that goes on?' I insisted.

He shook his head in bewilderment and sighed heavily. 'Ahh, I dunno – it's just me isn't it? You know what I'm like... I dunno.'

From this point on, it was a vicious circle. The atmosphere was terrible one day and the next he'd be telling me he loved me!

But I could see others had finally taken my place as a source of emotional support in Fred's life and I felt like an outsider. I said no more about matrimonial matters. The palpable air of disdain and bad atmosphere was by now fully apparent.

It was all beginning to make some kind of sense; pieces of the jigsaw finally seemed to be fitting together. People turned up in the garden and a month later they considered themselves bosom friends, wandering into our house without my permission, entering by the permanently unlocked back door without knocking, day and night, strolling into the living room as and when they wanted. If I locked the back door, they would come to the parlour or kitchen window and bang on that to be let in and Fred would later complain I was keeping him prisoner. They all seemed to be vying for his attention, like who could do the best work, carry out the most needed task, all wanting Fred to endorse their own sense of self-worth.

Too many small-minded, tap-room barristers were telling my husband what he should and shouldn't do about the troublesome relationship with his wife who seemed to be spoiling their fun and complaining about their intrusion. For some reason, call it charisma or whatever, Fred really did have the ability to cast spells over people – especially men of a certain age who strove to emulate him. Every word he said was always accepted as being one hundred per cent accurate and true. Not that he was a liar, far from it – but he could be given to considerable exaggeration in order to spin a good yarn and create a sense of drama. It was just his way, and really deep down he meant no harm. As I remarked earlier, the harm came from people taking what he said as the gospel truth.

Of course there are two sides to every story, and everyone was dazzled by Fred's uniqueness and fabulous skills as an engineer and storyteller. No-one questioned why he had been married three times, unsuccessfully as it turned out. It seemed to be always '*my fault*' and worryingly, the wicked things which I was supposed to have done increasingly became a topic of conversation between Fred and the regular gang of men, as well as casual callers to our home and people he met elsewhere.

I became a catalyst for his growing discontent. It shouldn't have surprised me, because he'd always been inclined to do this sort of thing in the past. This is illustrated by interviews such as featured in one magazine publication called *Pennine Magazine* in 1987: '*Fred went on at some length about the emotional and financial problems he's had to face since his divorce [from Alison] – ending with 'eh, you won't put all that down will yer?*'

It was a great pity that he didn't see any harm in talking about such personal areas of his life with the press or total strangers. The idea that Fred was embroidering our private affairs, and more than likely painting a very black picture of me to those who would have the time and inclination to listen, came as no great shock. But we did have big rows about it, which only added more pressure in the long run.

The black eye heralded a new attitude between us and the chasm widened; it was not spoken about but it was there, as real and as ugly as sin.

We muddled along from that point and I continued to look after him. Some days he felt very poorly but, as always, he still had the strength of two men. But now we were growing more apart and as I watched him fight the terrible illness, working on his engine and dealing with all the hangers-on and the subsequent effects on his mental and physical state, new changes slowly took place which would ultimately affect the rest of my life long after his death.

CHAPTER 14
'MBE ... My Bloody Empire!'

'I hope they hold up, or else I'll be showing me wedding tackle to Her Majesty!'

Fred continued to visit the Christie Hospital as an outpatient; even though the chemotherapy had not worked, he needed palliative care. By now he had a fixed urinary catheter in place and this was obviously depressing in itself. He kept getting reccurring bladder infections and had to go back periodically to the Royal Bolton Hospital for tests and treatment to replace the catheter, so this made him very subdued.

As well as these problems, filming had started with David Hall for what would be Fred's swansong series, *Made in Britain*. The concept of this series was for Fred to travel the country on his renovated Aveling & Porter Compound Convertible Steam Tractor. The steam tractor had originally belonged to Devon County Council, which had purchased it for £200 in 1912. In the mid 1980s, Fred paid £175 to its then owner, Peter Froud. You can see the original state of this engine in the second programme of his early series *The Fred Dibnah Story*, when he took poor Alison to Blackpool and made her ladder a chimney in the rain!

The tractor needed total renovation to make it into the beautiful engine Fred visualised. Being a perfectionist he wouldn't compromise, and it took many long years of sheer hard graft to bring it up to scratch – *and much hassle from three wives*! He made most of the replacement parts with the help of his steam-driven machinery in the back garden. He later designed and had made a hydraulic riveting machine, like the ones used in days gone by, and a massive, steam-powered radial arm-drilling machine was used to make the firebox. The engine was nearly finished towards the end of his life; very little was left of the original tractor, but because he had used all traditional machinery employed in the manufacture of traction engines, Fred boasted it was the only one in England, fully renovated by the power of steam!

The *Made in Britain* series would see Fred and his completed Aveling & Porter tractor visiting people and engineering works that used methods and traditional skills which reflect advances in engineering leading to the development and use of the steam machinery. Fred would explain to the camera how he renovated his own engine, and visit people who had helped him along the way.

It was a tough battle in the latter months. The engine was finally nearly ready for this epic journey and, apart from one or two setbacks and a few leaky rivets, Fred was raring to go. One day he came into the house and said, 'Bloody hell, cock, water's pissin' out o' boiler on that thing. Get me some eggs will you, when you go out next – about a dozen of 'em should do. I'm going to put them in't bugger to see if they stop t'leaks round the rivets. No matter how you caulk it, still some corrosion is needed to make it perfect, but we haven't got time, and all. Oh – and some porridge oats too, that might do the trick – used to use that sort of stuff in the old days to seal up the rivets, like.'

I didn't know if he was going to drive it or bake in it! Especially when a gorgeous smell of warm, toasting oats came wafting in through the open window a few hours later. However, we were in for some odours of a different kind a couple of days later when Fred discovered, much to his frustration, that the oat and egg method had failed to work and the boiler was still leaking. I should have realised something strange was on the horizon when I came in to hear Fred talking on the telephone to someone.

'Aye, mate – 40 gallons would do it, it corrodes the metal. You see once you're involved in it, you've gotta keep goin' until you find a solution an' all...'

Absent-mindedly I began putting things into the refrigerator, as Fred continued: 'Them eggs were a load of crap, mate, but I've got a better idea... It occurs to me that it should give a seal like it did in the old days and so we need about 40 gallons of cow piss.'

That got my total attention. He went on at length, eventually arranging for the curious consignment to be delivered. When he came off the phone he explained that a man from the abattoir promised to bring it here 'for nowt' in a big blue forty-gallon drum. Fred seemed pleased and went outside to tell Alf about his latest triumph.

Cow urine? What next?

However, the delivery never took place. The man rang back and said he could not get it, because of 'health and safety' regulations. Undeterred, Fred started to think along other, similar lines and in true style as an intuitive engineer...

'Here you are, mate, nip round t'back o' shed and piss into that big blue container, will you?' he asked any man who happened to wander into the garden. All the regulars were fully trained and obliged whenever the urge took them. Fred's idea was to harvest all of this human urine and then use it in the boiler! He seemed delighted with the idea, but I was a little concerned, especially since the hospital had told Fred that he should avoid dirty situations where bacteria may be present.

The stinking drum gradually filled up and Fred grew more excited until the day I dreaded finally came round, when he donned a pair of rubber gloves and ventured forth behind the shed with Ian and Alf in tow. The container was gradually hoisted up on the gantry alongside the engine and I watched, repulsed, as some of its contents splashed out over the boiler, over Fred and some of the others watching. 'Whoa, steady on, cock, yer spillin' it!' shouted Fred at one of the men.

The stream of dark, amber liquid continued flowing until the container was empty. Other members of Dad's Army began stoking the engine, and someone came over to turn on the outside cold water tap to top up the boiler with pure United Utilities drinking water. A few hours later, a ripe, pungent, vinegary and biscuity smell drifted in through windows and doors, mixed with the black smoke issuing out of the engine funnel.

I closed all windows, but the acrid smell pervaded the whole house. Nathan was upstairs. 'What the hell is that stink, Mum?' he shouted down.

Fred, features set in grim determination, wandered round the engine tapping and knocking here and there with a metal hammer when the engine was eventually in full steam.

'I think it's worked, Alf! I think we've cracked it.'

That night, because he wanted to work late on the engine, Fred treated himself to fish and chips – his favourite meal – going to the chippy in his fragrant work clothes. I wonder what they thought of this walking bio-hazard as he stood queuing. Only Fred could get away with something like that!

One day, he returned from a routine check-up at the Christie clutching some paperwork. 'It's for some newfangled Joseph Mengel stuff they want to pump into me, and because it's never been tested on humans before they don't know the effects, but so far it's worked on animals, like,' he said to everyone.

Avastin, Valtaxin, Pacis BCG, Valstar and Paclitaxel: these were drugs? They sounded like alien galaxies from another universe. And only tested so far on animals? It sounded horrific. I know someone has to be brave enough to do these experiments, or else no advances are made in the treatment of cancer. But as I glanced outside towards his sheds, looked at the pile of fan mail in front of him, noticed his healthy glow despite all he'd been through, I knew it wasn't for Fred. What if it made him so ill that he couldn't finish the filming schedule he was so eager to complete? What if he became totally bedridden and couldn't go to the Palace to meet the Queen for his MBE? I tried my best to dissuade him, but he said he'd think about it. We gave the 'Joseph Mengel treatment' as Fred called it, in reference to the doctor who experimented on Jews in World War Two. Thankfully, Fred decided to con-centrate on living the remainder of his life doing exactly what he wanted with his beloved steam engine on a tour of Britain.

The last ever chimney drop was on Sunday 9th May 2004 at Park Mill in Royton near Oldham. George Wimpey now owned the site after the recent demolition of the mill, and requested Fred's expert and famous method of felling the chimney. This particular mill had been built in 1913 and ceased its useful life as a spinning company in 1962. The usual team gathered and a friend, David Banks-Fear, Managing Director of Southern Springs & Pressings, came up from Bournemouth to lend a hand and worked hard alongside Eddie Chattwood, Mick Berry, Gordon (or 'Gordie') and several others. Fred oversaw the project with the gang of men preparing to fell the red Accrington brick chimney, all that was left now of King Cotton's temple. In the usual manner the chimney, a local landmark, was undermined with telegraph poles; a fire would be lit to burn these poles propping up the stack so consequently the chimney would fall. David Hall filmed the event. There was a sad, poignant feel to the day as I stood in front of the chimney at 12.34 p.m. and lit the final fire with Fred.

He was more apprehensive than usual, frustrated that the crowd would not disperse from the base of the chimney, and he kept rubbing his side where the tumour was. He was adamant it wasn't going to be his last chimney, however, and took his stance a short distance away as he always did, watching the seconds tick by on his gold pocket watch until the hooter sounded at 12.54 p.m. and the chimney collapsed. Afterwards, he clambered up the pile of bricks and stood posing for press photographs and interviews at the top of the mountain of rubble. Smoke and the smell of burning wood wafted up through crevices of the destroyed chimney as people stood around and coughed, but Fred was used to it and the glee on his face was captured by hundreds of cameras held by the press and the public.

It was a moving moment, and I often wonder what was going through his mind as he surveyed his handiwork, surely realising that this was his last job. We retired to the pub afterwards, and Fred swaggered in full of pride surrounded by his crew of tough men, also proud to be a part of this day. They all set about downing the usual pints of bitter and enjoying the moment.

As always, it was a job done with pride and expertise.

As he became more weary, Fred lost patience with some of the regular crowd. On Saturdays in particular, whenever he was at home, the garden would be full of men. He said that some 'didn't do a lot', just hung around talking to each other, distracting him from whatever job he was doing.

One of them had provided Fred with a pay-as-you-go mobile phone 'so we can speak to you whenever we want, Fred, even if you are away'. He didn't like it; he came into the house clutching the thing and immediately shoved it into a drawer out of sight. It rang a few times, peeling out its shrill call from the darkness of the drawer until finally the battery gave out. He said he didn't want to be at anyone's beck and call.

On a couple of occasions, he complained bitterly about the way some would follow him constantly with a camera – even to the point of capturing him eating or sneezing or reading the paper. He said it seemed to be a competition to see who could get the last picture before he dropped dead. Fred, never previously one for upsetting folk, did not broach the subject, but he was plainly disturbed by it so I took it upon myself to deal with the problem. I mentioned that I would have a word with the men in question, and welcomed the chance to assert myself. So cameras on a Saturday morning were banned and Fred seemed much happier; however, bizarrely, I later discovered that because of my actions in stopping the photographs, he was still moaning to the men about me '*interfering*'!

Fred and David Hall carried on with the filming of *Made in Britain*. The tractor was steamed onto a low-loader owned by Fred's friend Alan Atkinson and hauled to the next location, giving the impression to the viewing public that Fred and Alf were travelling the country on it. There were one or two occasions when he actually did 'road' it to a local venue, but by now Fred was becoming weak and tired all the time, and it would have been too much of an ordeal to travel far on the engine. Fred originally had the splendid idea of living on the road for months on end, travelling to each location under the power of steam, but it just simply was not possible. By now, he had to climb up on the engine by stepladder, assisted by Alf and other helpers, but he would not stop the trip. Jack and Roger were due to come over from the Isle of Man to accompany Fred and Alf on some of the filming dates.

Fred, getting gradually more and more out of touch with reality, even moaned about his pal David Hall. One day, returning home from a shooting schedule, he said that David had 'buggered off for the night with the film crew and left him stranded in the middle of a field with Alf, the engine and green living van, with only two sandwiches to eat all day between them...' He elaborated to the point that there was no doubt in my mind that the incident had occurred. He intimated he was fed-up with filming and annoyed by David who, he said, was not filming the stuff Fred wanted to do; he said he'd had enough.

I rang up to see what the problem was. David, being very fond of Fred, was upset. Nothing like that had occurred, David told me, and he could provide paperwork to prove he had booked a hotel room for Fred and Alf many days before the incident. I knew how two-faced Fred could be at times during his illness, but he'd always spoken highly of his pal. David explained how Fred, on this occasion, had refused point-blank to leave the engine in the middle of a field. Although Alf had offered to remain with it on his own so Fred could go back to the hotel with the filming crew for a shower, hot meal, a few drinks and comfortable night's sleep, he had steadfastly refused to leave. David and the crew had no choice other than to leave without him. Why Fred came back and started to criticise David, telling a different tale, can only be put down to his increasingly shaky grip on reality and the effects of the drugs he was taking. Whenever I raised the issue and tried to explain the situation, he insisted David had abandoned him in the middle of a field and was telling everyone he met about it. However, in happier times, Fred also said on many occasions, 'I'd be 'nowt without yon-mon and the magic lantern from the BBC.'

A few days before we were due to go to London for the MBE ceremony, Fred was feeling extremely unwell and stayed in bed all day, sleeping around the clock. We travelled down to London on Tuesday 6th July. I had to keep stopping the car because the tumour was pressing on him and causing discomfort, compounded by being in a sitting position for many hours. Consequently, it took us the best part of a day to get there.

I had been vigilant at finding a hotel close by the Palace. That night, I nipped round the corner to find a local shop, bought some goodies and we had an impromptu picnic in the room. We enjoyed the evening, watching telly, swigging red wine, eating smoked salmon, cream cheese, bagels, tomatoes, olives, salad, cream buns and fruit. We both deserved an early night, and so lights were out at ten and we both slept soundly.

Next morning Fred was first up, refreshed and ready for his big day. In a good mood, doing his tuneless singing 'de-de-da-de-da-daa-dee-dum...' and plodding around the room with his top hat in hand, trying to figure out a way to make it fit properly on his head. 'Nahhh – bloody thing's too big. Have you seen this – be down over me ears in no time,' he said, puzzling what to do with it.

Dear Sheila Thanks
very much for your letter it
really cheered me up. I remembered you very well the long
blond hair, Mum dad and
little lad, I would like to
say you are very welcome
to come and see me and
my yard anytime you want
also as you can see I am not
very good at letter writing
and spelling it really would
be nice to see you for a chat
and a cup of tea and a
look round the yard
wen heaver you wishe to
come round jest give me a
ring on Bolton 551303
Yours
Fred Dibnah

Shortly after meeting Fred in October 1996, he sent this letter inviting me down to see
his yard again.

The picture I sent to Fred after receiving his letter (see previous picture) and during our budding friendship. Fred was bowled over and said to his friends 'Where do you find a bonny bird these days interested in gas mantles and manhole covers?'

Fred visits my home in Blackpool, and, after fitting a new door, decides to put on a clean shirt – my blouse off the washing line!

Fred and me at a steam rally. I would spend all day with him selling merchandise and posing for pictures just like this.

A typical day on a steam rally. Fred would often have me in stitches with his observational humour and keen sense of fun.

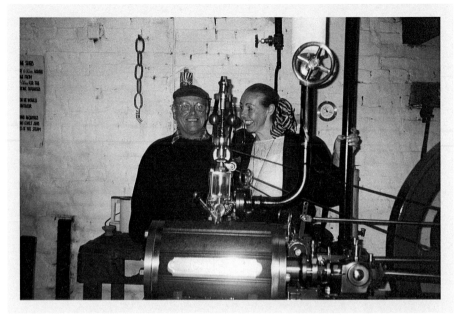

Wetheriggs Pottery in Cumbria with the stationary engine named 'Josephine'. Fred fully restored this engine to working condition before I met him.

My combined 40th Birthday and our engagement party. Fred secretly arranged a beautiful cake and told me how lucky he felt to be getting engaged to me.

One of my favorite pictures taken before we were married. There was a time Fred was very demonstrative in public and often would cuddle me like this.

Taken in September 1997 at Canvey Island, Essex. Fred had been commissioned by Sainsbury's to knock down the 450ft high steel reinforced concrete chimney. This later became known as 'The Great Canvey Island Chimney Disaster' because it fell down a day too early, almost killing Fred and his operatives.

A proud dad and his two beloved sons, Jack and Roger, at The Museum of Science & Industry, Manchester. We had gone there on a family day out.

© *Sheila Dibnah Collection*

© *Sheila Dibnah Collection*

A close moment shared between father and son, Fred's eldest son, Jack.

Taken at Doncaster Railfest during our visit with Fred's steam roller 'Betsy'. Roger (left) and Nathan enjoy standing on the footplate of the steam locomotive 'Mallard'.

Fred was fearless, but the stress shows on his face in this picture. He narrowly missed losing his left hand when it got stuck fast under a mechanical hammer in the workshops. He was making a dinger for a church bell. We both blamed the accident on lack of attention due to a man pestering him as he worked. It wasn't long afterwards I began suggesting casual visitors should be restricted whenever Fred had a difficult job to do in the workshops.

Fred loved nothing better than posing for photographs at the side of his Aveling & Porter steam-roller named 'Betsy' after his mother. The engine was originally named 'Alison' after Fred's first wife, but he changed it after they were divorced.

A relaxing moment with his steam roller. Fred restored this engine as a young man, and it is now owned by his two sons Jack and Roger Dibnah.

He then had the idea of using newspaper to make it fit, but was worried in case it started to slip down. 'Keep yer eye on it, cock, and give me a nod or wave if you can see owt happenin' when I get me medal.'

(What was I supposed to do, start gesticulating to the Queen?)

Then the next problem: the hired black formal trousers hadn't got any belt loops for his braces which, unlike normal braces, were something of an engineering feat and which Fred had designed all by himself. They consisted of two lengths of heavy rope tied at the back and crossed over, culminating in four large steel dog-hooks, like the ones you see on dog leads. These clipped on to the loops of his trousers, a bit like old Jed Clampet out of *The Beverly Hillbillies*. Fred had no time for regular braces, saying they always kept pinging off when he was in the middle of doing something unbelievably interesting.

He was fiddling and tussling with this problem for about ten minutes before he finally secured braces and trousers together in an ingenious fashion and again expressed his concern by saying: 'Bloody hell, I hope they hold up, or else I'll be showing me wedding tackle to Her Majesty!'

After breakfast, we met up with Jack and Roger in the reception area of the hotel. They had travelled from the Isle of Man for the event. The boys were excited and we all set off on foot. Although the day was windy, it was warm and bright as we crossed the road and strolled around to the big main gates at the front of the Palace where large crowds were gathered.

We walked across the gravelled perimeter and through an archway, entering the quadrangle where a few cars were parked. Then we followed the red cordoned-off walkway to a set of double doors, turned left and up a gold-leafed Rococo style staircase carpeted in red velvet pile, hung either side by elaborately framed portraits. Fred was ushered through another doorway, and we three were shown into the large ballroom used for state occasions set with heavy crystal chandeliers. Today, chairs intended for the award recipients covered the dance floor in formal rows; a tiered seating arrangement was quickly filling up with family and friends of those nominated to receive an award.

Jack, Roger and I took our places near the door and gazed about the huge, elaborate room. Two large gilt thrones and tables bearing many purple velvet cushions were at one end and, up on a balcony, a band played soothing light classical music. You could taste the splendour of the elegant ballroom. I decided to nip to the toilets, expecting something installed in Queen Victoria's reign, all high flush and flowered porcelain, but was dismayed to find average white fittings like in any hotel. Disappointing!

I returned just in time before the Queen was due to arrive.

Soon, a trumpet fanfare blared out and the Queen slowly entered the room on our right, preceded by men in red and gold livery, all carrying staffs and other formal accoutrements, walking in step to the music. The Queen was togged out in a lime-green outfit, which suited her well, set off by a large, striking diamond brooch on her shoulder. Her hair was immaculately coiffed, as one would expect, and she wore sensible shoes for the occasion.

The knighthoods were first, and the ritual of touching an individual on the shoulder with a sword was interesting. We sat there as these worthy people received recognition for all they had achieved in life. Eventually it was 'Our Fred's' turn. He entered the room in a small group, walking in single file across to the opposite doorway, then down a corridor around the back to enter into the room on the other side, ready to be presented to the Queen.

Fred stood in the doorway, proud, determined and bare-headed, dressed in his tailcoat and white cravat, looking like a latter-day Mr Pickwick. His moment had arrived, the announcement came: 'Dr Frederick Dibnah, for services to television and broadcasting.'

He strode purposefully across to the waiting monarch and, standing in front of her as directed, bowed down in a short acknowledgement. The room politely tittered as he cupped his hand and leaned slightly forward to catch what she was saying to him. You can just imagine it – 'Yer what flower, you'll have to speak up; I'm a bit deaf you know!' They exchanged a few pleasantries and she pinned the MBE medal on his chest. Fred bowed again quickly, and turned right to leave the room to healthy applause.

I asked him later what the Queen had said, and the answer was: 'Do you still climb chimneys, Mr Dibnah?' To which Fred responded, 'No, I'm getting a bit too old for that now, Ma'am.' She said she had seen his programmes occasionally on television.

The ceremony took just over two hours and the Queen left the room, regally walking down the centre of the ballroom between the rows of chairs and through the door on our left. She looked straight at us for a moment or two, and it felt funny making eye-contact with her, as she eyed up my four-foot long hair draped in a plait down one shoulder. Her eyes were very blue, I remember that, and her skin looked healthy and glowing.

Afterwards, we met up with Fred again and went out into the windy quadrangle for photographs and numerous press interviews. Tim Henman, the Wimbledon tennis star, had received his OBE on the same day, and the press wanted pictures of them together. I felt proud of Fred as I watched all the fuss and could see he was extremely thrilled and happy with the occasion.

Then, photographs and media interviews over, we left the quadrangle and walked back through the elaborate iron gates at the front of the Palace where David Hall was waiting to capture it all on film. We went back to our hotel and got changed. The engine had been brought on a low-loader a day earlier and was stored at the Royal Barracks across from the Palace. Once Fred had made certain the engine was fine it was time to celebrate.

Next morning, I left him in London with David. They were going to steam around London on the engine and, for the sake of a good programme, film the Buckingham Palace trip to make it look as though Fred had 'roaded' it all the way down from Bolton, sleeping in his living van during the journey. Fred had wanted to steam down the Mall but couldn't get permission; nevertheless he enjoyed his day, chugging around London holding up all the smart cars driven by 'men with long coats and briefcases with brass corners', as he put it.

The next auspicious occasion was his second honorary doctorate from the University of Birmingham on the 19th July. I was in the driving seat as usual, with Fred navigating. We got lost and ended up being late: a big roundabout, four lanes of traffic: '*Where next, Fred?* Of *course* we got lost – we always did! The map didn't seem to make any sense to Fred and I couldn't understand it either. Time was moving on and we had to be there in less than half an hour. The Vice-Chancellor and Principal, Professor Michael Sterling, had arranged to meet up with us outside for the brief and accompany us through into the robing room where Fred could get ready. I saw a sign for Edgbaston, where the university was located.

I said, 'There, Fred – a sign, it's the turning on the right through the traffic lights.'

'Eh up, wait a minute, pull over and let's ask this guy, he might be local.'

I drew up alongside an unwashed, shiny-headed youth sporting a white hooded sweatshirt and more jewellery than the Queen, who peered menacingly at the car. The lad immediately recognised Fred and patted his shaved bald head with a tattooed hand in excitement. 'Wow – man, you're that dude off telly with the steam machine! The old man has you on tape...'

'Do you know where the university is, mate?' Fred asked. 'We're lost, and I'm getting a degree given me for back-street mechanicing today, so you can tell your dad and I'll sign a bit of paper for him if you can get us there in time.'

The burly lad opened the back door and jumped in announcing, 'I can take you there if you want.' I stared ahead, gripping the wheel, slightly worried about the outcome of this unexpected encounter, wondering if I'd pushed my handbag under the seat and if we'd arrive with our throats intact. But the lad was so excited at seeing Fred that when we reached our destination, he asked for a picture of them together. I switched off the engine and got out of the car with Fred to oblige. The boy's name turned out to be Mark and he waltzed off into the blue yonder, clutching an elaborate autograph as promised, written on the back of a British Gas envelope.

We approached an aluminium doorway and pushed a red buzzer on the wall, explaining that we were here to meet Professor Sterling. We just arrived at the university in time ... except it was the wrong one! There are two universities in Birmingham! So now we were in big trouble.

I got out the mobile phone and rang through to the administration department and we were given directions to the right place. Fred had to stay on the mobile taking directions whilst I drove the car and, because of his deafness, he couldn't hear properly and kept getting it wrong. We went round the same roundabout five times, encountered road rage from a taxi driver, took a U-turn up a one-way street, nearly killing an elderly pedestrian in the process, but finally we arrived at the right university about three-quarters of an hour late!

We were met by a ruffled and slightly relieved group of academics who quickly accompanied us to the robing room and Professor Sterling. The ceremony went well, and Fred brought down the house with a speech that lasted about fifteen minutes.

As I saw him in his robes, clutching his diploma, amidst all those gifted young people and professors, it occurred to me that this indeed was a rare talent to be able to cross into other walks of life and not only be accepted, but also be respected for being 'his own man'. He never made excuses about his lack of education and, where others might feel nervous in the presence of highly educated and well-spoken individuals, he held the table enraptured throughout the meal. He committed a few faux-pas along the way but possessed the ability to laugh at himself. He could get away with such things as talking about his constipation troubles whilst we were on the soup course, and about how he had a fixed catheter so he didn't have to 'crenulate' any longer! I think he was so comfortable because deep down, although these were highly intelligent and accomplished people, he knew with absolute certainty that very few would ever be able to achieve anything like the skills, recognition and knowledge he'd acquired through sheer hard graft all his life.

CHAPTER 15
Love and hate

'When's that bloody Irma Stromberg coming again, then eh, cock
— frightens me to bloody death, she does!'

I loved Fred. No matter what anyone else thought, I truly loved him — but knew he was going to die soon. He had been good to me in so many ways; I knew by nature he was open and honest, never being furtive or secretive about things before he became ill. I knew he would never knowingly hurt anyone.

He had loved me once, of that I was certain.

I was flabbergasted to be cut of out his Will.

Time was running out. We could all see the deterioration of his body. I wondered just how long he could endure the gruelling levels of work he was subjecting himself to, working most days almost until he dropped.

The filming dates wore on endlessly, but public appearances and theatre work now had to stop. By late August Fred was feeling extremely poorly; some days were good, but most were bloody awful. I could do nothing right by now, and he fired off at the least little thing.

I was becoming depressed, increasingly dreading the prospects of what would become of the garden workshops and my life without Fred. I felt like I was on a sinking ship and wouldn't know what to do with his collection of steam artefacts. What, for instance, would happen if I couldn't get planning permission to turn the house into a heritage centre?

As usual he turned to his friends for comfort. They supported him relentlessly. Nathan and I nursed Fred single-handedly throughout his illness with no help from anyone, apart at the very end when everyone with a vested interest gathered around his deathbed.

By the end of August, Fred was on very strong painkillers and the doctors gave him something called Tramadol, which knocked him for six. He was spending longer and longer in bed. The Tramadol made him act bizarrely; it was like being with some mentally deficient stranger I didn't recognise. It changed his personality. He criticised and chided me cruelly each day saying things like, 'What have you done in your life, eh? BLOODY NOTHING!' Each episode would end with me in tears.

The morphine was also making him confused and disorientated. He often ranted at me during conversations with other people when I entered the room. He began to accuse me of 'slowly poisoning him with arsenic' and at times threw food at me, stating I was trying to kill him. It was my fault, he maintained, that Jack had originally left home, failing to see that it was due to the demise of his second marriage when his wife had left for someone else. He said I was using the occult to harm him, saying this frequently just to gauge my reaction. At other times he seemed genuinely frightened of me, afraid I would burn the house down around him or stab him in his sleep.

It was like living in hell with a complete stranger.

One hot sunny day, I came home after spending a few hours with my mum to find Nathan wearing only shorts and plastered in perspiration. The house was sweltering hot. He said Fred had put the heating up and been ranting that I was responsible for the house being damp. Nathan turned it off at one point, but Fred kept insisting he was 'in cahoots' with me to destroy the place, and turned the thermostat up again. On my return, there was a bizarre row where Fred cited me as an 'evil candle-worshipper', trying to bring forth demons into the house.

Fred was now bedridden on some days, even more confused and irritable. The flow of visitors to our home increased and they would stay until all hours. Despite everything, I wanted to be alone with Fred to recharge my batteries and think about the implications of what was happening. But it was as if I had ceased to be important. These visitors – they simply barged in, took over and gradually pushed me out.

All with Fred's blessing.

Frequently, he would sit up in bed steadily drinking alcohol brought by visitors. They seemed to disregard my need to spend time alone with Fred during the day whilst he was relatively animated and able to speak clearly before he became tired in the evening. As they had done whilst he was still mobile, they ignored my wants and needs.

You could feel the hostility on all sides.

I had no objection to visitors in general but I seemed to have lost the rights of a wife to say who, or when they were welcome in the home, and those rights never returned. Maybe I never had any? On reflection, I had seen it early in his illness when one 'close' friend of his rang our home while Fred was recovering from surgery after the removal of a kidney. The man told me he would visit Fred in hospital that evening. I politely asked him not to and to go the day after, since Fred would be just out of surgery and still drowsy from the anaesthetic. The abrupt response was, 'Listen, love, I've known Fred for over twenty years, and we are close.' When I went in to see my husband that evening, the man was sitting there at the side of the bed, taking up the only chair as he leaned in and made his presence known to Fred. I stood there amazed at his audacity and wondered why it was that, unlike other wives, I seemed to have no respect from this type of person. The answer? Fred belonged to his friends – his current wife wasn't important as far as they were concerned.

Early in September I had to ring the GP because Fred was refusing to drink anything I brought to him in bed, still stating that I was poisoning him. I was concerned about the effects of not drinking liquid on his remaining kidney. He was walking around the house, saying that I was trying to 'knock it down'. He was seeing people that were not there in rooms, and telling me off for doing things I knew his ex-wives had done while they were together. He wanted to know why I had taken his sons away and accused me of being unfaithful with other men whenever I went off to see and look after my mother.

Not recognising me one day, he asked about my long hair, saying, 'I thought you were a bloody hairdresser, cock – why's it long like that, eh – who are you, then – do I know you or what?'

His pal, Mick Berry, was present on one occasion and he too was anxious about Fred's state of mind. We sat beside his bed, observing Fred gibbering about nothing in particular not even noticing we were there. I liked Mick; he had known Fred long before he married Alison, working on felling chimneys with him. Fred once called him 'a tough man who you'd trust your life to'. Mick was visibly upset. I called the doctor to come over and have a look at Fred; he was getting very weak as he lay gasping in bed after his rant. By the time the doctor arrived, he was sitting up in bed, slightly more lucid, and wanted to get up to show the doctor around the yard!

Concerned, I rang the hospice later that evening to seek further advice because I was still worried about him. I spoke to one of the nurses there and, since Fred had a scheduled appointment there next morning, she asked if I could bring him in the car and they'd have a good look at him then.

We could all see the deterioration of this great man by now. It was just a question of time.

Next day, he was admitted to the hospice for the first time. He was dehydrated and was calling me names to the staff, telling them of the discord and growing chasm between us. I broke down in front of the staff, saying I was finding it increasingly difficult to cope at home.

One of 'his men', pretending to have my best interests at heart, asked me for a key to the top gate of the driveway 'so he could keep an eye on things in the garden whilst I was at the hospice with Fred'. But I changed the padlock instead and gave a key to Alf and Ian Thompson. Instinct was guiding me now and I felt uneasy, wary, that something was badly wrong; I did not know what exactly the problem was but felt no longer in control of my situation. I changed the burglar alarm combination, as I wasn't too sure who had a key to the house, and later changed the locks too. I thought people had been in the house during my absence; I knew someone had rifled through my office, and papers were removed that related to my property in Blackpool but I could not prove it.

On the 9th September, Fred was taken from Bolton Hospice to the Royal Bolton Hospital for further tests on his kidney function.

I went to see him that evening in hospital and for the next four days and nights whilst he was there, the bed was constantly surrounded by the usual visitors, Dad's Army and more besides, all coming in to see him, as they had done whilst he was at home. They all disregarded the fact I might want to spend time alone – no-one ever thought to ring and ask, 'Is it OK if we pop in to see Fred?'

On the 13th September Fred was transferred back to the hospice – and so was the legion of ever-present visitors. He developed a fixation for canned mandarin oranges, asking everyone who would visit to fetch some in. With his illness came the need to hike up the morphine levels but this did not prevent him drinking the large amounts of alcohol brought in by visitors. After he died, the hospice handed me a large, sturdy bag containing more than forty cans of Guinness and four bottles of wine.

On the 23rd September, I picked Fred up from the hospice and brought him home. Visitors started to arrive almost immediately, with two men waiting at the gate seeming to know exactly when we would be arriving home, and visits continued well into the evening. I felt exhausted, bitter and angry.

By now, one man in particular was constantly in and out of our lives. He called to see Fred as much as he could and made a special point of trying to befriend me, frequently calling my mobile to see how things were and if I was OK. I was very wary, but he seemed to be the only one who was anything like friendly towards me. The others gave off an air of hostility, stopping speaking whenever I walked into Fred's bedroom.

This man, whom I later considered one of the main ringleaders, seemed far too keen to establish himself as my pal. He was calling me up on my mobile three times a day or more at home, tracking me, asking questions like: 'Where are you today, Sheila – are you going to the hospital? What time are you visiting Fred tonight?' I assumed he was worried about me because I had to see to my mum as well, after the death of my father, and was compassionate about the terrible atmosphere at home that I was enduring.

It appeared he was in charge of the usual group of men, telling me who to trust and who not to trust and I gradually began to feel he was in charge of me too. But I was just too weary to object and my head swam as he told me who had said what about me, and who to be wary of. I was surprised at some of his observations and didn't know what to think or who was supportive of me by now. The trap was closing and I felt I was losing my mind.

'Don't rush back, Sheila, Fred is in good hands – you have a break...'

He encouraged me to see my mother and said he'd sit with Fred for a while. I certainly needed a friend; the atmosphere was strained everywhere I turned so I allowed myself to be guided by him. I felt at breaking point with my mother too, and trying to mourn my father became impossible. That in itself was all a great strain. My mother lived a twenty-minute drive away and had almost suffered a nervous breakdown after my dad's death in October 2001. As an only child, and not coming from a close-knit family, I was all she had and I needed to be there for her.

I wasn't sleeping or eating. Life had turned into a nightmare; I dreaded getting up in the morning. I could feel enmity all around and I didn't know why, so I spoke readily to this man, unguardedly revealing my innermost thoughts. I felt helpless and I needed someone who seemed to be rooting for me amongst Fred's friends.

He offered a touchy-feely kindness, which made me cry as he regularly gave me big hugs and told me not to worry; he would always be my friend and be there for me. He said I was welcome to see him anytime I wanted for a friendly ear. I clung onto him and his friendship, not realising that like the rest of the Steam Mafia - who now replaced the 'Dad's Army'- he was wielding the knife, ready to thrust it into my back at every opportunity. How could I know he had been urging Fred to change the locks and throw my stuff out into the street so that I would be forced to go back to Blackpool? How could I know he was encouraging Fred to divorce me a short while previously? How could I know he – along with others – had been encouraging Fred to cut me out of his Will? How could I know he was spokesman for the band of people trying to see me left without a penny from my husband?

At his suggestion I made a new rule with visitors that we would only accept them during the hours of 12.30 p.m. to 5.00 p.m., as I felt Fred needed more rest. Despite how cantankerous he was becoming, I ached to spend time alone with him. Also, I requested that from now on visitors get their own refreshments, as I was worn out seeing to all the endless cups of tea and coffee, running up and down stairs throughout the day, as well as nursing Fred.

The rule about visitors took no effect whatsoever.

Fred said belligerently that it was like being in a prison.

There were often fifteen to twenty visitors a day and an average of four around the bed at any given time. Lorna, Fred's middle daughter, started to visit more often. I noticed how much Fred was warming to her after many years of indifference towards his three daughters. I genuinely liked Lorna, indeed felt sorry for her – she needed to make her peace with her dad. They had only seen each other once or twice a year and Fred had never made any effort to contact the girls. I couldn't understand why he never bothered with his three daughters; they all seemed really nice girls. It was all a bit of a mystery, one Fred would not talk about, but at least they were around him now as he was dying and that must have been a comfort.

Their mother, Fred's first wife, Alison kept her dignity throughout my marriage to Fred and stayed away, getting on with her own life instead. I have always respected her for that and, having spoken to her a number of times, she appeared to be a gracious lady. When I invited her to make her peace with Fred as he lay poorly in bed, Alison declined; such was her self-respect and closure on that part of her life.

By now, I had started to go out regularly in the afternoons to get away from the dreadful atmosphere at home. Fred just called me 'the witch' and grinned manically with glittering eyes, shaking his head from side to side, whenever I entered the bedroom where he lay. I went to a place on the outskirts of Bolton where, as a kid, my parents would often take me to let off fireworks. It brought a sort of inner peace, speaking into the cold wind which whipped my hair around my cheeks.

I'd got into some kind of daily routine: making breakfast for Fred, changing his sheets and helping him take his medication, and if no visitors called, trying to read to him for a bit if he'd allow me to. When the afternoons came round each day, visitors poured in. One of them even had some spare keys cut to hand out, and people would go in and out of the house as they wished via the front door.

When Fred drew up a Will in the late 1980s during his second marriage, he omitted the three girls, leaving everything lock, stock and barrel to his second wife Sue and his boys. During my marriage, when he'd made another

Will at the advice of his financial advisor Richard Peppall, Fred again omitted the three girls.

When I queried his actions, he simply said: 'They buggered off and ran away, and never come back to see me or help me – so sod 'em!'

Everything was black or white to Fred. He took no prisoners, despite the fact his three daughters had grown up into women to be very proud of with good jobs and successful marriages.

I was exhausted, at my wits' end by now with all the visitors. Fred would rant, rave and still insist that I was 'poisoning him', saying how friends had warned him about not marrying me in the first place. I found it difficult to get any sense, because now he would hardly let me attend to his needs, insisting I was 'trying to kill him'. I could do nothing right.

I went back to the hospice, broke down in tears, and spoke to a member of staff. I cried hard – all the pent-up emotion came out. I said I couldn't manage to look after Fred at home much longer, because he was acting so abusively towards me. I told them how unhappy I was at home and that I simply couldn't cope with the influx of visitors each day. I felt at breaking point with everything, including my mother's dependence as she expected me to do errands and run her life for her as well. To add further to the problems, the completion of a large, almost derelict house I was buying in Blackpool came through. It had taken almost a year to complete on the purchase. The idea was to eventually bring my mother to live with me in Blackpool when Radcliffe Road was a heritage centre or, if the housing market was still strong, to sell it at a good profit. Fred, before he became extremely poorly, had wanted to ensure my future was secure, and we had decided on this particular property as an investment. He had given me some funds towards it, insisting: 'You'll get it all anyway, cock,' (meaning the money).

I returned home wearily around 4.00 p.m. to find more visitors clustered around Fred's bedside. They ignored me and left around 6.30 p.m. Then a fresh lot came around 8.00 p.m. and stayed until 10.30 p.m.

Everyone wanted to take a look at Fred like a peep show; when I took his lunch in, some even had cameras to take photographs of him. He told me to 'sod off' when more people arrived in the evenings, so I watched television alone in the parlour while upstairs people knocked on the front door to be let in or used a spare key until about 11.00 p.m.

At the end of September, one of the social workers came to see us at home to discuss Fred's care plan, and told me she was aware that there were marital problems. I asked her where that had come from, and she said Fred had told her that I hated him and wanted him dead.

I was shocked.

It is true to say, life had not been particularly happy since we learned that Fred's second session of chemotherapy hadn't worked. Now he was dying – but this? Yet on rare days he was relatively fine. Sometimes I could see the cloud had lifted as soon as I walked into the bedroom. His dry sense of humour would return and so would his wonderfully accurate perception of people. He nicknamed the social worker who came to see him 'Irma Stromberg' saying she was 'too bossy' and he would joke: 'When's that bloody Irma Stromberg coming again, then eh, cock – frightens me to bloody death, she does!'

I looked at this frail, bedridden man and still, at times, could see his inner strength and the steely determination behind the character. He bore the dreadful pain he was in with great dignity, still trying to do things himself, such as getting up and having a shower. He didn't like to be a burden, and wanted to be up and about again, but by now he was fully bedridden. It wasn't like Fred to complain, and so he astounded us all with his bravery and sheer courage. A tough, proud fighter, still in his flat cap, the engine driver's blue twill jacket now replaced by a pair of cotton pyjamas in a similar shade, he was determined to see it through with tenacity to the end.

On the 8th October, Fred had to be rushed into hospital. He'd suffered renal failure. Around 7.00 p.m., one of the staff nurses took me into a private room and explained that he was by now a very poorly man and had insisted he didn't want to be resuscitated in the event of an emergency.

She said that as next of kin I needed to be informed of his decision. I started to cry uncontrollably. In that clinical room, I heard what I'd been dreading for some time: the end was almost here. I went back to sit quietly at his side whilst he slept fitfully, holding his work-worn hand, looking at the syringe-driver pumping a high dosage of morphine into his body, catheter bag and tubes, wondering with dread when it would be and how I'd cope with the terrible news.

Within five short minutes, my thoughts and peace were shattered by the unexpected arrival of Dad's Army turning up for the evening visit, but I sent them away, angry at the intrusion, needing this special time alone with my very sick man.

Next day, I went back up to the hospital during the afternoon visiting time but there were far too many people there and so, frustrated again, I left after about fifteen minutes. I didn't bother going at night, because I had received so many calls during the day from casual acquaintances asking how Fred was, adding they would 'go in later'. I knew there was simply no point.

That same night, I received a mysterious call around 10.45 p.m. and it sounded like an elderly man's voice. It was particularly nasty; the caller told me that Fred hated me and wanted me out of the house. I listened to this tirade quietly for about three minutes, and then simply said, 'Have you finished?' I put down the telephone, not wanting to give the caller the satisfaction of knowing they had really upset me. Despite being shocked and feeling desperately sorry for myself, I thought carefully about what had just happened. It was obviously someone in Fred's circle, because he knew too much about our home situation, and some of the comments had referred to Blackpool and my property there.

I immediately reported the incident to the police and the man was warned off. The silly fool had omitted to block his number!

CHAPTER 16
Alone...
'Thanks for looking after me'

F red was moved from hospital back to the hospice on the 12th October 2004. I would visit; he would look away, a flickering look of hatred on his face. Three days later, he changed his Will to disinherit me.

One of the reasons cited was because I had bought a brand new BMW with his money! Back in April 2003, we had decided to renew our car. Fred said it could be my car, because he loved his battered old Land Rover. So I chose a sporty silver Peugeot 206 diesel turbo model. It was zippy and eco-nomical on fuel, with comfortable leather seats.

But Fred hated it on sight, saying it was like a tin can, a product of the modern world. Despite only having had the car a month, he wanted to sell it and get something different. Asked what he thought we should buy, he said, 'I dunno, why don't we get something big and comfortable. We can afford it – go and have a look at the posh garage at the bottom of Halliwell Road, but I'm not riding around in that silver thing any more.'

The 'posh garage' was the Mercedes dealership. Fred liked the engineering reputation of Mercedes but later, over tea, I said it might be less showy to see vehicles at the BMW dealership.

However, I soon became aware he was receiving an awful lot of flack from his pals for driving a prestige car even though it was a relatively modest second-hand one. He started to tell people, 'It's the wife's car, 'nowt to do with me that, I'm only interested in steam engines!'

This resentment amongst certain individuals was just another illustration that I was 'changing' him, and astonishingly, I overheard him on several occasions saying to people that I'd made him go out and buy a big, swanky motor vehicle.

The cloth cap image did not sit comfortably with the shiny car in the driveway, so it became easier and far less embarrassing to say I had bought it. I don't think there was any malice at all on Fred's part – he was just not comfortable with any show of success or money.

As he became poorly, I didn't realise he was telling people I had forced him into buying the car, because by now that is what he believed.

On my return from the hospice, I came across an opened letter from the same solicitor consulted previously about 'matrimonial matters'. The letter was addressed to one of the Steam Mafia.

This letter concerned Fred's Will. From reading it, I could see that he had made arrangements in December 2003 to draw up a new one. I found a draft copy of the new Will. Again, the letter was addressed to the same member of the Steam Mafia. This letter was a request for Fred to make an appointment to visit the solicitor's office in order to make it legal. I searched around and found further letters hidden in his workshop.

Reminders had been sent on 26th July, 31st August and 4th October 2004. But remember, Fred didn't disinherit me until 15th October 2004, shortly before he died on the 6th November.

Hospice medical notes from two days before, on the 13th October, state: *'Bright and cheery although gets muddled'*; *'Gets a little muddled'* and *'Requested to speak to solicitor tomorrow'*.

The day before he signed the new will, 14th October: *'Got out of bed overnight and nephrostromy bag became detached...'* Later that same day: *'Muddled at times'*; *'Seen by solicitor this morning'*; *'Pain in abdomen'*; *'Remains quite muddled'* and *'Difficulties continue in relationship with wife'*.

There was no doctor present at the time of signing the Will but because of the ambiguity of the medical notes, suggesting that Fred 'knew what he wanted' that day, I would have a very hard time taking on the medical profession and *proving* Fred was not in his right mind at the time, which I would have needed to do beyond all reasonable doubt. However:

Day of signing new Will: 15th Oct: *'appears to be in more pain'* and 'also anxious re Solicitor visiting today - wife visited early am.'

18th October: *'Fred was very confused about what he wanted, and couldn't seem to make up his mind'*; *'Feels out of control of his situation'*, and *'Seems frightened'*. (I bet he did!)

I recalled the prescription drugs, increasingly heavy drinking, then the rows and afterwards, always: 'I'm so sorry, cock – you know I didn't mean it, I'm just frightened to death and all with what's happenin' here like... I don't want to die yet, I've got too much to do out there ... you know I'd be lost without you, I'm f***ing hopeless on my own. You know what a pillock I can be at times!'

The Steam Mafia and other family members started to make plans for the funeral. I offered no resistance and my home began to feel like unfamiliar territory as they came down and took over the yard.

Fred: poorly by now, awful to see.

My uncle on my father's side had died of cancer when I was a child, but they had kept me away from him during his final months. Now I knew why. It wasn't Fred lying in the bed, but something like a wax effigy and, as he lost the power of reason, he faded into another dimension, surfacing only now and then to look around and hold on with grim determination to what was left of his sad existence. Now I could see the terrible effects, worse than any horror film, the cancer pushing through his abdominal wall with diabolical determination, making his leg swollen and his breathing shallow and laboured.

I prayed for the end. No one deserved to suffer like this.

I had one last, memorable evening. I visited the hospice at 7.00 p.m. one evening shortly before he died. (He would have signed the new Will by then.)

I was alone with my husband. He could barely speak and stared unblinkingly out into space towards the wall-mounted television. *Coronation Street* was due to start; we would watch this together at home without fail. He mumbled something incoherent like, 'Guinness... Guinness...' I saw the distinctive black can on the bedside table, poured some into a yellow plastic feeding cup perched at the side, and held it gently to his lips. No resistance now as he sipped his favourite tipple from me. Slowly and deliberately, he took the liquid and then finally pushed it away with a trembling hand.

I pulled my chair closer to the bed and, as the programme started, Fred stared at the television, unblinking, unseeing, weakly grasping my hand as we settled down together for our final time alone in that small claustrophobic room.

I reached up to the monkey-handle dangling above the bed and grabbed his cap hanging from the apparatus, placing it upon his head. His features looked gaunt and thin, his skin waxy and unreal, but with his cap on – he was still my Fred. I laid my head gently upon his shoulder and he tightened his grip best as he could on my hand. He said something. I couldn't quite catch what, but he said it again, straining, trying to turn toward me. I leaned forward and I heard it.

'Thanks for looking after me, cock, thanks for looking after me,' he whispered, and a fleeting smile flickered across his face.

It took a great deal of effort. The last words he ever said to me: 'Thanks for looking after me.' A tear appeared at the corner of my eye but I did not want him to see, so I blinked it away and replied, 'Come here, you daft big Hippo. It's taken all this bloody nonsense to get a quiet moment alone with you, you awkward bugger!'

He smiled again slightly, his eyes unfocused, and held my hand in his as we gazed at the television together until he fell asleep ten minutes later. His grip slackened and he slipped off to dream, no doubt of times when he was a tough young man out with his steam engine, or knocking down some factory chimney.

I removed the cap, kissed his pale, vulnerable head and left him sleeping peacefully alone.

All the love was still there between us at the end but it was buried under fear.

November 5th: Bonfire Night. Nathan was having trouble coming to terms with everything and, in denial, decided to light a bonfire at our home, with fireworks in the usual tradition. Fred had always made the most of that particular night and we always had a roaring fire, black peas, baked spuds and treacle toffee with the family. Then, late at night, Fred and I would some-times sneak out for a walk round the neighbourhood. We'd smell the familiar odour of burning wood and call for a drink or two at a local pub, before walking back home seeing who could find a burned-out sky rocket on the road first, dashing off like a couple of kids to retrieve it and take it home. Bonfire Night was always special to us. November 2004, however, was to be entirely different.

I'd invited my mum and Nathan went through the motions of lighting fireworks, but as the phosphorescent flares periodically lit up the sky and crackling orange flames from the bonfire illuminated our faces and cast glow-ing shadows over the quaint back garden landscape, our icy hearts failed to melt.

At around 8.00 p.m., I got a call from the hospice, telling me that Fred was deteriorating and we should come in. We arrived about twenty min-utes later. Lorna, Jayne and Caroline were already there and Graham, Fred's brother, arrived. We sat beside the bed for a long time, leaving the room once while the doctor examined Fred. He was not aware of us. A nurse came out and said he was now more stable and we could return to his room.

We all left around 10.30 p.m., as Fred was sleeping peacefully by then.

Next day, I could not get my head around anything and, similar to a lightbulb that burns brightly before it pops, I ran around manically doing everything and anything to prevent me from thinking too deeply. I remember feeling very afraid, somehow angry at Fred for leaving me all alone. I'd been up since 5.30 a.m. and rang the hospice at 7.30 a.m. He was still stable and sleeping peacefully, they said, the danger was over and could I come in later?

Fingers tapping, head spinning, the room seemed too quiet and I paced the floor relentlessly. I wanted to do something to keep busy. I thought I should drive over to see my mum, then stop off around lunchtime at the hospice, and spend the rest of the afternoon with Fred.

That is what I did.

Nothing was going to be right for a long time again after that day.

I had recently had a slow puncture and was keeping the tyre pumped up with air before each journey, and now I had completely forgotten about it. I sat in the waiting bay of a local tyre repair depot when a call from the hospice came through asking if I could come in. Fred had taken a turn for the worse. I sat there, contemplating my stupidity in setting off on this ill-fated journey. The tyre fixed, I drove at breakneck speed for the hospice.

I got a call.

Fred had died.

I arrived just minutes too late.

I was now a widow. My Hippo gone, slipped away without me...

Lorna and Jayne had been with him. I was shown into a side room. A member of the staff explained that I could see Fred once the doctor had been in to issue the death certificate. Numbly, I spoke to his daughters; we were all in shock and hugged each other.

Eventually, I was ushered in to Fred's little room, where he lay peacefully on the small bed with his eyes closed for the final time. His features no longer contorted in the grip of fear, he looked as he did a few months back before becoming so poorly. He had lost a lot of weight by now, of course, and one leg looked withered and pitifully thin under the bedclothes but apart from that, yes, he was 'Our Fred' again.

I touched his bald, defenceless head, still nice and warm, his hands still soft to hold. I turned his hand round and round in mine stroking it, kissing it, examining it, pondering about all the hard work it had achieved in its lifetime. The realisation that it would never work again, nor touch a steam engine, made me cry hard. But despite my grief, to be with him like this brought some inner calm and I was glad he was finally at rest and at peace. I had lost my lovely husband ages ago; this was just his earthly shell, a sad portent of more bleak things yet to come.

I had nothing to organise. I felt numb. Lost, empty and numb. The garden filled up each day with the Steam Mafia and the men now clamoured around the garden like some fevered infestation of devoted followers after losing their god, polishing, fettling, fussing, cleaning, making sure both steam engines were fit to be seen in all their glory at the funeral. Plans were made, arrangements discussed between them. I felt like an outsider, no involvement or power over my own husband's funeral except to suggest that his favourite piece of music, 'Don't Cry for Me Argentina', should be played.

Fred had not been fully stable since learning he had cancer years previously and that it was incurable when it returned after the second cycle of chemotherapy. He turned more and more to his group of men, and his mood swings, drinking and depressive episodes became gradually worse. He blamed me for a lot of things, and yet deep down I know through it all he loved me. However, as he lost his grip on reality in the final months of his life and the clarity of his mind gave way to irrational flights of whimsy, Fred's fears focused on his hatred of all three of his wives and how he perceived we had each treated him. He started to accuse me of 'poisoning him' and 'spending all his money'.

In fact *he* had been busy systematically poisoning *me* to the real toxic issues present in his life: those claiming to be close to him during those awful last months of his life who apparently had it in for me out of misguided and blinkered loyalty to Fred.

I had got rid of some of the men in the yard, their associates and people whom I considered were taking advantage of my trusting husband in the early days.

Now it was payback time as far as my enemies were concerned, and the whole episode turned into nothing more than a witch-hunt. If Fred was disloyal and scathing about me then they would follow their leader.

But serious questions still remain unanswered.

Why did the ringleader who had befriended me telephone the solicitors offices on the 14th October to arrange a meeting at the hospice for the following day at 2.00 p.m., then later, still posing as my friend, say he knew nothing at all about what had happened?

When the solicitor came into the hospice to see Fred on the 15th October, this was the third visit for the legal representative; Fred had previously turned them away on two separate occasions refusing point-blank to sign anything.

A reliable source present at that fateful meeting in the hospice says, it was alleged by those present (members of the Steam Mafia and several others) to the visiting solicitors clerk that I had spat in Fred's face while he was ill.

Also...

I had stolen all his money.

I had bought myself a swanky car.

I had said, 'I'll have everything.'

I had abused him.

I had threatened him.

I had marketed him.

Fred wanted me to have nothing.

It seemed Fred was eager to express before the signing of the new Will, just what kind of person I was. He turned searchingly to his friends as the paperwork was held in front of him to sign during this third visit – he'd refused to sign the paperwork on two previous occasions, remember – and asked his friends to tell the solicitor's clerk how awful I was. He also urged the clerk to contact other friends not present to verify the type of person I was. He seemed keen to have their opinion to justify his actions of cutting his wife out of his final Will just days before he died. The clerk firmly pointed out it had to be his wishes and not those of his friends if he wished to disinherit me.

I shall never know why someone did not come forward to tell me what was happening to Fred at the end of his life, although I do not blame his close pal Alf for not doing so. I also feel some of the ones who were beginning to feel guilty about the situation were bullied into 'keeping his trap shut' by the Steam Mafia just the same as I feel strongly that Fred was bullied into changing his Will.

I urged my own solicitor to go ahead with litigation to try and overturn the new Will, because I knew I'd been set up. However, I was told it would be virtually impossible to do so, since I would have to 'prove' beyond all reasonable doubt that, at the moment of signing the new Will, Fred was mentally incapable of making his own decision. As an alternative, I brought a reasonable provision claim against the Estate. I was sick to my stomach when I did this, because by then several independent people (including one who witnessed it first hand) disclosed what had happened on the day Fred signed the new Will and the lead-up to it. I was shown several official letters spanning over a period of months and they had been sent to the ringleader's address. One of the official letters concerned divorce and tellingly pointed out that the decision must be that of Fred's and not his friends...

All those who were part of this close-knit situation gathered around the bed like a dark cloud, the duplicitous ringleader having made certain that I, along with certain other people, wasn't going to be there that particular afternoon by calling earlier to suggest I come in to see Fred in the evening instead after spending an afternoon with my mum.

Fred wearily signed the legal paperwork before him, muttering that he wanted this over and, as usual, grumbled about me to all present. That done, those assembled celebrated by cracking open a bottle of champagne, toasting each other above my husband on his death bed.

So, did he know exactly what he was doing? Was his mind crystal clear, not fogged by the high doses of morphine delivered by syringe-driver – or was he simply manipulated and bullied into it by so called 'friends' and those with their own agenda who gradually wore him down?

Fred died just ten days later on the 6th November after lapsing in and out of consciousness for a number of days. By then he hated me during his increasingly limited wakeful hours, as death gradually released him, finally, from pain and misery.

'*Thanks for looking after me, cock,*' he had said ... those words of love.

Words I came to cherish and shall never forget as long as I live.

Tuesday 16th November 2004. My famous husband was being buried today.

The garden began emptying of people as the two Aveling & Porter engines, Betsy and the new, unnamed tractor, by now in full steam outside on the street with the flat-bed trailer, bedecked in ladders and flowers, looking like something from a street carnival, waited to take Fred's coffin to church when the hearse arrived. Four more steam engines waited to join the cortège, having arrived earlier on low-loaders at Fred's request for the event. The house was full of flowers and people, and thousands more waited outside, forming crowds along the streets on route to Bolton Parish Church, where the service was to be held. More, throughout the country, would watch the procession on television.

The funeral cars arrived, and I stepped out through the front door into the dreary, fine rain just shortly after 11.00 a.m. Someone held up an umbrella for me. Faces turned and looked enquiringly in my direction. A few flashes went off, and I put my head down to avoid people's curiosity.

The funeral director, John Howarth, came across to speak with me. 'Shall we now move over to the car, Sheila?' he enquired. It was like speaking with a concerned friend. The car, a cream-coloured vintage Rolls-Royce, set off behind the flat-bed trailer pulled by Fred's steam tractor. This was driven by his son, Jack, and Michael Webber. Michael had known Fred since he was a little boy, and later became a brilliant friend to me. Behind us, two black limousines carrying other family members and friends took their places. After the limousines, Betsy took pride of place, pulling Fred's green living van and Land Rover. We were accompanied by the Royal Artillery Band of the 103 Regiment from the Bolton Barracks as we slowly made our way through the streets. Faces constantly appeared, resembling moving wallpaper through the misty windows of the car, and we were flanked either side of us by people accompanying the procession on foot. The windscreen wipers made their own noisy accompaniment.

The tissues, strategically placed in my handbag, remained unused through-out the entire journey. In the car, in private, we discussed Fred, spoke quietly about how well loved he had been and what a tragic shame it was that he died so young, when he had so much to do. My friends supported me, and Mum gave me a heartfelt hug, slightly dislodging my aubergine-coloured formal hat with her concern.

We arrived at the church to a round of respectful applause. Fred had worked on the Bolton Parish Church about thirty years ago, one of his first big jobs when a welder friend of his father mentioned that Canon Norburn was looking for someone to gild the weathervanes. He had gone round on his old AJS motorbike to have a look and meet with the Canon to discuss it. Fred worked on the church again in 1996, once more gilding the four six-feet-four-inch high weathervanes. Each one weighed more than sixty pounds, and it was a mammoth task.

The church also featured in one of the early programmes. A fearless Fred had captured the viewers' imagination as he stood there, almost in free space, totally at ease on the Bolton skyline. Now, at his funeral, he attracted atten-tion in a far different and more sombre way and the coffin became the centre of the crowd's focus as we disembarked from the car beneath this prominent landmark for Fred's service.

We followed the coffin, carried by pall-bearers in black suits, through the heavy wrought-iron gates into the churchyard. They were led by Mr Howarth, the funeral director, in his sombre black morning suit with top hat and brass-topped cane. The respectful crowd parted, allowing us access into the church accompanied by the melody of 'Don't Cry for Me, Argentina'. Down the centre aisle to the front of the church where Canon Michael Williams waited.

We were seated in the family pews and still my tissue remained dry for I could not cry. It seemed so far removed from my own memory of Fred: the simple soul who hated all manner of fuss and ostentation. Still, it is what he wanted, you see; he had not said it to me, of course, only expressed his wishes to others. Personally, I would have liked a simple, dignified family service in a small, humble church after the grand procession, where we could all cry in private, followed by a large public wake afterwards.

I looked at Fred's oak coffin to the left of me, sitting on its trestles, and I couldn't imagine my husband beneath that lid, dressed as I had said he might like to be in his blue engine driver's jacket, waistcoat, collarless granddad shirt, black trousers and oily flat cap.

It passed in a blur, this very public service. I thought about better times with Fred as I listened, from a distance, to people speaking about the man I loved. Watching his larger-than-life eloquent friend wearing oily overalls, the same one who said he'd got the last photo of Fred in existence, take the podium and speak in glowing terms about our dear, departed Fred, sharing his personal experience of those last days in the hospice with all people present, I felt totally alone...

We finally rose from the pew to follow the coffin back up the aisle. Looking ahead, I clung to Nathan's arm and held my head high. Outside, cameras popped and countless eyes peered at us for any signs of emotion. The coffin was loaded back and secured onto the trailer. Back in the relative privacy of the car, we continued on to Tonge Cemetery.

There was no mistaking where Fred was being buried. Huge crowds had already gathered and steam engines waited; the rain continued and the sky was dull grey as I stepped down from the car. Mr Howarth led me through the throng to the side of the open grave. My first impression: shock. I hadn't been to a burial since I was a teenager and the sight of that cavernous hole with its mound of earth covered by a bright-green tarpaulin resembled a sleeping giant ready to be operated on by a surgeon in a theatre. It was a hospital colour I'd seen far too much of over the past few years; so stark against the natural tones of stone, earth and grass, it was almost menacing.

I walked up to where Canon Williams was standing where the coffin, held by the pall-bearers, waited to be entombed forever.

The Canon started the graveside service...

'*Man who is born of woman has but a few short years to live...*'

Cameras flashed, someone started to load a film and the winding, mechanical noise jarred my ear. A man holding a television camera dodged around the grave for a better view. A few onlookers nudged forward to look into the hole; someone released a shutter close to my face and a windproof microphone periodically invaded the space between me and Canon Williams

'*Ashes to ashes, dust to dust.*'

I took the proffered box, scooping a handful of soil.

Across the grave, as the coffin was being lowered into the ground, a cacophony of steam whistles rent the air, underscoring the finality of the scene. I became vaguely aware of a large news camera on a sturdy tripod, intent on getting every nuance of the graveside service and images of the coffin being laid to rest. I remembered Fred once saying the BBC had turned up with a big camera that resembled a Howitzer and now a similar one caught me on film, throwing soil onto my late husband's coffin. Others present, strangers, took the soil from the box, and I set off through the crowd, finding an ashen-looking Roger close by, looking forlorn and weary. With a bit of gentle persuading, we accompanied him back to the graveside and he threw down a handful onto his father's coffin, his tears scoring rivulets through the oil and soot upon his small face that so resembled a youthful Fred.

I turned, steeled myself and walked into the crowd, away from the grave, away from the cameras, the fuss. I got into the waiting car with my family and close friends, grateful for the tiny windows of the vintage vehicle as the car picked its way through the mayhem. For now it was all over.

I had to face the next battle alone.

A letter came within a few days from the solicitors saying they held my husband's Will at their offices. Now the lengthy legal process began. All Dad's Army had gone apart from Ian Thompson, Jimmy Crookes and Alf Molyneux, who still came down to the yard to tidy up and look after Fred's workshops.

I considered Jimmy, who was one of the very few consistently nice to me during the Dad's Army days, to be exactly like Alf – basically a good, decent bloke with his heart in the right place. He felt sorry for me and explained that I should be strong, and not let it get me down. He reassured me that Fred was not a bad person and had made a mistake because he was ill and fearful.

Most of Fred's other closest friends were supportive. 'John Wayne' – Peter Lidgett who now lived in France – called regularly whenever he was in the UK to see how I was coping. Eddie Chattwood, the amiable steeplejack, and his wife, Margaret, made sure I was OK. Derek Roscoe from Kirkbean, with whom Fred and Alison had nearly stayed in Scotland the night before their wedding, contacted me, and Alan McEwen, the master boilermaker from Yorkshire, offered his unstinting support. An astute businessman with a keen, enquiring mind and long-time devoted friend, Alan thought the world of Fred, respecting his ability to mend and make boilers and sharing a passion for chimneys and steam. Many casual friends came forward too; people who had known Fred for many years and had loved him, offering me their full support.

The first spectacular grief, not in public but in private, happened on a parallel with sheer desperation about my predicament. Full of sorrow, wracked with my terrible loss, I spent each evening sitting in our cosy parlour in the Victorian gatehouse where Fred had lived for the last thirty-five years during his two previous marriages and later with me. It seemed unreal, like watching a horror film unfold, as though Fred, through the very act of death, had sucked out all the life from the room. It was stone dead.

Wandering around in the cold atmosphere, I handled the beautiful, shiny, familiar objects not only in this room but throughout the entire house. These artefacts, so special to Fred, lovingly rescued from skips and dustbins many years ago then restored by him, now felt totally lifeless. So close to him, yet so far apart, I could not feel or smell him, yet they were here, these chattels – and he was not. Heartbroken, I could only speculate what would now become of them – and me for that matter. All I had left of him were these cold, inanimate objects. But they didn't belong to me, his widow, nor did our marital home in which I lived with Nathan. I mooched around this cold, alien territory, my home of seven years, pondering the enormity of what was happening and how the dream had turned out to be a nightmare.

So what went wrong? In March 1999, he'd said during an interview with a national paper when asked what his perfect idea of happiness was, 'Achieving my dream of having a working mine in my back garden, finishing the restoration of my steam tractor, and remaining happily married to Sheila for the rest of my days.' Another newspaper had asked what his favourite fantasy was and, cheekily, he'd replied: 'Black nylons and suspenders on my tall, leggy wife, Sheila.'

More cynically, when asked the month before about his lack of wealth by a local northern newspaper, he'd said: 'All me bloody women have had all me money anyway!'

Three long hard years of mental and physical suffering through an incurable illness, and this was it? The dark spectre of coldly worded legal letters started to arrive amidst the hundreds of sympathy cards. The Estate wanted access to conduct a valuation of the house contents, and had wasted no time in arranging it. My time was spent between crying, feeling helpless and seeing my own solicitor, Tony Percival, who listened to the whole sorry story of the past few months.

By contrast, kind strangers stopped me in the street to offer their condolences: 'So sorry about your loss, he was such a lovely man, Fred, such a pity; you'll have to remember the good times, love.' Oh yes indeed! He *was* a lovely man, passionate about everything – including me, once. It seemed light years ago now.

It's not the passion I remembered most from when Fred was healthy, but the vulnerability and the unexpected sensitivity: a sudden hug after a long day, a kiss, a kind word; the spontaneity: 'Let's go out for tea, cock'. A joke, shared ideas, plans for the future, a laugh together; precious things we'd take for granted within the safety net of marriage. Underneath he was only a human being with all that entails: wants, needs, wishes, faults, fears and pains – but outwardly, to his public, he was this larger-than-life, egotistical, tireless icon, inspiring hearty devotion in everyone he met. It was a lot to live up to. He wore this steely macho image like a shell but beneath the tough veneer lurked a damaged and quite sensitive soul, one who didn't like to show tenderness towards his women in front of his gang of men, because of what had happened during his two previous marriages.

He feared being ridiculed by these 'alpha males' making constant comments that he was going soft in his old age. No woman would ever fully understand or know how to make him want only her, for his heart belonged to steam.

'You love those engines more than me! If we can't go on holiday together, then you can forget it Fred, it's over!' I fumed at him once during a terrible row, an echo no doubt of past exchanges in his marriage to Alison.

'OK, cock, if that's how you see it; but I'm not going on any bloody holiday to some fancy beach sitting with a load of dickheads in sense-of-humour shorts! I've too much to do in me shed. Not seen all of England yet – so there!' he retorted good-naturedly, without missing a beat.

I recall his deeply loving moments. When he fleetingly bared his soul, it was like dealing with a helpless fluttering little bird, one that you wanted to love and keep forever warm, safe in the palm of your hand. But for only so long before the call of the wild eventually beckoned it back into the flock, leaving you with only a memory as he ambled off to accomplish yet another task in the yard.

He was a true, gentle, kind and loving man, but just couldn't help himself because there was a dark side too, brought about by illness. He was a paradox: Fred, on his own was really terrific at times, but when he was faced by the choice of being 'with the gang', talking about or doing manly things, the woman in his life stood no chance at all. You had to realise that even though he loved you, he adored his own company and relished the chance to 'get things done'. Gifted, productive and driven by a necessity to create, Fred would never see recreational time as anything other than something for 'those buggers wi' nowt else better to do'. How else could he have achieved so much in one lifetime, if not by working every given waking moment?

In his way, he loved all his three wives, but simply could not understand the concept of women wanting to occupy that special place of being the most important thing in his life. And sadly, we never were – through no fault of our own. He *needed* us, and that was that. Wore his heart on his sleeve, spoke frequently about his 'three wives' to all who would listen, like we were all part of a harem. It didn't make him any less of a man, merely less of a husband at times.

I once had a conversation with Alison, for whom I have always had the upmost respect and continue to do so to this day, since she is a dignified, gentle lady. I could see she had loved Fred with all her heart but at times had found him a little too bombastic and insensitive with the things he told people about his marriage. He didn't mean to be, it was just his way, a small design fault! He'd say: 'This is the current wife' or 'This is wife number three'.

It's likely, however, that Fred felt vulnerable and couldn't understand the female psyche; thus he would moan and tell 'his men' everything that was happening in his personal life. And because there were these conflicts of interest due to feelings of neglect on my part and opposition to what project he was currently on, the many problems were magnified out of all proportion as he became increasingly ill.

Fred had not been completely stable since learning he had terminal cancer. Only I know how afraid he was, saw him weep in private; I lived with his fear for three years. His erratic mood swings, drinking and dark, depressive states started then. It was an upside-down, see-saw existence. He increasingly lost his grip on reality in the final months of his life, and the clarity of his mind gave way to irrational flights of whimsy due to medication. His fears also focused on his hatred of all three wives, how he perceived we had each treated him badly in our own ways.

This repetitive moaning about his current 'problems at home' to whoever would listen, liberally sprinkled with dramatic exaggeration for effect, is where I consider the evil seed germinated back in 2001. And because of it, certain misguided people were a little too eager to show me the door after Fred died, and complained bitterly about my actions to everyone *they* met – never once considering that from a wife's standpoint, Fred Dibnah as a husband might be almost impossible to live with.

Fred needed the security of marriage, but in general he tended to be self-centred and somewhat uncomfortable because of his lack of confidence with women. He did not really understand us and dealt with the problem by shutting us out emotionally as and when it suited him. But he inspired true love in all his relationships and was at times surprisingly tender; he reciprocated love when the mood took him, so I am left with some very special memories ... they keep me going. Articulate, animated – this larger than life 'man's man' so full of life with energy to burn, the highly skilled and charismatic Fred whom we dearly loved blinded us all: family, friends, fans and foes.

Perhaps one of the most fitting testimonials to what was happening during those final months and the sad, unpleasant outcome, came from Fred's devoted and long-time acquaintance, his 'right-hand man' and friend of twenty years, Ian Thompson. Ian and I always got on very well. He was devastated by Fred's death and during a conversation with me, said some startling things. He said he wanted to be interviewed on film to record what was said, as he wanted people to know what was going on. I arranged with film producer Paul Donoghue of Rallyscene to visit the yard. I knew he was a good, impartial friend of Fred's of many years and he interviewed Ian and provided me with a copy of the resulting interview.

Among other things, on film, according to Ian, Fred had at times cried and broken his heart complaining that life was no longer his own and he was fearful of what would become of him. He felt his life being taken over by illness and was beyond his control. Ian mentions many other terrible things that went on behind my back, which, for legal reasons I cannot go into because that would involve naming and shaming people in print. But it's harrowing to discover what allegedly went on; and if what Ian says is to be believed then those responsible should hang their heads in guilt and shame. To this day I cannot watch that interview without feeling sick. In extracts of the conversation with Ian Thompson, recorded with his full agreement, are some general worrying observations:

(I ask Ian in response to a comment he makes): 'So, Fred would get upset at times then, and was he crying, actually crying you said?'

Ian (replies) – 'Yeah! Yeah, bloody hard thinking about it just now, to see him like that, when we are sat on our own, just talking...'

'So he'd confide in you, tell you things?'

'Yeah, he would. Like, he didn't know what to do. He was like stuck in the middle – these guys are saying "do this/do that, tell her to get out, and never come back" and all that and all the rest of it. I can't say exactly who said that, but I can imagine the whole lot of them saying it even when I've not been here.'

This simple soul, 'Our Fred', a man loved and adored by the nation, recognised by royalty after a lifetime of hard toil, had sat all alone in his precious sheds in Bolton, amidst his treasured artefacts and wept in sorrow at the sheer futility of it all.

CHAPTER 17
Life without Fred
'A Much Loved Steeplejack'

The headstone I chose for Fred's grave was made by a traditional stonemason called Mark Stafford from Nottingham. The Estate legally tried to prevent me from organising this final tribute, stating I had 'no rights' over the plot where Fred's grandparents were buried and where I wished also to be with Fred when my time came. They demanded that I return the deeds to the grave. It seems one of the Steam Mafia had been appointed by the Estate to design Fred's monument, but I just wouldn't give in and carried on liaising with the stonemason. I felt this was the only part of my Fred which I had left. The monument is simple and quietly dignified, bearing the inscription: *'A Much Loved Steeplejack'*. It was placed on Fred's grave on Friday the 4th November 2005 just two days before the first anniversary of his death.

The house and grounds began to fall prey to the effects of time. Without

Dad's Army to put them right, the sheds started to leak, taps dripped, the toilet stopped working properly, the central heating broke down, the damp walls began to make everything mouldy, the garden became overgrown, things went rusty and the burglar alarm stopped working. All this was reported to the Estate, but nothing was done to rectify these problems. I felt I was being 'smoked out', so to speak. I struggled on through lengthy legal wrangles and stayed at the house for as long as I could, but it was truly awful and I felt like an intruder in my home.

Matters were still far from settled with the Estate when the house was broken into and the workshops ransacked. Every cupboard, nook and cranny was searched. Thieves had even gone up into the loft! Treasured items collected over a lifetime were stolen or destroyed. Betsy and the new Aveling Tractor both sustained minor damage.

It had happened whilst I was away collecting a cheque for £2,500 for the Memorial Fund from Lorna Bailey Artware in Stoke-on-Trent. Since Fred's death I had concentrated on raising money to erect a bronze statue of him in Bolton. On the eve of 16th December, coming back from Stoke, I received a chilling telephone call from Alan McEwen. 'I've been past the house in Bolton today, Sheila, and seen stuff in the garden which I consider should not be there.'

Total chaos met me when I opened the door. Copper piping had been roughly removed and brass plaques from both engines stolen. We surveyed the shed floor, scattered with broken and discarded artefacts and office papers taken from the house.

As if this wasn't enough, the thieves returned several days later for a second go, further ransacking the sheds and causing more damage to the engines. I shook my head in dismay, as I noticed that the brass plate from the little stationary engine called Caroline was missing, along with lubricators and its steam valve.

It was becoming impossible to stay in the house; the electricity had to be turned off due to problems with dampness. The cold was bone-numbing and the damp was so severe by now that light switches had started to 'arc' with a blue flame and threatened to burn the place down. I looked around the trashed room, its damp and mouldy walls, fungal growths discolouring the Victorian-style wallpaper. Taking in the broken ornaments, I thought of Fred sitting in this room smiling at me all those Christmases ago, when I examined the calloused hand which he was very proud to show me. I could see him with a pint of Guinness in hand, avidly watching *Last of the Summer Wine*, perched on his green chair (which was now mouldy), sporting his blue dressing gown and oily cap, smelling of coal tar soap and creosote.

The traction engines left Bolton for the very last time on Boxing Day 2006. Fortunately Michael Webber, Fred's long-time mate, was up from

Sussex visiting his parents. A Bolton lad, he'd grown up knowing Fred and his family. When he learned of the burglary, he took matters into his own hands and quickly organised for both traction engines to be moved and stored in nearby Preston.

But none of this awful outcome has made me think any less of my husband. Illness and drugs finally changed Fred. I'm not left with any bitterness towards my husband; nothing can take away the special man I knew as my 'Hippo'.

Friends, if you are lucky, are real, true, loyal and worthwhile friends.

To date I've discovered my husband didn't really have that many real friends. He was, surprisingly, a loner to whom people readily attached themselves.

Fred, it seems, was less discriminate about those he confided in.

Only the genuine people are important to me these days.

They are the ones who have stood by me...

So did I learn anything from this tragic situation?

Would I have done anything differently?

The answerer to both questions is yes. I've learned it pays to be very careful whom you trust; for not everyone has your best interest at heart even if they seem to genuinely care. There may be a hidden agenda. And perhaps if I had my time again, I would be far more assertive and not allow our marriage to become overgrown and strangled by those hidden agendas as I tried to grieve for my father and later watch my husband die. The real tragedy is not being cut out of Fred's Will, but that he possibly died in misery and fear, surrounded with torment unable to be left in peace during his final days. Those responsible should be ashamed of what they did to us as a family with their interference, but above all – ashamed at what they did to Fred.

Paul Donoghue said when he and Colleen, (his wife at the time) were supportive of me during my monumental legal battle with Fred's Estate, *'you took your eye off the ball, Sheila, so why didn't you just throw them out? You were his wife after all...and just who the hell were they anyway?*

It's a good point.

I've written this book because, hopefully, it will help Fred's memory to remain untarnished by what some would consider his bitterness against his wife; it is my absolute firm belief that Fred was manipulated and went to his grave craving peace and quiet at the end of his life, and signed that new Will in a desperate bid to stop all the 'mithering' as he'd call it.

It's been cathartic for me as well – but also serves as a stark warning to others that when a loved one is seriously ill, they may cease to be themselves because of medication and other people's influence, and that can have a devastating effect on those left behind ... so be warned: don't take your eye off the ball whatever you do.

As Fred's legal spouse I was entitled to a provision from the Estate. Acknowledging that fact would have made a great difference and I would not have had to go through years fighting a bitter legal battle; unfortunately, those who were resolute that I should get nothing would never listen to reason. As part of my final terms of settlement, I had legal restraint placed upon me by the court. It's something called a Tomlin Order so I cannot publicly discuss any detail of the settlement from my 'reasonable provision claim' against Fred's Estate. It really doesn't matter – the story is about how the case came about, and not the 'nuts and bolts' of it, so to speak.

But I can say this about the outcome: there are no real winners ... just consequences. Once you start an important legal case it escalates and there is no turning back. You have to carry on; see it through to the bitter end. Not matter what. The costs in terms of fees and emotional upheaval are monumental.

After failing to attract any bids at open auction the previous month with a guide price of £250,000 to £300,000 the house, yard and workshops were sold by the Estate through a sealed bid in October 2009 for £185,000. The site was later turned into The Official Fred Dibnah Heritage Centre by new owners Mr & Mrs Pownsey who placed it back on the market as a going business concern in 2012 for £1.2 million. Fred's steam tractor went to be sold at auction in Cambridgeshire on 24th July 2010 with a guide price of £120,000 to £140,000. It sold for £240,000 to a Mr Michael Oliver, a Cheshire businessman, who kindly allows Fred's sons to display and use it at steam rallies and events alongside Fred's roller 'Betsy' which they now own. Would Fred have changed his final Will just days before he died if he could have foreseen the future with a clear mind devoid of all illness and pressure, the irony of his extended family being split apart and at war as I battled for my legal rights as his widow?

As for the naysayers – even if you've read this far – you'll never know the truth because you didn't live through it. Gossip gives ignorance freedom of speech without any roots in fact. I wouldn't for one second change my years as Fred's wife. The time shared, the fun – sometimes tears – the uniqueness of the man. Those times I now celebrate and choose to remember with pride as any loving widow should.

The rest they say, is history.

These days, to earn a modest living undertaking after-dinner speaking engagements across the country, I clock up more mileage annually than Fred did. Such is his appeal still after almost nine years since he passed away. I'm lucky to have my stage experience to fall back on, which comes in handy with this line of work. I enjoy talking about my life with Fred and some of the amusing antics we got up to, and was voted the Best Speaker of the Year for two consecutive years at the Annual National Conference of Ladies

Luncheon Clubs, at Harrogate. The biggest audience I have addressed so far is for the Dorset Federation Autumn Council meeting at the Lighthouse Theatre, Poole in Dorset where I entertained over 1,500 members of the W.I for just under an hour. Ann Widdecombe was the morning speaker, and as I sat and enjoyed lunch with her and committee members from the W.I, looking forward to this showcase event, I realised Fred would have been proud of me. He knew I was tough and I had finally made it through the hard times. To speak about the good times, relive the funny tales, puts it all into perspective. My talks mean my love and celebration of Fred and the happy moments we shared go on and on, and the bad ones gradually fade away into the background.

In the play *The Demolition Man*, Michelle Collins portrays all the sadness, frustration, fear and disbelief I felt during my bleak time as Fred's third wife but also the love and joy that he brought into my life before he became ill. When we met, Michelle had already read the back story of my memoirs, along with Aelish Michael the playwright, and she was horrified at what I'd been through. The play brought Fred alive again before an audience and I recall once more the loyalty we all feel for Fred.

And of course for the 6.5 million viewers who enjoyed watching my late husband on television at the height of his fame, his true legacy remains alive not only in David Hall's excellent BBC 2 programmes but perhaps best in his own flesh and blood. Fred's two sons, Jack and Roger, both dedicated 'steam men' in their own right, show their dad's traction engines each year on steam rallies throughout the UK together with their three half-sisters, Lorna, Jayne and Caroline who own and display Fred's Land Rover alongside them. People flock from all over the world to see *'The Fred Dibnah Collection'*.

As for my own son Nathan ... the pain has been far too great, and he's chosen to close that chapter in his life on a man who he once treated like a father.

My biggest thrill is being able to walk past the bronze statue of Fred located in the town centre of Bolton. The statue was unveiled on the 29th April 2008 which, had he survived, would have been his 70th birthday. On the square plinth of the 8ft statue one of the four plaques reads:

Fred Dibnah was a Bolton lad and proud of it.
He spent his life working on many of the town's landmarks and
shared his love of steam engines with millions of television viewers.
After his death in November 2004, it was decided to launch a fund
to pay for a lasting tribute to recognise his achievements.
Thousands of people, locally and nationally, made donations.
Thank you to all those individuals, organisations, companies
and steam enthusiasts who helped pay for this statue to
"OUR FRED".
It has been an honour to be associated with this appeal and
the committee is rewarded by its success.

The Bolton News
Mrs Sheila Dibnah, widow of Fred and fund-raiser
Miss Wendy Close: Fund raiser with her cap badge sales
William R. Greenhalgh: Friend, fund-raiser and memorial designer
Brian H. Tetlow: Chairman, Bolton Civic Trust &
Chairman of the Appeal

As I stand gazing at it someone will frequently say something like: '*Fred Dibnah, there'll never be another like him you know.*'

I agree and feel happy sharing the moment. I can look back and remember the good times as I stand on my native soil. I have finally come home.

Back to Fred, back to my roots, back where I belong.

One of the treasured moments I often reflect upon is a time in Wales shortly before illness and bitterness blighted our lives. A date had been arranged for his show *An Evening with Fred Dibnah* at Cardiff New Theatre and we'd travelled down the day before, having been booked into the prestigious five-star St David's Hotel & Spa in Cardiff Bay. Arriving at the white, modern, steel structure akin to something off the Blackpool Pleasure Beach, we parked the car to find a reception fit for a king awaiting us. The management offered us champagne on ice and the hospitality you would expect reserved for Hollywood royalty. I expected Fred to start moaning about the plush, modern and sophisticated hotel, but he didn't. Our smart, air-conditioned room overlooked Cardiff Bay, and we ordered a bottle of wine and smoked salmon sandwiches, enjoying a snooze together afterwards, locked in each other's arms for a couple of hours.

I left Fred watching telly and went to enjoy the spa facility, returning to the room in the early evening to find him dressed and ready to go out.

'Do you fancy a walk roun't bay, like, cock?' he asked. 'We can have our dinner out, might be a bit pricey in this bloody joint, like – and I don't reckon there'll be any fish and chips around this neck of the woods. But we can have one of them Chinese things if you like, with green peppers, or summat, eh?'

I walked over to him, and slipped my arms around his waist.

'Mmmmm ... sounds good, Hippo – come here, give us a big kiss!'

'Bugger off you daft sod ... yer after me body again,' he chuckled, and gently pushed me away. 'Wait 'til later, else I'll be knackered up again an' all.'

We strolled around the bay, arm in arm, taking in the warm, early evening sun and all the cosmopolitan eateries at our disposal. We eventually came across a bijou Italian place near a museum, with smart forecourt, good menu and wine list. The clientele were bright young things and ignored us as we entered, giving only a cursory glance to the old-fashioned man in a flat cap and the younger woman with long blonde hair towering above him. The waiter lit the candle and Fred deliberated over the large menu: 'Bloody hell! I thought we were still in Great Britain! What the hell does this lot mean, then, eh flower?'

'Let me order, Fred. You know what you're like in these places.'

'Get some of that garlic bread, and I want some chips as well...'

'Might have to have pizza or pasta ... there's no chips here, Fred.'

'Bloody hell, knackers up me teeth that stuff, cock.'

'You like it when I do it...'

'Aye, it's not so bad. Remember that time when I asked you how to cook a black puddin' and you said you were going to learn me how to cook pasta instead?'

'Yeah, and you were frightened of eating salad.'

'Christ. Bloody rabbit food! I fancy a pint, cock. Is it all that bottled fizzy stuff that makes you burp – no Guinness either?'

'Wine instead?'

'Aye, order a bottle of the good red stuff.'

That conversation was typical of countless times we'd dined in nice places, which deep down Fred secretly enjoyed but didn't like to admit. Waiting for our food, we sat there across from each other in the crowded, intimate res-taurant with the bottle of red wine. Later, he looked into my eyes and told me that, despite the fact I was an awkward cow at times, he really did love me.

He leaned over towards me, displacing a side plate and, resting his elbows on the table, squeezed both my hands, peered into my eyes and continued: 'You know, it's a funny bloody life really, but me mam would have been proud o' me, I reckon. They never had owt, me mam and dad, only a life of bloody hardship and drudgery. And here's me now ... in a posh grub shop with a beautiful young wife, plenty of money in the bank and everything to live for.'

I looked at him. Painfully outspoken and so excruciatingly dogmatic at times that I could kill him – but something lurking there behind the image was irresistible and far better than any other relationship I'd ever known. He was a life force, my Fred.

I truly loved my husband, my Hippo, the wonderful, indefatigable Fred Dibnah, with every fibre of my being. Despite the frequent rows, frustrations, bad tempers, fame, steam engines, broken marriages, kids, ex-wives, hangers-on and certain misguided, back-stabbing from so-called friends – I loved him through and through, warts and all...

And as always, the last word belongs to Fred:

...Like years ago, when I just climbed up chimneys to mend them, the future looked pretty grim because the main occupation was destroying them. There weren't only me doing it either, but quite a few others too in Manchester, and the surrounding area. We were all looking for the next one to knock down. It was very obvious, the speed that they were going

at – the days of the boiler with a chimney were over with. It was quite a worrying thing to me. Lots of steeplejack companies that I knew about went bust. I really were one of the lucky ones, in so much that along came the BBC just to make one twenty-minute film – about twenty-six or seven years ago – and they've never gone away!

Life has completely changed: if I had to survive now by doing chimneys, I'd be hard-pressed. The 'celebrity' business and more TV work has saved the bacon, in a way. Yeah, really, the pressure of being a celebrity and the fact that everywhere you go people want to talk to you is a bit of a strain. I suppose I myself have got quite used to it over the years, but my first wife didn't like it. I rather think it sowed the seeds of destruction in my first marriage. My second wife partially wore it – but she didn't like me talking to people. Then of course, my third wife – she's not over keen on all the glare of being on show all the time, everywhere we go. It has without a shadow of a doubt changed my life, you read about all them showbusiness types, and their divorces sort of style – and I think they have something happened a bit similar to how it was for me as well...

I reckon it's all a bit of good luck – this fame thing – but really, I suppose in the past, there were a lot of good opportunities that went by the board. Lots of things now, where I can see I were really exploited. But now, things seem to be running on a better keel. I now get to spend a bit more time with the wife, and Sheila is very protective of me and can be a bit bossy with folk who ask me to do stuff for 'nowt' sometimes! Before, it was very hit and miss – people just wandered up and said 'Will you do this – will you do that?' gave me a few bob and I did it with no sort of thought of what could possibly happen in the future.

Now I am always more wary of things of that nature, I've got lots more to do and look forward to yet ... and, life is better now than it's ever been...

Bolton, Lancashire. Spring 1976

I looked up from my kneeling position. Since leaving art school at 17, I had been employed as a window dresser for the large Co-operative department store at the side of the Town Hall in Bolton. I was concentrating on part-time modelling work for the Lucie Clayton Agency in South King Street, Manchester. I was also taking singing and dancing lessons and belonged to an amateur dramatics group, with a view to becoming an actress. I dreamed of having a glamorous exciting lifestyle, travelling the world and meeting interesting people far away from Bolton. But for the time being, we had twenty large picture-window displays at the town centre Co-op to refurbish and redesign and it was sheer hard graft. Bored, confined and bogged down with petty rules and the endless routine of shop work, I longed to escape to a better life, a better future.

And now, almost lunchtime, I noticed that the Town Hall clock, sporting its recent addition of scaffolding tubes and funny lolly-stick planks, had stopped once again. A tiny flat-capped figure dangled from the pinnacle of the building, perched on a bosun's chair, swinging, tapping away merrily at the masonry; the third time this week. His battered old red truck bearing ropes, ladders and other strange tackle was parked across the road from where we stood.

Muttering to my fellow window dresser Christine Jones (who later decorated my wedding spanners and bricks) I grumbled: 'Why do they always seem to keep stopping the clock? What time is it now? That bloke's been at it for ages. I wish he'd get a move on!'

Not missing a beat, she quipped back: 'Awww ... leave him alone, it's only some poor workman earning a living like the rest of us.'

And it *was* beautiful for as long as it lasted, the journey of his life.